Performance Management in Schools

SCHOOL LEADERSHIP AND MANAGEMENT SERIES

Series Editors: Brent Davies and John West-Burnham

Other titles in the series:

Performance Management in Schools

How to Lead and Manage Staff for School Improvement

Edited by
John West-Burnham
John O'Neill
Ingrid Bradbury

PEARSON EDUCATION LIMITED

Head Office:
Edinburgh Gate
Harlow CM20 2JE
Tel: +44 (0)1279 623623
Fax: +44 (0)1279 431059

London Office:
128 Long Acre
London WC2E 9AN
Tel: +44 (0)20 7447 2000
Fax: +44 (0)20 7240 5771
Website: educationminds.com

First published in Great Britain in 2001

© Pearson Education Limited 2001

The right of John West-Burnham, John O'Neill and Ingrid Bradbury to be
identified as authors of this work has been asserted by them in accordance
with the Copyright, Designs and Patents Act 1988.

ISBN 0 273 65487 X

British Library Cataloguing in Publication Data
A CIP catalogue record for this book can be obtained from the British Library.

10 9 8 7 6 5 4 3

Typeset by Pantek Arts Ltd, Maidstone, Kent.
Printed by Bell and Bain Ltd., Glasgow

The Publishers' policy is to use paper manufactured from sustainable forests.

About the Contributors

■ ■ ■

Derek Bowden is lecturer in Educational Leadership, International Leadership Centre, University of Hull. He has been a headteacher of a Cheshire Comprehensive School and Consultant for Local Education Authorities on Leadership Development, Appraisal and School Effectiveness. His teaching experience includes work in Britain and Nigeria in secondary schools, a sixth form college and a further education college. He spent a period of time seconded to industry researching management training. He has taught educational management with the Open University, Leicester University and Manchester Metropolitan University and was a Senior Lecturer at the University of Lincolnshire and Humberside.

Gill Bracey is a freelance consultant, following 11 years as a senior manager in two different secondary schools and seven years managing a national development project for a group of local education authorities. Gill is currently contracted as Education Adviser to Workplace Learning Division, Department for Education and Employment, for the three-year Investors in People Strategy for Schools. Other work includes consultancy with individual or families of schools on a range of topics including self-evaluation, the development of quality standards for community schools with the International Community Education Association, and Investors in People assessment and advice services across the education and business sectors.

Ingrid Bradbury was deputy head of a large special school and head of an infants' school in Slough and has had 28 years' teaching experience. She now works as an Office for Standards in Education inspector in special and primary schools, as a Threshold Assessor, an information and communications technology trainer and an independent educational consultant.

Michael Brearley was the head of two large secondary schools. He is the author of *Emotional Intelligence in the Classroom* and has designed and run workshops on performance management and dynamic leadership for both business and education. He has been actively involved in Performance Management in both the primary and secondary sector.

Peter Brereton taught for 15 years in inner city secondary schools in Liverpool before a secondment to Liverpool University. From here he joined UBI (Understanding British Industry) as a regional director for the North West and set up the Teacher Placement Service (TPS). In 1996 he launched his own company and during this period initiated the Partners in Leadership programme as part of the Leadership Programme for Serving Headteachers. Since 2000 he has been a business development executive for Nord Anglia Education plc.

John Clark is a senior lecturer in the Department of Social and Policy Studies in Education at Massey University, Palmerston North, New Zealand. As a philosopher, he has a particular interest in administration, curriculum, policy and research. He has published in a variety of journals including *Educational Administration Quarterly*, *Educational Management and Administration*, *Educational Research* and the *New Zealand Principal*. He is the author of *Educational Research: Philosophy, Politics, Ethics*.

Graham Collins is a senior lecturer in Massey University's College of Education, Palmerston North, New Zealand. In 1995 and 1996 he served on the New Zealand Ministry of Education's performance management development group, charged with developing the framework for performance management that was introduced in February 1997. In 1997 and 1998 he was responsible for co-ordinating the training and support for schools implementing performance management in the Massey University College of Education region. Recently he has researched the impact of performance management on the 'teaching' principal.

Maureen Doyle is the headteacher of Servite Roman Catholic Primary School in Chelsea. She is in her 14th year of headship, having served in two different London schools during that period. Maureen also taught in Scotland and Liverpool before moving to London.

Tony Gelsthorpe has worked in UK secondary schools, community colleges and the education department and advisory service of a local education authority. University tutoring and international consultancies in Germany, the Middle East and South East Asia have contributed to his working life as principal of a community college for 18 years. He has authored *Managing Community Education*, *Towards a Community Curriculum* and is joint author of *Transforming Schools through Community Education*. Chair of Examiners for a national awarding body, he is now consultant to the Community Schools Network supported by the Department for Education and Employment, a member of the national Investors in People Strategy for Schools Advisory Group and continues his long association with the Oxford Consortium for Educational Achievement (OCEA) Partnership working on school self-evaluation for improvement.

Howard Kennedy is Managing Director of the London Leadership Centre, Institute of Education, University of London, where he has made a significant contribution to leadership thinking and learning. He contributes to an International MBA in Leadership. Howard has been an adviser to the UK's Teacher Training Agency, and the London Leadership Centre is presently responsible for writing the new National Professional Qualification for Headship. Howard has had 17 years headship experience in the primary sector and led a beacon school with a national reputation for high achievement and innovations in learning.

Mike Mayers started teaching in Staffordshire in 1972, and was deputy head-teacher of King Edward VI School in Lichfield from 1984 to 1990. He served, as headteacher of The Pingle School from 1991 to 1999 and in September 1999 became headteacher of Chaucer Technology School. While at The Pingle the percentage of pupils gaining five A–C grades at GCSE rose from 19 per cent to 47 per cent and the average A-level point score rose from 10 to over 20. A recent Office for Standards in Education report noted that under his leadership the school had made significant improvements, particularly commending the high and improved quality of teaching and learning, and very effective systems for monitoring classroom practice.

Alan Murphy is headteacher of St Edward's School, Poole – an 11–18 Denominational Comprehensive School. However, he was recently seconded to act as headteacher of another local secondary school placed in special measures by Her Majesty's Inspectorate. He has been a tutor for the Leicester University MBA in Educational Management for over five years. He is an experienced management trainer having led courses at home and abroad for a variety of providers. He specialises in leadership and team development. Alan Murphy is also a web site developer and has been running The INSETnet for over three years.

John O'Neill teaches and researches in educational management at Massey University, New Zealand, having previously held a similar post at Leicester University, England. Prior to that he spent ten years teaching children with special educational needs in primary and secondary schools. His research interests are in educational policy and teacher development. Publications include *Effective Curriculum Management, Co-ordinating Learning in the Primary School* (with Neil Kitson) and *Teacher Appraisal in New Zealand: Beyond the Impossible Triangle.*

Ken Thompson is principal of Gladstone Park High School, Victoria, Australia. He has wide experience as teacher, principal and education officer and adviser. He is a regular contributor to the University of Hull MBA in School Leadership.

David Weller is a professor in the Department of Educational Leadership at the University of Georgia, USA. He has been a high school teacher and a middle school principal. He serves as a consultant to public and private schools in the area of organisational development and total quality management. He is the author of *Quality Middle School Leadership* and *Quality Human Resources Leadership.*

John West-Burnham is Professor of Educational Leadership, International Leadership Centre, University of Hull. John worked in schools for 15 years before moving into higher education. He has worked at Crewe and Alsager College, the University of Leicester and the University of Lincolnshire and Humberside. He was also Development Officer for Teacher Performance for Cheshire local education authority. John is author of *Managing Quality in*

Schools, and co-author of *Effective Learning in Schools* and *Leadership and Professional Development in Schools*.

Mike Wintle has been a headteacher for a number of years in a variety of authorities and has worked for a number of local education authorities as a consultant. His experience ranges from rural situations to extremely challenging schools in Nottinghamshire and South Yorkshire. He is currently head of a large, very successful primary school in Lincolnshire. He has worked as a consultant for Manchester University for over five years and is a senior marker for a large examining group. Mike has undertaken in-service training provision in a large number of local education authority and individual schools. He is author of *Assessment Leading to Target Setting* by Falmer Press.

About the Series Editors

■　■　■

Professor Brent Davies PhD is Director of the International Leadership Centre at the University of Hull. Brent works exclusively on headteacher and senior staff development programmes in the UK and in Australia, New Zealand and the USA. He has written 11 books and published over 50 articles.

John West-Burnham. See above for details.

Dedications

■ ■ ■

John O'Neill: for Kirsty and Isobel

Ingrid Bradbury: for Reg and Annette Barker

Contents

■ ■ ■

Introduction

■ ■ ■

Performance management has emerged as one of the dominant themes in education systems throughout the world. It is a manifestation of the changing nature of accountability in all public services where the emphasis has switched from internal professional validation to external measurement and judgement. Historically, education professionals were largely responsible for determining and defining the criteria for success in schools. The challenge to this hegemony has resulted in the introduction of public, quantifiable and comparable measures of the outcomes of schooling. This has facilitated a greater emphasis on the performance of the individual teacher based on their contribution (or otherwise) to the achievement of organisational outcomes.

This trend has led to a new regime of inspection, monitoring and reporting, which runs counter to many perceptions of professional accountability. This book is designed to be informative and supportive but also to raise issues and concerns about performance management.

The stimulus for the book lies in the widespread policy, bureaucratic and regulatory changes in the areas of 'standards' and 'performance management' in England since 1997 (*see* Chapter 17 for a discussion of these). These changes have included:

- the establishment of a powerful, centralising 'standards and effectiveness unit' within the Department for Education and Employment;
  <www.standards.dfee.gov.uk/seu/>
- a 'standards fund' that targets financial resources to local education authorities and schools within closely defined central government priority areas in education;
  <www.dfee.gov.uk/standardsfund/>
- the specification of 'national professional standards' for classroom teachers and those in all positions of responsibility;
  <www.canteach.gov.uk/info/standards>
- for experienced teachers at the normal salary bar, a system of voluntary 'threshold assessment' linked to further salary increases;
  <www.dfee.gov.uk/teachingreforms/rewards/perfthresh/>
- a revised mandatory framework for appraisal and performance management that, for the first time since the long discredited Revised Code of 1862, links teachers' pay progression explicitly to pupil performance outcomes.
  <www.dfee.gov.uk/teachingreforms/rewards/perfmanage/>

The contributors are practitioners, consultants and academics who bring a range of experience and multiple perspectives to the issue of performance management in schools. There has been no attempt to create a consensus about performance management – each contributor has a distinctive perspective.

The book brings together contributions from both advocates and critics of performance management. The aim of the collection is twofold. First, to challenge the assumptions and values that underpin this new, emerging hegemony of 'performance', 'standards' and 'accountability' in education. Second, to provide intelligent ethical and pragmatic signposts for those who are charged with the implementation of mandatory frameworks at school level.

The book is organised in three parts. Part One focuses on the theory and practice of performance management, raising issues about the principles and best practice of managing performance in schools. Part Two offers a series of case studies in which a wide range of effective practice is described. Part Three offers the opportunity for the reader to draw comparisons between four interactional perspectives.

We are very grateful to the contributors who worked to very tight deadlines.

We hope that this book will provide reassurance and support to those responsible for performance management in schools, serve as a resource to those studying the many aspects of school improvement and contribute to the debate on how best to sustain the professionalism and commitment of teachers.

John West-Burnham, John O'Neill, Ingrid Bradbury
April 2001

Part One

■ ■ ■

The Theory and Practice of Performance Management

1

■ ■ ■

Perspectives on Performance Management

John O'Neill and John West-Burnham

The purpose of this chapter is to provide an overview and synthesis of the issues associated with performance management in schools. The themes discussed in this review will be developed in subsequent chapters and given more detailed analysis and exemplification.

At the heart of this introduction is an attempt to map out the issues that need to be considered in terms of principle and practice in the application of performance management systems to schools. Politically driven policy innovations are beguilingly simple to the politicians and civil servants who design and implement legislation. Performance management is particularly susceptible to the rationalistic fallacy – the seductive belief that the articulation of policy will necessarily lead to change in practice. This neat linearity is not reflected in actual experience; performance, especially in schools, is too complex a topic to be amenable to legislation. It requires a profound reconceptualisation of many basic assumptions concerning the nature and purpose of education, the definitions of educational achievement and success, the nature of the school as an organisation, the role of the teacher and many other related issues. Equally relevant are concerns about models of accountability, how success and failure are to be measured, and by whom, and what rewards and sanctions are to be employed.

This chapter is structured around a number of fundamental questions about performance management. Our intention is not to provide definitive answers but, rather, to clarify the issues for debate and to provide a conceptual framework to facilitate review of the specific discussions that follow.

What is performance?

Central to our conception of 'performance' is an understanding of the power of language and of the social contexts within which teaching, management and leadership are practised.

The essential point to be grasped here is that the language we use to describe teaching and learning, and other practices in schools, conveys assumptions about the nature of the processes it describes, their value and their purposes. The language we employ also infuses our actions and strategies. To talk about 'performance' in a particular way immediately opens up some possibilities for 'performing' and 'managing' performance, and simultaneously closes off others.

For example, if we define 'performance' as the successful completion within a given time frame of the variety of definable, observable and measurable teaching or management actions that may reasonably be expected of an individual who has specific, statutory and contractual responsibilities in any given school setting, we are making particular assumptions about the nature of performance and, from this, related assumptions about how performance should be assessed, when and by whom.

In contrast, we might conceptualise 'performance' as a disposition to exercise one's professional judgement in ways that enhance the pursuit of collectively and broadly defined longer-term educational goals while taking into account the needs and socio-economic circumstances of members of the school community in order, pragmatically, to resolve day-to-day dilemmas of practice.

In this second example, the assumptions that underpin the conception of performance are quite distinct from those expressed in the first. Moreover, in this second example, performance is conceptualised as both an individual and a social activity. To the extent that it is defined, performance is the practical embodiment of the school community's aspirations. In the first example, it is possible that performance is defined by one individual, enacted by another, observed and assessed by a third and rewarded or sanctioned by yet another. In the first example, it might be appropriate for one person to assess another's performance against a written descriptor of the desired behaviour or standard. In the second, it may only be possible to evaluate the degree of consonance between action and goal by deconstructing the narratives recounted by the individual and workgroup concerned.

Without wishing to labour the point, in the first example, the conception of performance is one based on assumptions about occupational competence; in the second, it is based on assumptions about professional ethics. In the former, management of performance relies on empirical data and claims of objectivity, in the latter on values and claims of trust (Codd, 1999). Rather than arguing that performance management should be based either on generic competencies or shared moral purpose, we would suggest that some aspects of 'performance' in schools lend themselves more readily to the former, others to the latter. The important point is that in developing systems and processes, we should be centrally concerned with performance and not 'performativity' – the employment of 'judgements, comparisons and displays' of performance 'as means of control, attrition and change' to improve productivity or output (Ball, 1999: 1). Ball illustrates the perverse effects of performativity using the analogy of the train that in order to arrive at its destination on time and help the operator meet its punctuality targets, fails to stop at the stations along the way to pick up passengers waiting on the platform. Similarly, we feel that performance management in schools should not leave frustrated students or teachers waiting vainly on the platform. The management of performance in schools must, in our view, serve educational purposes.

Those in schools who have the responsibility for the development of performance management systems and processes need to recognise from the outset that the language they deploy will significantly influence the ways in which staff think, act and interact. Thus, at a very basic level, whichever definitions of performance are articulated within classrooms, workgroups and staffrooms, they must be consistent with the values and practices of all those to whom they apply (i.e. students, teachers, associate staff, senior management, governors, parents and caregivers) if they are to have any prospect of successful enactment.

We need also to distinguish between individual and collective performance. Although the practice of classroom teaching may still at the beginning of the twenty-first century be conducted in isolation from other adults, most other aspects of teaching, management and leadership are social activities. More than this though, individual teachers are members of functional workgroups: the subject department or pastoral team in secondary schools, the Key Stage 1 or Key Stage 2 teachers in primary schools, and the senior management team in both of these. Teachers and senior staff interpret their surroundings, organise their work and gauge their performance against the norms and expectations of immediate colleagues among whom they develop both professional and social relationships.

Workgroup and, to a lesser extent, institutional cultures therefore exert a powerful influence on individual practice. They both elaborate and constrain the possibilities of individual action. Thus, in attempting to articulate our definitions of performance, we need to be clear about the areas of activity in school where individual performance may appropriately be evaluated, and by whom, and those where collective professional judgement and behaviour should be the focus of attention. To concentrate solely on the performance of the individual is to ignore the social context of schooling in which individuals work and learn.

5

Why is performance management in education an issue?

During the 1990s most education systems in the English-speaking world moved towards some notion of performance management. This is largely attributable to the cumulative and increasingly widespread perception that education systems were underachieving or failing to perform. This perception was almost entirely derived from comparative, quantitative measures of educational outcomes.

This anxiety was reinforced by the increasing amounts of data available, which allowed more and more specific and detailed measurement of various components of school performance. The contrast within educational systems, and between schools and between educational systems (e.g. English-speaking systems and the countries of the Pacific rim) revealed significant discrepancies. The anxiety was reinforced by the general observation that high-performing education systems were usually found in high-performing economies. A neat, but simplistic, causal relationship was established between educational performance and economic performance.

Underpinning this economically motivated concern was a growing sense of unease, particularly in England, about the integrity of the social infrastructure. Youth crime, teenage pregnancy and a general sense of social malaise were felt to be at least partly attributable to an educational system that had lost its way.

The 'discovery' of educational underachievement coincided almost exactly with a growing consumerism in society, which in turn lead to a challenge to historical patterns of accountability. Traditional models of accountability had largely been internal and circular. The professions, notably education and medicine, had been responsible for both defining and judging accountability – using internally generated criteria and validating their own judgements.

This situation changed radically with the introduction of externally (i.e. government) generated criteria, external judgements as to the extent those criteria were met and the publication of data which allowed implications, however fallacious, to be drawn. The practical manifestation of this has been the introduction of standardised testing in order to generate the data to allow comparisons to be made between institutions and over time. Once the system had been created for organisations it was a natural corollary to extend it to individuals.

Performance management had therefore emerged as what might be described as a functional accountability, relating judgements about individual performance to an essentially economic model based on measurable outcomes rather than a professional model judged on what might be termed moral or ethical criteria. This change brings with it a shift if what constitutes appropriate recognition – quantitative measures of quantifiable outcomes are accompanied by quantified rewards, i.e. pay. All of this in spite of Barber's (1997: 227–8) contention that

The research evidence on merit pay in general is mixed. In education worldwide it is largely negative. It appears to have worked only where three conditions have been met: where teachers are already well paid and the merit pay is a relatively small addition; where there are clear, published criteria on the level of performance required to gain the merit pay; and where everyone who meets those criteria gets the pay.

The debate about performance related pay is returned to below. What is inescapable is a changing definition of accountability and increasingly robust view that in the public sector, as much as in the private sector, organisations and individuals are maintained and employed not so much to work as to perform to set standards. This is in direct contradiction to the prevailing ethos in education that perceived performance as a professional, i.e. quasi-moral, imperative subject to many variables outside the control of the individual. The extent to which that remains valid is a key component of the debate in this book. However, even raising the issue for debate is important given the realisation that teachers under the age of approximately 35 in England and Wales will not have taught anything other than the National Curriculum, those under 30 will only have worked in schools with a statutory appraisal scheme, and only those over the age of 40-something will have trained and worked in an occupation that took arms-length government support and its own professional autonomy for granted. The occupational conception of performance as something other than instrumental technical competence is, arguably, disappearing from teachers' collective folk-memory as each year passes. There is, as a result, a moral imperative on us as writers to articulate other conceptual and practical possibilities in volumes such as this.

How is performance to be defined?

This is at the heart of the debate about performance management; the definition of performance will determine both what it is to be measured and how it can be measured. This leads on to further issues, most importantly, who decides what constitutes performance and how authoritative their definition is. Defining any non-mechanical level of performance is difficult; the classroom presents a range of complex factors which would appear to militate against the sorts of models of performance management that are possible with easily quantified outcomes subject to minimal interpretation in the context of easily controllable variables. Consider the variables impinging upon the success of a lesson in the secondary school:

- the relative complexity of the topic;
- the skill and experience of the teacher;
- the ability range of the pupils;
- what happened the previous lesson;

- the time of day;
- the day of the week and time into the term;
- the prior knowledge of individual pupils;
- the resources available;
- parental commitment and expectations;
- the overall culture of the school.

The list could be extended almost indefinitely. Some factors will clearly be directly under the control of the teacher, others will be totally outside their control. As Davies (2000: 29) argues: 'The evidence is overwhelming that the single most important factor in a school's performance is its intake.' In the context of Davies's study, performance is defined as measurable outcomes of academic attainment. Although these have recently become the preferred indicators of 'successful' schools and schooling in both policy and research in Britain, their unquestioning use overlooks the central problem in defining performance in education – what are the significant outcomes that performance will be measured against. The problem is that any mode of assessment will inevitably determine and constrain that which is being measured.

If the political imperative is to measure, then significance will be attached to that which can be measured – the intangible, the elusive, the complex and the problematic, which are not amenable to easy measurement, will thus be marginalised. One of the major concerns with any performance management system is that it will, of necessity, be reductionist, instrumental and will tend to simplify to facilitate comparative measurement and so judgement. And yet, if we are talking about education, then we are talking about the full range of human experience from 'that which can be easily measured' to that which is diffuse, personal and where the significance will only emerge over time. The anecdotal evidence is that the emphasis on performance tends to drive out the latter in favour of the former. As Apple (2000: xii) bluntly puts it:

> The seemingly contradictory discourses of competition, markets and choice on the one hand, and accountability, performance objectives, standards, national testing and national curriculum have created such a din that it is hard to hear anything else.

This is not to argue against performance management but to revive concerns about the implementation of a performance management system based on limited and functional definitions which ignore either higher-order purposes and values or the immediate socio-economic circumstances of teaching and schooling that delimit 'the art of the possible' (Thrupp, 1999: 103) in material ways. In schools where students' intergenerational educational aspirations are low, where 'the diseases of poverty' are endemic, where children do low-paid work each day to contribute to the family income or take time off school in order to care for younger siblings, or where it is impossible to find a warm, dry and quiet place to do one's homework (Hawk and Hill, 1996: 89), performance is a very different phenomenon from that in classrooms, schools, families and communities where individual and collective schooling success is taken for granted. Ours is not a fatalistic assessment of the potential of performance management, merely a realistic one.

Performance management is easy in a genuinely open market, with a product that is totally consistent and where it is possible to establish a precise correlation between individual effort and defined outcomes. Even the most reductionist view of education does not lend itself to those criteria.

A further complicating factor is whether performance is to be measured in terms of outcomes or behaviours or a combination of the two. A significant example of both strategies being used in education is found in the management of headteacher performance in England. As part of the annual performance management cycle headteachers have to agree with their governing bodies a range of targets, which might well include quantifiable outcomes. The Leadership Programme for Serving Heads (LPSH), although it is a 'one-off' event focuses on the diagnosis of performance against a range of specified characteristics, i.e. behaviours.

The behaviours approach recognises that not all aspects of a job are capable of being reduced to specific targets or outcomes. However, the essential issue remains the same – an individual is held accountable, or their performance is evaluated against a set of criteria, which may or may not be relevant, appropriate or valid. Drucker (1993: 189 and 190) captures the essence of the tension:

> But schools are becoming much too important not to be held accountable – for thinking through what their results should be as well as for their performance in attaining these results.

and

> ...the greatest change – and the one that we are least prepared for – is that the school will have to commit itself to results.

However, in the chapter that precedes this conclusion Drucker argues for a very different notion of what constitutes a school. Unless there is an overarching agreement as to what the core purpose of a school is, then measurement of outcomes or behaviours will inevitably reinforce a limited and marginal view.

How is superior performance to be rewarded?

The associated question to this one is, of course, how is unacceptable performance to be penalised? The issue is essentially the same in both cases – the integrity of:

- the definition of performance;
- the accuracy of the measurement of performance;

- the credibility of the judgement about that performance;
- the perceived validity of the action taken.

As Barber indicated above, merit pay only works when there is money available to pay it and this encapsulates the problem. Any performance management system that offers tangible rewards has to ensure that those rewards are available for all who qualify, that they are available over time but, crucially, that they are significant and valued. It is this last point that is pivotal to any reward system; we doubt if there are any teachers who would feel recognised and reinforced by a commemorative tie, a brooch or access to the head's personal coffee-machine for a week.

A significant complicating factor, discussed in subsequent chapters is the aspiration that most teachers share, to work in a context that is concerned with values, a sense of social justice with a focus on the development of young people. It is this aspirational and altruistic component of the work of a teacher that confounds and confuses the notion of reward. On the one hand, teachers have historically been poorly paid and any form of financial recognition is welcome; on the other hand, it is unclear as to the extent to which financial recognition would actually serve to enhance performance. For some it would undoubtedly serve as a significant incentive but for others it would be marginal, trivial, if not actually demeaning. For many teachers time and a reduction in paperwork, rather than money, would be the real incentive. For some, public recognition, as in the recently established annual teachers' awards, would be the culmination of their career, for others it would be worse than death. For some educationalists the award of an OBE would be valid recognition by a society that they have faithfully served, for others it would be an inappropriate symbol of the system that they work to change. What is crucial is that any reward is valued and significant to the individual, generic rewards do not work in this context unless there is a very strong team-based culture.

The converse argument also applies here – if meeting or exceeding requirements is to be rewarded then, for the sake of credibility and consistency, less than satisfactory performance has to be penalised. Putting aside the quasi-legal procedures of competence and capability, which should not be included in this context, there is a real issue in either not rewarding or penalising an individual. Failure to perform to a required standard is a highly complex situation. The problem centres on the ability to demonstrate, without doubt or ambiguity, that it is the sole and exclusive responsibility of the individual and not in any way subject to external variables. Any other approach contravenes the most basic principles of natural justice.

We would therefore suggest that any system based on the notion of reward would have to meet the following criteria:

- clear, up-to-date and agreed definitions of the actual job;
- identification of outcomes which are personal and specific to the individual;

- clear and agreed criteria as to the nature of evidence that will be used to make judgements;
- a formal, consistent and transparent system to judge individual performance;
- experienced and credible staff to actually make the judgements;
- recognition expressed in ways that are valid, personally significant and consistent;
- a clear differentiation from parallel but distinct procedures, e.g. promotion, capability etc;
- consistent application of the scheme over time;
- monitoring and evaluation of the effectiveness and efficiency of the scheme.

Unless these criteria are met it is difficult to see how any reward-based performance management scheme will gain acceptance, credibility and be valued. The pivotal issue is the development of a scheme that has generic equity but individual significance.

How does performance relate to the school?

One of the key variables influencing individual performance is the organisational context. An important component of this is school culture, which will be discussed in a subsequent chapter. A number of contextual factors other than culture will have an impact on individual performance. Of these perhaps the most significant is organisational design. The case studies in Part Two will develop and exemplify this point in much more detail, but at this stage it is worth stating that individuals' capacity to perform effectively is shaped by the context in which they work and socialise. Hock (1999: 71–2) captures this issue in discussing teams:

...whose performance transcends the ability of individuals. The same phenomenon can be observed in the symphony, the theatre, in fact, every group endeavour, including business and government.

...countless (people) have tried to explain, and reduce to a mechanistic, measurably controlled process, that which causes the phenomenon. It has never been done and never will be.

There is an overwhelming consensus that teams are conductive to high performance – the whole is greater than the sum of the parts. Many organisations have redesigned themselves, moving away from historic hierarchies based on command and control structures to flexible structures based on autonomous teams. How far this is possible in schools remains a moot point. What is clear is that there is a high correlation between individual performance and membership of a group and that an organisation that is designed around, and systematically facilitates, the development of teams is more likely to create an environment that is propitious for high performance. Indeed, in a number of studies of secondary schools, it is the immediate workgroup or subject department culture that has been shown to exert the most significant influence on the work, strategies and values of its members (Siskin, 1994).

This makes sense, particularly in larger secondary schools where teachers' loyalties are to the workgroup, not to the school, and their affiliations are to the particular subject and epistemic community, not necessarily secondary school teaching in general. Equally, teachers within a subject area may have divergent views on the nature and purpose of their subject (Siskin and Little, 1995). This fragmented, subject-specific view of teaching, its development and its performance has practical implications for the definition, evaluation and comparison of performance within and across groups of teachers. If some teachers of English conceptualise their performance differently from others, and teachers of English differently from science or mathematics or humanities teachers, both the aspects of performance to be measured, the instruments used and the judgements made, may also have to be very different from each other (Nolan and Francis, 1992).

Directly related to organisational structure is the way in which resources in the organisation are managed. Resources, whether hard or soft, are a key determinant of performance in the extent to which individuals are able to control and deploy the resources they need to function and perform effectively. Perhaps the most significant resource in a school is time, but space, materials and money are all significant to varying degrees according to context. Another important factor in organisational terms is the place of planning in the organisation. In many ways planning is one of the crucial determinants of any organisational definition of performance as it sets the generic outcomes that will have to be translated into individual targets.

What are the criteria for effective performance management?

In this introductory chapter we have outlined some of the philosophical, conceptual, political, statutory and practical issues that need to be recognised and addressed as schools seek to develop worthwhile performance management systems and processes. Teachers, managers and leaders in schools tend to adopt pragmatic approaches to their work in the sense that they seek practical resolutions of human problems and dilemmas that are consistent with their values and ethics. Their implementation of new statutory requirements for performance management in schools will, we suspect, be addressed no differently.

Nevertheless, in a volume that seeks to provoke debate and reflection, as well as providing functional signposts for those engaged in the practicalities of implementation, we would be doing our readers and fellow contributors a disservice if we were not to locate this discussion of performance management within a wider debate about purpose and moral agency in teaching, school management and leadership. A challenging starting point for thinking about how we wish collectively to mould schooling practices and performance to help further our educational goals is provided by Hargreaves and Goodson (1996: 20–1) in their elaboration of seven principles of post-modern teacher professionalism:

- *increased opportunity and responsibility to exercise* discretionary judgement *over the issues of teaching, curriculum and care that affect one's students;*
- *opportunities and expectations to engage with the* moral and social purposes *and value of what teachers teach, along with major curriculum and assessment matters in which these purposes are embedded;*
- *commitment to working with colleagues in* collaborative cultures *of help and support as a way of using shared expertise to solve the ongoing problems of professional practice, rather than engaging in joint work as a motivational device to implement the external mandates of others;*
- *occupational* heteronomy *rather than self-protective* autonomy, *where teachers work authoritatively yet openly and collaboratively with other partners in the wider community (especially parents and students themselves), who have a significant stake in the students' learning;*
- *a commitment to active* care *and not just* anodyne *service for students. Professionalism must in this sense acknowledge and embrace the emotional as well as the cognitive dimensions of teaching, and also recognise the skills and dispositions that are essential to committed and effective caring;*
- *a self-directed search and struggle for* continuous learning *related to one's own expertise and standards of practice, rather than compliance with the enervating obligations of* endless change *demanded by others (often under the guise of continuous learning or improvement);*
- *the creation and recognition of high task* complexity, *with levels of status and reward appropriate to such complexity.*

The criteria for effective performance management will and must vary from school to school. Although they may work within common curriculum, assessment and credential frameworks, each school is essentially a unique and idiosyncratic social community, shaped by its own history and circumstances. Beyond conformance with broad statutory requirements, schools will seek to develop systems and processes that are consistent with their cultures, aspirations and capacities. Such diversity is necessary and to be welcomed.

We hope that the discussion here and in the chapters that follow will contribute in quite tangible ways to the development of meaningful, purposive performance management processes in schools; processes that help develop and enhance the professionalism of educationalists who work within them on the basis of clearly articulated educational and moral values.

References

Apple, M. (2000) 'Preface' in J. Smyth, A. Dow, R. Hattam, A. Reid and G. Shacklock *Teachers' Work in a Globalizing Economy*. London: Falmer.

Ball, S. (1999) 'Performativities and fabrications in the education economy: towards the performative society?'. Keynote address to the AARE/NZARE Conference, Melbourne, December.

Barber, M. (1997) *The Learning Game*. London: Indigo.

Codd, J. (1999) 'Educational reform, accountability and the culture of distrust' *New Zealand Journal of Educational Studies*, 34 (1), 45–53.

Davies, N. (2000) *The School Report*. London: Vintage.

Drucker, P.F. (1993) *Post-Capitalist Society*. Oxford: Butterworth-Heinemann.

Hawk, K. and Hill, J. (1996) *Towards Making Achievement Cool. Achievement in Multi-Cultural High Schools (AIMHI)*. Report prepared for the Ministry of Education. Albany, NZ: Massey University Educational Research and Development Centre, December.

Hargreaves, A. and Goodson, I. (1996) 'Teachers' professional lives: aspirations and actualities' in I. Goodson and A. Hargreaves (eds) *Teachers' Professional Lives*. London: Falmer.

Hock, D. (1999) *Birth of the Chaordic Age*. San Francisco: Berrett-Koehler.

Nolan, J. and Francis, P. (1992) 'Changing perspectives in curriculum and supervision' in C. Glickman (ed.) *Supervision in Transition*. Alexandria, VA: Association for Supervision and Curriculum Development.

Siskin, L. (1994) *Realms of Knowledge: Academic Departments in Secondary Schools*. London: Falmer.

Siskin, L. and Little, J. (eds) (1995) *The Subjects in Question. Departmental Organization and the High School*. New York: Teachers' College Press.

Thrupp, M. (1999) *Schools Making a Difference: Let's Be Realistic*. Buckingham: Open University Press, ch. 7.

2
■ ■ ■

Creating a
Performance Culture

John West-Burnham

The purpose of this chapter is to explore the tension, inherent in all organisational processes, between the formal, structured and systems-based approach to management (the formal domain) and the approach concerned with beliefs, motivation and engagement (the affective domain). The central proposition is that while the formal domain is necessary it is not sufficient, and that engagement with the affective domain is essential for significant and sustainable change.

It is relatively easy to change structures and systems, and doing so often creates a beguiling sense of having 'made a difference'. However, for performance management to make significant changes over time it is not enough to introduce a new policy with associated documentation, to redefine roles and introduce new processes, rewards etc. Systemic change is essentially cultural change and, if performance management is to become 'the way we do things round here' rather than a short-term essentially bureaucratic exercise, it will have to address the fundamental issues of school culture.

Culture is an elusive and, by definition, intangible concept (and there is a strong connection between structures and cultures) but a focus on cultural change is a fundamental component of moving an organisation into different modes of operating which are embedded and lead to significant changes in behaviour and expectations. There are numerous definitions of culture available but all point to the same organisational phenomenon:

> *. . . it is likely that an influence more powerful than that of any particular teacher, school policies or indeed behaviour of dominant pupils is at work. This overall*

atmosphere, which pervades the actions of the participants, we call ethos.

(Mortimore et al., 1988: 68)

I am taking 'ethos' to be synonymous with culture and there are a range of other terms employed in this context, e.g. 'climate', 'atmosphere', 'tone' etc. The semantic nuances are less important than the significance that most writers attribute to this aspect of organisational life.

Culture implies the commonality of assumptions, values and norms. They are shared by the majority of staff, although not every member of the organisation will share all values and norms. However, even if teachers do not share specific assumptions, these will still influence their behaviour, because they comply with the expectations of others, or resistance against these expectations. School culture can therefore be defined as the shared assumptions, values and norms of staff that influence their functioning.

(Visscher, 1999: 20)

It is Visscher's notion of commonality that is central to this debate – performance management will never go beyond the superficial level of engagement if it does not become embedded in assumptions, values and norms, and this points to a distinction between the management of a system and the leadership of a process. The debate about the relationship between leadership and management is littered with semantic distinctions but, for the purposes of this discussion, leadership is seen as creating the cultural perspective, management reinforcing it with an appropriate operational infrastructure. In this sense they are symbiotic; which is worse, management without leadership or leadership without management? Both situations are dysfunctional but it is leadership that secures engagement, commitment and creates significance, and this is what makes the difference in an area as complex as performance management. This view is reinforced by Senge et al. (2000: 325).

A school's culture is its most enduring aspect. The explicit roles of the school, the policies and procedures, feel much more 'tangible' but they are also much easier to change. An administrator can change the roles with a decree. But you can't tell the staff of a school to 'change your culture!' Culture is deeply rooted in people. It is embodied in their attitudes, values and skills, which in turn stems from their personal backgrounds, from their life experiences (including their professional experiences) and from the communities they belong to (including the professional community of any school).

Figure 2.1 seeks to represent the tension between the formal, structured approach to performance management and the affective approach. Of course, any diagrammatic representation will create an artificial dichotomy between these elements; they should not be seen as polarities but, rather, as parts of a continuum. The precise location of any particular performance management approach will be determined by a range of complex interchanges between variables. It is the purpose of this discussion to consider the implications of particular approaches for the effectiveness of any attempt to enhance performance.

	The Formal Domain	The Affective Domain
The performance imperative	*External policy driven*	*Internal morally driven*
Definition of performance	Policies and procedures Performance criteria Job descriptions Focus on conformity	Values and norms Images and metaphors
Organisational processes	Managerialism Short-term planning Line management Focus on consistency Functional training	Leadership Shared meaning and practice Dialogue and debate Focus on improvement Personal development
Motivation	Extrinsic, for reward	Intrinsic, for growing
Culture	Individualistic, competition	Co-operative, collaboration
Measurement	Objective, quantitive, imposed	Subjective, qualititive, negotiated

Figure 2.1: A typology of performance

Any organisational system, structure or process will inevitably have to seek to reconcile two, potentially conflicting, imperatives: in essence the generic and the individual. By definition organisations have to work in the realm of common denominators, the shared, public and generalisable experiences which constitute organisational life. This is often in tension with the individual's subjective view of self and how this relates to, and engages with, the public domain. In one sense organisations only exist to the extent to which individuals are willing to surrender personal perspectives to the collective consensus. There is thus a continual interplay between individual and organisational imperatives, but in the final analysis, as Senge (1990: 211) expresses it:

> *Organisations intent on building shared visions continually encourage members to develop their personal visions. If people don't have their own vision, all they can do is 'sign up' for someone else's. The result is compliance, never commitment.*

This is at the heart of the creation of a culture that enhances performance – it has to be based on commitment, not compliance. This is central to the tension in Figure 2.1 – the extent to which any system is based on commitment rather than compliance. Senge (1990: 219–20) goes on to produce a hierarchy of attitudes towards a shared vision, which illustrate the implications of enforcement as opposed to engagement:

- Commitment — purposive engagement.
- Enrolment — positive will to implement.
- Genuine compliance — positive acceptance.

- Formal compliance   – acceptance and adherence.
- Grudging compliance   – minimal acceptance.
- Non-compliance   – rejection.
- Apathy   – neither for nor against.

Clearly commitment and enrolment would appear to be the most significant and desirable characteristics of individuals in an organisation which is seeking to create a performance culture. A balance has to be achieved between organisational and personal imperatives so that neither is compromised and both are enhanced. If this state of equilibrium is not achieved then it is almost inevitable that the deficit model of a control-based, hierarchical, machine bureaucracy will emerge – if only because it is relatively easy – the formal is always 'simpler' than the affective.

The rest of this chapter is devoted to an examination of the conditions necessary to create a culture where there is high individual commitment to organisational goals. Such a culture will need to meet the following criteria:

- depth, i.e. in forming fundamental attitudes and values;
- sustainability, i.e. capable of enduring over time;
- authenticity, i.e. relating to fundamental concerns;
- credibility, i.e. perceived as valid and relevant.

The elements that need to be explored in depth to understand a culture based on performance are vision and values, social relationships, learning and motivation. Linking these factors is the notion of leadership and, in particular, the behaviour of the leader.

Vision and values

The interaction between the vision of how the organisation *could* be, and the values that decide how it *should* be are fundamental to any definition of culture. According to Senge (1990: 207 and 208): 'A shared vision, especially one that is intrinsic, uplifts people's aspirations' and 'Visions are exhilarating'. Or, at least, they can be and perhaps should be. This is the very heart of performance management, the creation of a sense of purpose that informs all aspects of organisational activity and is personally compelling.

The synthesis of values and vision often expressed in an aims or mission statement is the essential prerequisite to performance management because it both defines the outcome and articulates the level of expectation. However, this is not always the case; too often mission statements are expressed in terms of clichés and pious aspirations without any reference to what constitutes an acceptable level of performance.

To be of any value in the context of performance management, a mission or aims statement should meet the following criteria. It must:

- focus on the core purpose of the school;
- be written in clear and compelling language;
- be accessible to all members of the school community;
- be comprehensive, i.e. refer to all aspects of the school life;
- inform all management processes.

It is this last point that sees the important interaction of the formal and the affective. There is no doubt that a compelling vision is a powerful force for creating a performance-based culture. However, it has to be translated into specific manifestations which serve to both exemplify the vision and show how it is to be translated into appropriate behaviours. The analogy with the highly effective classroom is precise. A teacher will articulate high expectations but these will also be translated into specific and defined behaviours, routines and practices. The overarching characteristics are consistency and clarity.

Culture is a complex interaction between deep-rooted assumptions and concrete actions. A school's aspirations for high performance have to be written in compelling and convincing language. They also have to be expressed through:

- strategic planning and target setting;
- policies, syllabuses and schemes of work;
- job descriptions;
- staff handbooks.

Fundamental to the creation of a high-performance culture in this context is the language that is used. Language is one of the most significant expressions of culture and the use of appropriate vocabularies, metaphors etc. is an important reinforcing factor. Language which is positive and celebratory, and metaphors that are positive and aspirational help to reinforce and consolidate the sense that high performance is the norm.

The case studies in Part Two of this book provide clear examples of the deliberate choice of specific vocabularies to reinforce the emphasis on a performance culture. What is very clear in the case studies is that the visions and values of the schools have very real and specific outcomes. It is not enough to inspire – inspiration has to be guided to a defined purpose. It is in this context that the notions of being a professional or having a vocation became significant. If the school has shared values, which are expressed as a consensual vision, then individuals also need a higher-order sense of purpose which provides in personal terms what the mission provides in organisational terms.

There is probably nothing as potent in creating a high-performance culture than engaging with the sense of purpose, vocation and commitment of the individual. From the greatest works of art and literature to the noblest examples of courage and self-sacrifice, the most significant outcomes of human endeavour and interaction have been inspired by that which is significant and profound – rarely by promotion or incremental adjustments. This dimension is exemplified by Sergiovanni (1992: 53):

> *Commitment to exemplary practice means practising at the edge of teaching, by staying abreast of new developments, researching one's practice, trying out new approaches and so on . . . Moving towards 'valued social ends' means placing oneself in service to students and parents and to the school and its purposes. The heart of professionalism in teaching may be commitment to the caring ethic . . . The caring ethic means doing everything possible to serve the learning, developmental and social needs of students as persons.*

The implications of these propositions are profound and wide-ranging but, in essence, they point to the moral basis of performance as the authentic and sustainable imperative for guiding professional practice.

A high-performance culture, therefore, requires a complex interaction between collective and individual values and aspirations. Managing the tension between the ideographic and the nomothetic is one of the most significant characteristics of effective leadership. Such leadership has many attributes, of which one of the most important is the context of this chapter in the creation of effective social relationships.

Social relationships

Sergiovanni (1992: 90) demonstrates the importance of the link between relationships and values: 'Congeniality, in the form of interpersonal loyalty and affection, has its merits. Indeed, congeniality, in combination with the professional ideal, contributes to the establishment and nurturance of collegiality, and its absence is not necessary for collegiality to be present. What is necessary is mutual respect.'

Mutual respect, often expressed as trust, is both a prerequisite and an expression of a high-performance culture. If the individual is to perform to optimum effect then there has to be a positive, supportive and nurturing environment. According to Deal and Kennedy (1999) there are four important aspects here: the social side of work, fun and adventure, challenge and fellowship at work. They go on to stress the importance of:

> *redefining the workplace as a meaningful human environment with high potential for top productivity. [Managers] can help to make work an attractive place to be. They can recapture the spirit of employees and channel this energy into furthering*

the goals of the business. But they can only do so if they recognise the mutual
dependencies of employees and employers and the need to create a cultural milieu
that benefits all. (Ibid.: 282)

Work is a social experience that extends far beyond the geographical and
chronological boundaries of the school. For most of us social relationships are
how we define work. In essence, the more positive the relationships the more
likely it is that individuals will be able to perform, and the more negative, the
less likely. In terms of social relationships a 'cultural milieu' is likely to be created through the following:

1	Trust	– genuine regard and respect with recognition of the individual's expertise, experience and professional authority expressed through support rather than control.
2	Fellowship	congeniality, warmth and affection; important in themselves but even more significant in that their absence militates against high performance because it diverts energies and focus.
3	Fun	– we tend to remember, and want to repeat, the positive experiences in our lives. Nothing is as positive as success and fun, nothing is more conducive to sustaining high performance.
4	Emotional intelligence	– Goleman (1998: 310) provides a detailed definition: 'Being a team player, having self-confidence, presence and style; being empathic and a good listener, maturity and integrity' and 'Having the qualities of a friend, colleague and partner; being honest and adhering to ones values, being sociable, with "sparkle" and a sense of humour'.

The combination of these factors adds up to the positive aspects of the affective side of any organisation – they are the tangible expressions of a
high-performance culture. Cooper and Sawat (1997: xxxi) express this aspect
of performance most convincingly and compellingly:

No matter what the product, idea, service or cause, we buy – *or buy in –* based on
feelings; and then, if possible, we rationalise or justify our choices with numbers and
facts. No one talks about the rationale *of a passionate relationship or hobby, or brags*
about a reasonable *marriage or* logical *vacation, or requires a* statistical analysis
of deeply felt human longings and dreams. By and large, the passions *– the word*
the ancient Greeks used for emotions – are more honest than thought or reason.

(Original emphases)

Performance is born of passions, compassion, belief and conviction – to talk of
managing it is to diminish or trivialise its essential integrity. It has to be recognised that the formal aspects of performance management may be necessary

but are not sufficient to the creation of a high-performance culture – in the same way that a marriage ceremony does not guarantee a passionate or lasting relationship. We ignore the affective dimension of performance at our peril.

Learning

Sustainable performance is the product of the complex interaction of many variables; central to the notion of sustainability is continuing professional learning. It is fundamental for a number of reasons:

1 It models the central definitions of performance in education – optimising individual learning.
2 It enhances the knowledge, skills, qualities and experience of the individual so as to sustain improvement.
3 It supports the development of consensus.
4 It reinforces the understanding of performance and helps to create individual models.

The term 'learning' has been deliberately chosen to emphasise the distinction with training – learning is affective, training is formal. Training does have a contribution to make to the creation of a high-performance culture but only within the context of a culture focused on learning. By definition training is unlikely to be sustainable with regard to the significant aspects of a performance culture and it is difficult to see how generic training can be individually authentic.

If a sustainable and authentic performance-based culture is to be created then learning in the context of professional development needs to have the following characteristics:

1 It is focused on the individual learner.
2 Information and experience are mediated to create personal meaning and mastery.
3 The motivation to learn is intrinsic and moral.
4 The optimum time and place for learning will vary according to the individual.
5 Learning to enhance capability, and so performance, has to be work focused.
6 To change practice and behaviour learning strategies have to include reflection feedback and coaching.

It is very easy to underestimate demands and the impact on the individual made by moving from self-defined appropriate or adequate performance to organisationally defined high performance. Teachers in particular spend much of their professional lives isolated from their colleagues – definitions of performance have often been personal, historical and self-legitimating. The move from individual performance to organisational performance requires individual learning within the context of organisational learning. Although learning is an individual, subjective and unique process, the context in which it takes place has to be a macrocosm of effective learning for the individual.

Senge et al. (2000) offer three core concepts about learning in organisations:

1   Every organisation is a product of how its members think and interact: 'effective school reform cannot happen until people move beyond superficial conceptions of educational systems and recognise the unseen values and attitudes about power, privilege and knowledge that keep existing structures, regulations and authority relationships in place' (p. 19).

2   Learning is connection: 'all learners construct knowledge from an inner scaffolding of their individual and social experiences, emotions, will, aptitudes, beliefs, values, self-awareness, purpose and more . . . Increasing students', teachers' and other people's awareness of these connections strengthens the process of learning (p. 21).

3   Learning is driven by vision: 'Lifelong learning . . . is the fundamental means by which people engage with life and create their desired futures . . . Improving the numbers and providing safe learning spaces are legitimate goals, but they can't replace the power of a larger vision, personal and shared, as the driving force behind improving schools' (p. 22).

The three extracts powerfully reinforce the notion of culture as the product of individual and organisational learning. The relationship is symbiotic – each is diminished by the absence of the other. Effective schools are created by effective people, improving schools are created by improving people and learning cultures are created by people learning.

Cultures are created and sustained partly by intentions but more significantly through the significance that can be derived from language and rituals; the status accorded to professional learning will be a major determinant of the value placed on it and, so, its contribution to a school's culture. Clues as to the existence of a performance culture based on learning might be found in:

● references in the school's aims to the learning of adults;

● reference to learning and teaching and knowledge rather than curriculum;

● job descriptions which refer to the right and responsibility to learn and support the learning of others;

● reference to professional learning rather than training;

● the celebration of the successful learning of all adults – whether an MBA in School Leadership or a Food Handling Certificate.

Motivation

Motivation is the glue that binds all the previous elements together. Central to enhancing the potential for high performance in a school is the creation of a culture that supports and reinforces the motivations of the individual to achieve and sustain high performance. It is in this area that some of the greatest myths about performance management are promulgated. The relationship between performance and reward is a complicated one and is not amenable to simplistic bureaucratic strategies. Nothing is so beguiling to policy makers and administrators as to find a 'one size fits all solution' to the problem of motivating the individual working in a complex organisation.

The policy-driven approach to motivation has generally been to pay lip-service to the affective dimension of performance but to put all the resources into the formal dimension. Thus performance related pay, or a variant, has become the norm based on a simplistic model relating reward to outcomes and by a negative corollary not rewarding those who fail to achieve specified levels of performance. This approach raises all sorts of issues and tensions:

1 In assuming that performance can be measured by quantifiable outcomes it automatically operates within instrumental and reductionist outcomes (that which can be measured).

2 It also assumes it is possible to isolate (to the exclusion of all other variables) the contribution of one individual.

3 There is a fundamental assumption that financial recognition actually motivates.

4 It has to be accepted that those who set targets, and then judge the extent to which they have been achieved, are both capable and credible.

5 The criteria on which judgements are based, and the means by which performance is assessed against those criteria, have to be perceived as valid and reliable.

In practical terms these issues produce many anomalies – recognition for the teacher in the special school classroom but not for the other adults providing care and support, recognition for the A-level teacher but not for those who taught the students before Year 12 etc. In a profession that is systemically underpaid any sort of financial reward is welcome, but the cost is often too high, especially in a context of public accountability that only recognises and rewards achievement within a narrow and contrived definition of educational outcomes.

It is a truism to state that financial recognition may produce short-term gratification but is not appropriate to creating a culture of sustainable and authentic performance. Sergiovanni (1992: 57) encapsulates the problem by distinguishing between three motivational rules:

1 What gets rewarded gets done.
2 What is rewarding gets done.
3 What is good gets done.

In terms of motivation the three levels can be classified as extrinsic, intrinsic and moral. The extrinsic is not sustainable; it is in the intrinsic and the moral that the authentic motivators of educators are to be found:

> *The evidence seems clear: self-interest is not powerful enough to account fully for human motivation. We are also driven by what we believe is right and good, by how we feel about things, and by the norms that emerge from our connections with other people; we are driven . . . by morality, emotions and social bonds.*

(Ibid.: 23)

What emerges from this discussion is the imperative to create a culture which, while recognising the external reality of accountability and performance management systems, creates value in the intangibles such as recognition, achievement, engagement, autonomy, growth, learning, fulfilment and engagement with the higher-order purposes of education and teaching children and colleagues.

The external, constraining, imperatives are very powerful and they can create an instrumental and reductionist culture. However, there is clear evidence in the case studies in Part Two of other factors, notably moral purpose, retaining high significance. Motivation will always be a complex and contingent topic – many will work to excellent effect for financial reward and status. However, the issue remains – to what extent in education can the end justify the means? Simplistic outcome–reward models of performance management do work, but in simple systems which create a culture of competition, individualism and short-termism. Such a model cannot be justified in an education setting. Models of motivation both create and reflect culture – in schools, surely, performance should enhance collaboration, community and the pursuit of long-term, higher-order values.

Conclusion

It is difficult to try and summarise the essential characteristics of a culture that creates, sustains and facilitates high performance. However, certain generic propositions may be derived from this chapter. A high performance culture is:

- created and developed by the school;
- firmly rooted in values;
- expressed through shared language;
- reinforced by sophisticated social relationships;

25

- enhanced by collaborative learning;
- sustained by intrinsic and moral motivation.

These six propositions are directly related to the quality of leadership. In fact, they could be descriptions of some of the key qualities of leaders. There is an absolute correlation between sustained, authentic high performance and leadership. Performance management will undoubtedly provide the formal infrastructure that ensures targets are achieved and outcomes delivered. However, leadership is fundamental to achieving performance that will endure in all aspects of school life.

Leadership is one of the pivotal determinants of organisational culture; in Deal and Kennedy's (1999: 211) terms.

> *Culture is about embracing deeply held beliefs about what it takes to succeed and excel. Strongly held and consistently practised beliefs give culture its power to raise human expectations and performance to truly extraordinary levels. . . [Those who seek] to recapture superior performance must hold strong beliefs themselves and be willing to stand up for cherished values. It takes leadership to believe in something passionately enough to inspire others.*

Leadership behaviour is one of the most powerful agencies in changing a school's culture and then sustaining that change. Culture is a content-free concept – the nature of the culture of a school has to be decided and created. An emphasis on performance management will create a culture of conformity and compliance; leadership for high performance will foster the creation of a totally different culture, one focused on values, relationships and the core purpose of educating young people rather than schooling them efficiently.

References

Cooper, R. and Sawat, A. (1997) *Executive E.Q.* London: Orion.

Deal, T. and Kennedy, A. (1999) *The New Corporate Cultures.* London: Orion.

Goleman, D. (1998) *Working with Emotional Intelligence.* London: Orion.

Mortimore, P., Sammons, P., Stoll, L., Lewis, D. and Ecob, R. (1988) *School Matters: The Junior Years.* Wells: Open Books.

Senge, P. (1990) *The Fifth Discipline.* London: Century.

Senge, P., Cambron-McCabe, N., Lucas, T., Smith, B., Dutton, J. and Kleiner, J. (2000) *Schools that Learn.* London: Nicholas Brearley.

Sergiovanni, T. (1992) *Moral Leadership.* San Francisco: Jossey-Bass.

Visscher, A.J. (1999) *Managing Schools towards High Performance.* Lisse: Swets and Zeitlinger.

3
■ ■ ■

Developing School-Based Performance Criteria

Derek Bowden

Introduction

Any job or role within a school (or indeed any organisation) can be taken through a process of clarification with the aim of producing a number (maximum ten) of short statements which describe doing it well. The description is of the whole job, core and space. Our experience of working this process through with schools is that it:

- recognises the unique nature of the particular school;
- enables the school to develop its own language of quality through a rigorous examination of meanings;
- celebrates the variety of teaching approaches and styles that facilitate quality outcomes;
- uses the statements as a springboard for dialogue about performance rather than a static defined standard to be measured against.

In so doing, the process addresses the main objections to sets of standards, which are identified in earlier sections of this book. It also meets the need, argued by Peterson (2000: 5), for an effective performance management process to be owned by the teachers.

Make evaluation a task managed by a teacher and not a thing done to a worker.

He comments on experience of teachers in the USA:

Current practice is more something done to workers, rather than something done by professionals.

(ibid.)

Creating a job/role clarification statement

An example is given below. It was produced by the teaching staff of an urban Catholic infants school. It is not offered as some model of excellence but as a real working document designed to be used by colleagues for discussing the quality of the work at their school.

1 Implement and foster a Catholic ethos in accordance with the school Mission Statement.

2 Plan, deliver and assess all subjects of the National Curriculum in a way which allows each child to develop to the full, the whole range of his/her talents.

3 Provide a safe physical environment with adequate freedom to foster confidence and skills to work with a range of materials and resources.

4 Create an emotionally secure atmosphere, conducive to learning, that meets the needs of individuals and builds the self-esteem of each child.

5 Create an attractive, stimulating environment including displays which value and celebrate our children's work.

6 Provide and maintain good quality resources, easily accessible to the children, encouraging care in their use and storage.

7 Develop relationship with colleagues, support and advisory staff and work with colleges and local agencies to supervise and train students as necessary.

8 Foster a relationship with parents, enabling parents and school to act in unison for the benefit of the child. To implement statutory reporting requirements in a way which secures appropriate action.

9 Be active and reflective on any steps needed to further his/her professional development in a way which leaves a space for one's own life and family.

Stage 1. The staff working in groups of three, with the Head in one of the groups, were asked to identify the key tasks of a teacher in the school. The maximum was set at ten so that the final product would fit on a side of A4 paper and be a realistic tool.

Stage 2. Each group of three came up with bullet points which were then displayed to the other groups and discussed in plenary until the final nine were agreed. They would have been something like:

● Catholic ethos;

● National Curriculum;

● physical classroom;

● children's needs;

● display;

● resources;

- colleagues and other professionals;
- parents;
- self.

The staff then 'tested' the nine bullets to ensure that every aspect of their job could be located in one of them.

Stage 3. The key task bullets were divided between the working groups by a process of barter and negotiation. Now the groups were asked to expand each bullet into a statement which described:

- the task;
- the purpose or outcome;
- quality or success indicator(s).

In writing the task, the verb used is critical. There is a world of difference between creating or maintaining, providing or developing, fostering or ensuring and so on.

Draft statements were then considered by the whole staff for question, challenge and refinement until there was general agreement on the wording of the nine items. This process took several hours of hard discussion, argument and (essentially) humour. During this robust professional debate values, aspirations, anxieties, frustration and, most importantly, personal visions of the job were brought out, explored and tested. It was at this stage that a staff language was developed in the specific context of that school.

Work was still needed to tidy up the style and system but the heart of the working document was in place.

Use of the statement

We have experience of supporting this process in a number of schools of varying types and sizes. With a larger school, the organisation is more complex with, probably, the need to consider separate subject areas but the principles, working in trios and then plenary consensus apply. Various roles can be tackled including new teaching staff and governors. The process has been used by bank employees, a group of clergy and a medical practice. It takes time, at least half a day, and needs careful organisation, preparation and presentation.

The completed set of statements can be put to governors for approval (or, even better, have some governors involved in the process; a more powerful way of getting on wavelength than the usual induction courses). If the school is really into partnership, the statements can be sent to parents. An interesting topic to liven up the annual parents' meeting would be the writing of a set of statements for good parenting.

They can also be used as part of the staff recruitment and selection process. Professional discussion based on the statement can offer more insight than the typical formal interview where structure and protocol prevent deep exploration between candidate and school.

The statements should be revisited annually and, if necessary, revised so that all current staff have a sense of ownership.

The main use, however, for the purpose of this chapter, is as a tool for managing performance. The brevity of each statement within the set and the fact that is was written by the people using it provides a bridge for entering the previous 'no-go' area. That area is, of course, critical dialogue about what people are doing in their classroom and around the school. We must also remember that 'critical' feedback includes the giving and receiving of positive comments.

As an illustration of the power of the model we can refer back to the example job classification. The fourth item includes the phrase 'conducive to learning' because the teachers recognised that in meeting the needs of children from a deprived background they might concentrate on nurture at the expense of challenge. The sixth item tackles the issue of resources which are beautifully maintained, because they are so difficult to access they are rarely used. The ninth one gives the teachers a better chance of avoiding the distress caused when good results are obtained but at the expense of the quality of the teacher's personal life – a sacrifice increasingly common in the league-table mentality of the education system today.

Summary

The purpose of this chapter is to describe a process which works and which offers schools a way of 'managing performance' within the requirements of current legislation and the constraints of historical and cultural barriers. For brevity, the illustration focuses on the role of a classroom teacher in an infants school but the process can be applied in any organisational context to any role within it. For us, a key benefit of using this approach to performance management is that it recognises the professionalism of everyone involved and allows people to retain their confidence and dignity. We see the job clarification process being entirely consistent with the model of the effective leadership identified by Harris, Day and Hadfield (2000: 21) reporting research on the characteristics of leadership in 12 primary, secondary and special schools regarded as successful by heads, staff, parents, governors and students:

> In their schools people were trusted to work as autonomous, accountable professionals; there was a *strong emphasis upon teamwork and the achievement of agreed standards and participation in decision making* emphasis added.

References

Harris, A., Day, C. and Hadfield, M. (2000) 'Effective leadership – challenging the orthodoxy', *Management in Education*, 14 (2), 19–21.

Peterson, K.D. (2000) *Teacher Evaluation*, Thousand Oaks, CA: Corwin Press.

4

Target Setting: Science or Fiction?

Peter Brereton

Introduction

In discussing with a recently retired headteacher how I intended to approach this chapter, he commented, 'Teaching is an art and not a science, you cannot teach by numbers'. The same principle and practice, I suspect, is also true for target setting; to a point it can be regarded as a science, especially when setting targets that have clearly measurable outputs in a given time span. However if we were only to set targets in those areas that are easily measurable and not target other areas of importance, then education would be very myopic indeed.

So what are we talking about?

It was with some trepidation and humility that I approached the writing of such a chapter. In the past, why has 'target setting' been 'less than popular' with teachers and managers? It is clear to me, having worked with schools on target setting and action plans for Investors in People for many years, that many have approached the area with some reluctance and a certain cynicism. For some it has been a distraction from teaching; having to commit to paper what they did naturally anyway. It has been a bit like medicine, we know it is not pleasant to take but we also know that in the longer term it can do us 'good'. This drive from our emotional intelligence might be enough to get most to the starting gate but I doubt it will give us the momentum to reach the finishing line. Target setting is still perceived by some as a mechanism for piling more work on already laden professionals, but I hope to demonstrate that it could also work in reverse; by allowing individuals to target what is important. On reflection, my more recent experience in business has crystallised the need to pay special attention to 'winning hearts and minds' for the long-term process of target setting rather than getting bogged down in the debates around paperwork and implementation issues. We rarely make a conscious choice to undertake any activity without an outcome in mind. The intended outcome requires conceptualisation and forethought and the 'mileposts' which relate to it on the journey all need planning. We also need to commit to the process. If your ambition is to be more healthy, then a milestone may be to get fit or drink less alcohol. To get fit, you join a gym, arrange a fitness assessment and plan a fitness programme. If you merely talk of getting fit and cutting down the drink then it is not a target, just a diversion.

The process of target setting takes us 'out of our box', it touches people's values and attitudes and opens us up to close professional scrutiny as well as being a challenging process to accomplish fully. Like any systematic and scientific practice it requires research, the gathering of information and data, discussion, agreement, honesty, enthusiasm and a willingness for the process, the perception of the potential benefits and, crucially, quality time. It requires whole school policies and systems of monitoring and evaluation to recognise, review and measure the effectiveness of the outcomes. If all the components of target setting are not present, then it can become just another exercise, it will be denigrated, sidelined and doomed to failure. For some individuals the perception is that target setting is the first brick in the wall of competency procedures. The implication is that if targets are set they will be measured. If schools are not prepared to tackle the contentious issue of teacher and management underperformance then they should not set targets.

A perception of target setting amongst many teachers is the imposition of even more bureaucracy and paperwork to demonstrate competency. Many in the profession, and outside, firmly believe in the underlying principle that the output of schoolteachers, that is, the education of their pupils, is multidimensional, not easy to measure and dependent upon a plethora of external and imperceptible influences. Teachers will resent being held professionally accountable for targets that are at the mercy of so many variables beyond their control. It is also interesting to reflect that in business the same external influences can affect achievement of targets. I found that the best way to manage these external influences was not to pretend otherwise, but to recognise this inevitability 'up front' and to identify what potential outcomes these influences may have. The over-riding issue is the ongoing dialogue of review and target setting.

At the same time, it is widely recognised in the profession that through educational processes like records of achievement and individual education plans for pupils with special learning needs, there are distinct benefits for children's learning; it is a truism, but if you do not know where you are going, then do not be surprised if you do not get there. So, if the processes of time management, prioritisation and target setting for pupils push them towards a more organised and systematic approach to lifelong learning and are deemed to be valuable for them, then perhaps it really is time to 'walk the talk' and embrace target setting.

Clearly all the evidence points to the fact that school improvement does not just happen in a vacuum, it needs to be planned for carefully. Performance management will help schools to improve by supporting and improving teachers' work. For this first time ever, it provides a framework for both teachers and the team leader to agree and review priorities and targets within the framework of the school's development plans. Monitoring progress towards the achievement of objectives is a key part of the performance management cycle. Therefore, setting targets is at the very heart of the process and is crucial if the process is to operate effectively with the least disruption to the core task of teaching. The trick in setting and agreeing targets is to create a positive and purposeful learning experience. For some time the process has been happening in a great many successful schools, so how is performance management influencing this?

'Objective setting' and performance management

First, the terminology has changed: the *Performance Management Framework* no longer refers to 'target setting', being replaced by 'objective setting'. 'Semantics' some may say, but I believe the difference, albeit subtle, is key to achieving a pragmatic solution for busy professionals.

Targets	Objectives
Specific	Clear
Measurable	Concise
Achievable	Measurable
Realistic	Challenging
Time related	Flexible

Within the *Performance Management Framework* this process is exclusively referred to as 'objective setting'. I really cannot see any difference in the process from 'target setting', but the latter is usually now referred to in the process of whole-school targets. Having spent half my working life in schools and the other half in business, it appears to me that the term 'objective setting' has a somewhat 'softer' edge. Targets are more commonly associated with overarching, hard-edged business objectives, for example sales or market growth targets, and are considered either 'hit' or 'missed'. On the other hand while objectives are orientated towards both process and results and still demand measurement, they have a somewhat more qualitative aspirational notion and leave open the period for achievement. The *Performance Management Framework* illustrates this perception in these two respects:

> *Teachers should never be discouraged from setting challenging objectives which are not quite met, or not met for reasons outside the teachers' control . . . furthermore . . . a teacher who has not quite achieved challenging objectives may have contributed as much as, or even more than, a teacher who has met less challenging objectives in full.*

This appears to be illustrated by the subtle change in definition. The reader will be familiar with the SMART acronym in relation to target setting (I can hear from here the collective staffroom groan at this business training import) but you will recall that the 'T' relates to the need to have targets time-related. For example, Class 7 will achieve 95 per cent punctuality for morning registration by Christmas, is a SMART target. It meets all the criteria but clearly has a very specific timescale.

In contrast, when setting performance management objectives they need to be:

- clear;
- concise;
- measurable;
- challenging;
- flexible

with the caveat that they should also be 'challenging but realistically achievable'. So, has the need to time limit the objective gone, and what is the meaning of 'flexible'?

The *Performance Management Framework* guidance for objective setting for teachers links their current job requirements, their career aspirations and the school's priorities. This in itself may present quite a considerable challenge. The timescale for each of these will be different, school development priorities may have both annual and longer timescales, current job requirements may be on an academic year basis and career aspirations could have a much longer-term focus. The key here is that objectives will have to be measurable and, therefore, they need to be clear and concise. At some point, they have to be measured. The review cycle process will therefore dictate this review and assessment point. The appraisal process and review cycle will be annual and, therefore, if the objectives are longer term, they will also need to have key milestones with which to monitor progress.

For example, a pupil progress objective may be:

> *By next year to increase the percentage to (45–50 per cent) of the class as a whole that will be able to do all of what the Numeracy Framework states that they should be taught over the year (currently 40 per cent).*

How will you know if this objective is on course for achievement at the next review meeting in February? If objectives span more than one year it would be helpful to identify milestones to assess progress at the performance review.

However, some objectives might coincide with the review cycle, for example this professional practice objective:

> *By the end of the review cycle to have completed the training for a positive reward scheme for good attendance, and disseminated the information and knowledge to colleagues, so that the new system is in place for all pupils from 2001.*

Flexibility is the key. Objectives should be *flexible* as they may need to be amended or even replaced during the year. The reader will notice from these two examples that these objectives have not itemised every activity, but have merely picked out the main expectation and yardsticks. There is an amount of work still to do to create an action plan to deliver these objectives. When an objective becomes redundant or is superseded by circumstances, then the teacher and the team leader will need to review the situation and the action plan.

For example, in a particular class, some children with very challenging behaviour, were giving the teacher particular problems. The teacher had agreed objectives referring to professional development and classroom management strategies together with techniques to minimise disruption and maximise the teaching and on-task times. During the course of the year the school implemented a withdrawal unit and one of the most challenging pupils was permanently excluded. The conditions with which the teacher was faced changed almost overnight and, as discipline was not now the primary focus, new targets on providing a broader range of teaching and learning strategies to cater for some of the more gifted and talented pupils were implemented.

Nowhere is this more relevant than in those schools catering for pupils with severe or complex learning difficulties. In such schools, the objectives will probably fluctuate widely. If we accept this premise at the outset, and build into the monitoring process a mechanism of regular sampling in order to ascertain the current impact and progress of the objectives, then given the very challenging nature of such schools, we should still be able to provide a focus for action.

The over-riding purpose of objectives is not to make comparisons with the performance of others, but to develop the mindset that when we have an outcome in mind, we can act in ways which will impact on the realisation of that outcome.

The nature of objectives

It is important to recall from the *Performance Management Framework* that objectives should:

- cover pupil progress and professional development;
- emerge from the team leader/teacher discussions;
- have scope appropriate to the teachers' responsibilities;
- be clear and precise to allow measurement;
- be based on knowledge of prior attainment of pupils;
- relate to particular ways teachers can help their pupils.

Schools are already very familiar and practised with target setting related to the attainment of pupils. Objectives used in industry, as I mentioned earlier, are usually a combination of results and processes. Therefore, in education, it would be difficult to argue that pupil achievement should have no place in the consideration of the effectiveness of teaching and learning. The danger lies in just considering test and examination data as the only source of evidence and excluding the use of other indicators. These 'other indicators' may be comparative or normative and may take account of improvement against similar pupil cohorts elsewhere, or the value added in year-on-year test and examination performance, rather than absolute results. Indeed the Department for Education and Employment's (DfEE's). *Performance Management Framework* does frequently use the term 'pupil progress', which can be interpreted in this way. Such indicators do not have to be confined to academic performance. Many other issues are monitored in schools, for example, those relating to behaviour, key skills and unauthorised absence:

Pupil Progress Target

> *By the end of Year 5, increase from 60 per cent to 75 per cent the number of pupils who can swim unaided 25 metres and ensure that all physically able pupils can swim, unaided by floats, one width of the swimming pool.*

Objective setting is a bit like flying a plane; there are two critical and probably 'stressful' points for both the aircrew and passengers, one at take off and the other at landing. However the analogy stops there, as the nature of the objectives will emerge from the discussions between team leader and teacher with the school circumstances varying enormously. Performance reviews are not an isolated activity, but link to other aspects of performance management including the day-to-day role of giving feedback, coaching, reviewing and modifying objectives during the year. Team leaders or line managers need to have the understanding, knowledge and skills to review progress effectively, agree meaningful and challenging objectives, and give feedback on performance. The emphasis is on management style and interpersonal skills rather than the mechanics of the scheme. Another aeronautical analogy may help illustrate the need for the development of managers and team leaders involved in this process: when the oxygen masks drop from the ceiling of the plane you are instructed to place it on yourself first and only then your children, the rationale being that without 'oxygen' you will be unable to help those in your 'care'.

If there are doubts about whether a teacher's performance in the classroom can be fairly judged by a 'team leader' whose main contact with them has been outside the classroom, then the individual needs the opportunity to be able to discuss and agree the process and mechanics of the review. In my time in business, working almost exclusively with professional people, the most effective appraisers were those whose training, management style and relationships with their staff were based on observation, questioning and monitoring of outputs rather than expertise in a particular discipline. The further requirement of lesson observation skills, a complex and all too easily subjective area, and the skills of feedback are key in this process. It is easy to underestimate the need for skills training for both the teacher and team leader in this sensitive area, and in particular in objective setting. Authors such as Daniel Goldman, Martin Seligman, Stephen Covey and Peter Senge all argue, in their own ways, that the capacity to conceptualise a positive goal, relate patterns of behaviour to that goal and demonstrate a willingness to move towards that goal in a self-supported way can be correlated to success in life. How we may wish to define success in life is beyond the scope of this chapter, but it is enough to conclude that those people who are most successful professionally set clearer objectives than those who meander through life. This raises the question of whether individuals can develop or rekindle such skills and, to my mind, the answer is undoubtedly 'yes', if motivated to do so. If we are motivated to achieve, we do set clear and challenging objectives and successful people follow through. This is probably the most crucial function of school leadership and the greatest challenge for some.

A health warning

'*Setting* the bloody target doesn't mean I am going to reach it' was the one-liner I overheard in the office which leads me to reinforce some words of caution or 'health warning' for managers and team leaders who have a key role in helping to identify and set the objectives. Challenging or ambitious objectives will require equally strong support. There is little to be gained in agreeing a set of challenging objectives if the team leader or manager cannot commit the support, guidance or time to adequately champion the individual. Failure and frustration will be built in. If the process is perceived by the teacher as a form of management by institutionalised, devolved target management, then the likelihood of a positive reaction is minimal. The objectives, above all, have to be owned by the individual learner. It was clear from the conversation overheard in the office that my friend neither owned the 'target' nor saw herself as a learner! The capacity to achieve the objective must be within the grasp of the individual and if the objective is too abstract, too remote or not within their experience then they will likely not engage.

Objective setting cannot happen in a vacuum; there is a trinity of information sources needed. First, the teacher's job description needs to be an accurate summary of the main responsibilities, roles and competencies necessary for the job. Availability for the task of objective setting is key. If it is, in effect, an indeterminable list of things 'to do' that never gets finished, then its value is very much reduced. Second, the need to have the school's development objectives, and in particular the objectives for the key stage or department, is also central. These can vary in complexity and size but in my experience they need to be concise, relevant and specific. To have the data and information on prior attainment of pupils or comparative statistics is the third core requirement for effective objective setting. For those schools approaching objective setting for the first time, the challenge is to have this management information readily to hand, accurate and up to date, and for it to identify precise performance information to show the achievements of children. The existence of accurate and meaningful job descriptions may be an issue and therefore some schools may need to take stock of the school's assessment criteria. Data collection systems and record keeping can be improved or tailored to support this purpose in future years. As with good teaching, the secret of successful objective setting lies in thorough preparation.

Who has to have objectives and how many?

Under the new appraisal regulations headteachers and teachers must be set objectives that focus their work during the year. For both, it is suggested that there should be no fewer than three objectives and no more than five or six. Objectives are set and agreed at the review meeting at the beginning of the review cycle. However, should the headteacher's objectives come before those of the staff, or should the staff's objectives reflect those of the headteacher? The answer is not straightforward. Take the objective on pupil performance. The only way in which the headteacher's objective on pupil performance can be achieved is through the efforts of the whole staff. Unless staff objectives are in alignment with that of the head's then the 'target' will likely be 'missed'. The leadership objective is not so critical, but in effect it has to support the staff in working towards the school's collective aims. The need, therefore, is to have 'joined up' objectives between management and teachers, each mutually supporting or facilitating the other.

I mentioned previously that teachers need to develop objectives in relation to current job, career aspirations and school priorities. If these alone were accomplished it would result in three objectives. However, life is never that simple and what tends to happen is that the objectives are multidimensional and overlap these discrete areas (Figure 4.1).

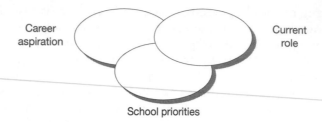

Career aspiration

Current role

School priorities

Figure 4.1: Multidimensional objectives

To illustrate this, consider a school which has identified that the quality of teaching and learning in Key Stage 3 in the afternoon period is being detrimentally influenced by the poor standard of behaviour at lunchtime. Therefore, the head of Year 7, has agreed to take a lead on the following objective:

> *To implement, as part of the school's behaviour policy, a lower school playground management system with the break and lunchtime supervising teachers and support staff, to meet the health and safety requirements and ensure that the pupils comport themselves in an orderly and courteous way in preparation for lessons after break and lunchtime. It is expected that these new measures will reduce by 50 per cent the numbers of children reported for poor behaviour at break, lunchtime and on entering the school as well as contributing to a conducive atmosphere for effective teaching and learning following these breaks.*

Quite clearly, this example of major system implementation, for this teacher, complements their current job as head of year. Further, it develops their experience in designing and implementing a new playground management system, gives an opportunity to demonstrate team-building skills with other teachers beyond the year group and support staff (preparation for senior teacher role) and links directly to a whole school priority of behavioural management. In fact, it fits all three circles in Figure 4.1.

This multifaceted example also throws into sharp contrast the sheer size and scope of a potential objective; when does an objective become a major project? This also revisits the question of how many objectives an individual can competently tackle; there can be no hard or fast rule about this and clearly the judgement of the headteacher, in reviewing the agreed objectives in the performance review cycle, must equalise the balance of responsibilities for individuals across the whole school.

Giving enough focus and time to each target, in order to stand a good chance of achieving success, is motivational; to underachieve or not achieve in especially challenging objectives can be demotivational and even lead to dysfunctional teachers and managers.

Objective setting is a journey that will never end because, no matter how effective the teacher, department or school, they can always improve. Improvement may be more dramatic when starting from a low base, yet reach a point when only fine-tuning as opposed to a major overhaul is required.

Who sets the objectives and what should they cover?

It is crucial that the teacher or manager is encouraged to construct his or her own objectives. The *Performance Management Framework* states:

> for the headteacher a small group of appointed governors, with the advice and support of an external assessor, is responsible for setting the objectives and for monitoring progress towards their achievement. At least one objective should relate to school leadership and management and one to pupil progress. For the teacher, the objectives will be negotiated and agreed by the team leader, appointed by the school, who will also be responsible for monitoring progress towards the objectives. The objectives should cover pupil progress and professional practice.

The crucial element here is who 'owns' these objectives rather than who 'sets' them. The team leader clearly has a role to focus discussions and ensure the objectives are concurrent with the job role and aligned with the school development priorities. Teachers have rightly pointed out that it is very difficult to disentangle an individual's contribution within a team and, since teaching is very much about teamwork and co-operative effort, performance management could potentially reduce co-operation between teachers. I believe the opposite will happen. In order to achieve objectives teachers will need to draw even more heavily upon the team and enlist the help, support, encouragement, coaching, professional development and championing from the line manager or team leader. This raises the whole issue of the changing nature and role of the middle manager in schools. Huge expectations and increasing demands can have a negative effect on these increasingly influential people, and they, like all within the school environment, need effective support to enable them to operate efficiently.

So what makes a not-so-good objective?

Let us consider the following teacher objectives for pupil progress.

Example 1

For the teacher of a Year 6 class, based upon the information on prior attainment of the class (27 children) in the optional Year 5 Standard Assessment Tasks, where 30 per cent of pupils performed significantly above average:

Objective: Therefore the proportion of pupils reaching level 5 in the national tests in Mathematics at 11 will be at least 35 per cent.

This objective meets most of the criteria, it is clear, concise and very measurable. However, it is not sufficiently challenging as the improvement in pupil performance only extends to approximately two pupils when prior attainment is taken into account.

Example 2

For a teacher in the Reception class, based upon information drawn from baseline and continuing assessment in the nursery where a large proportion of pupils show very limited personal and social development:

Objective: The pupils will show significant improvement in their social skills and will develop a sense of personal responsibility.

Here again the objective meets most of the criteria. It is clear, concise and challenging but lacks measurability. It fails to set out any criteria (such as Early Learning Goals) against which the children's progress could be assessed.

Let us now consider some example objectives focusing upon professional practice.

Example 3

For a Key Stage 3 teacher who is keen to extend their use of information and communications technology (ICT) in modern languages as well as develop their own skills:

Objective: To attend the local authority ICT course for modern linguists in using the Internet for language development and e-mail friends abroad.

This objective is clear and concise and can be measured by way of attendance on the course. However, there is insufficient attention to the impact of the training in raising the teacher's skills or ability to use the knowledge effectively in school. Consequently, there is not enough challenge built into the objective.

Example 4

For a Key Stage 4 teacher (Year 10) in a school whose recent Office for Standards in Education (Ofsted) report confirmed the school's own view that high attainers were not being challenged in mathematics:

Objective: To make a contribution through more effective teaching to raise, by 10 per cent, the proportion of pupils who attain grade C and above in two years' time in GCSE examinations.

This objective, while being concise and clear in terms of the final measurable outcome, has two inherent problems.

First, the 'contribution' which the teacher is expected to make is not described with any clarity. This might seem a contradiction as the *Performance Management Framework* states, 'agreeing objectives does not mean itemising every activity but picking out key expectations and yardsticks'. However, it is advisable to focus on precisely which aspects need developing in the teaching of mathematics to higher attainers.

Second, the Year 10 teacher will not be the only member of staff who influences the outcome, so it will be difficult to attribute the extent of the teacher's input in raising standards.

The examples reinforce the need for teachers and managers to think long and hard about the objectives being set, to set aside time to discuss and agree the wording, and even reflect upon the objectives before confirming the final text.

The reader may recall the system in the former Soviet Union of quota setting within a seven-year economic plan. If, after four or five years of the cycle, the targets were in any danger of being reached, the bureaucrats would 'back off' and 'soft pedal', aware that if the target were met too easily or too early then the next seven-year plan would set even more stretching quotas. Getting the balance right is more a question of good judgement than a scientific principle. To saddle the unsuspecting individual with additional objectives because of outstanding progress could also be demotivating.

I support the notion that objectives have to be rationed. The *Performance Management Framework* states a minimum of three and maximum of five or six. This implies that objectives need to be few in number focused on school priority areas and of significant value to the individual teacher.

It was a US Secretary of State who said, 'We should make the important measurable, not make the measurable important'. This is a salutary observation in relation to objective setting. For example, does this objective merit a specific description?

> *By the end of Year 5, ensure that all children have developed the skills necessary to log on to the Internet and send and receive e-mail.*

This is not to imply that ICT skills in the use of the Internet are not valuable, but are they really important enough to merit a discrete objective in this way? Are there more pressing and core objectives that may merit a higher priority than this? Is there an alternative strategy of achieving this objective or could it be encompassed within a broader objective in ICT and literacy?

It is an issue laden with values and judgements but the general rule of thumb is one of 'significant importance'.

So what does an effective objective look like?

Following a self-review process in the science faculty, the objective for a member of the science staff with responsibility for physics is as follows:

> To increase the number of students achieving A*–C grades from 86 per cent to 90 per cent in line with students' prior progress in this subject. Strategies will be undertaken which increase the skill set to be developed, extension activities to be undertaken, additional resources required and the focus of external experiences (visit to science and industry museum). In particular homework completion checking and coursework monitoring will be key indicators.

I will simply leave the reader to review this against the specifications for setting objectives and reflect upon its status.

I stated at the start of this chapter that objective setting has the potential to reduce teacher stress and this was vividly illustrated for me when a female headteacher described her job as 'multitasking on the run'. She was making the typical comparison between the way in which male and female brains work, the female having a greater capacity for 'parallel processing'. Irrespective of the neurological or gender basis for this statement, it did ring a note of truth in respect of objective setting for people who are already very busy.

Objectives could revolve around the process of reducing this form of stress that will lead to 'burn out' if left unchecked. It is important that objective setting needs to be a tool for management and teachers to focus more clearly on the important things, teaching and learning, and in effect relegate the peripheral areas of work. Targeting fewer objectives, but in sufficient depth and clarity, may assist busy colleagues cope more easily with what appears to the external observer to be an ever increasing workload and differing priorities.

A real danger here is in giving specific examples; it is for the reader to examine the context of these examples and extract the generic attributes in order to help them conceptualise the desired outcomes.

Goals agreed, targets made, objectives set, so now what?

Objectives in large measure still aspirational, mainly expectations, with some yardsticks. As we have said, objectives without related task are merely a diversion. There is now the imperative to commit them to paper, add some detail and identify strategies, tactics or new approaches to deliver the desired outcomes. There is little new in schools and education in this respect; the real issue is finding the most appropriate, pragmatic, tried and tested strategies that work for pupils and do not reinvent 'school improvement wheels'.

There is little point in setting objectives if no one knows about them! Clearly, the process will have been discussed and agreed with the team leader who will be crucial in supporting the learner achieve the outcomes, but there are others who should also know about them.

One would argue that other team members should be aware, not in order to compare with their own objectives, but to be able to contribute tried, tested and successful strategies that they may have used in the past and also to understand the direction taken by others within their team. After all, once individuals in a team know which way they are collectively heading it would be ridiculous to find everyone aligned in a different direction!

Where objectives relate to pupil progress there is little value in setting them if pupils have no idea what they are. Obviously, the older your pupils, the more sophisticated your sharing of information will be. Year 11 pupils on the C/D borderline will need to know that performance in the GCSE assessment in a subject area is part of someone else's target as well as their own. The impact this can have may be dramatic; to understand that the teacher really does care, has strategies to help them along the way and knows their destination all contribute to raising pupils' esteem and aspirations. Even for younger children in primary school, who are familiar with the layout of the National Curriculum and understand the levels they are aiming to achieve in the Key Stage 2 standard assessment tasks (SATs), there is evidence that they are much more composed and show less anxiety about testing than their counterparts who do not share such knowledge.

So, we have in place the process of setting objectives, working towards those objectives, measuring progress, reviewing the progress and creating a positive climate in which reflection is encouraged on all elements of the learning cycle. But there is still something missing. Children's learning should be permeated with encouragement, praise, reward and celebration. As adults our capacity and motivation to celebrate our achievements seems to diminish: 'Work hard and play hard' was a phrase that I heard more than once in my years in business. A clear difference between the cultures of school and business was the latter's keener focus on celebrating success. However, on hearing that the headteacher was going to announce to the staff after school the outcome of the 'threshold review', a teacher in one staffroom suggested that they might be 'down the pub'. A colleague asked if the member of staff was a bit presumptuous in assuming that he had 'passed' the 'threshold'. 'Not at all, I'm going to be celebrating with those who have!'

Full marks to the teacher! Let's make the time and the effort to recognise team and personal successes and celebrate them.

5
■ ■ ■

Skills for Performance Management

Ingrid Bradbury

Introduction

Performance management is about recognising achievement as well as areas for development. It should be supportive as opposed to pejorative. If teachers do not understand the process and the rationale for performance management it becomes a 'sledgehammer to crack a nut' rather than a positive experience. It is about enhancing performance, celebrating that which is good and excellent, and ensuring that teachers are able to develop skills where necessary. It is about making judgements, but only as part of a developmental process, where time is given for discussion, reflection, target setting and support. The majority of teachers, until the introduction of appraisal and inspection in the early 1990s, had not been seen working by other adults except for parents who were helping or classroom assistants who were working with individual pupils. Initially appraisal was seen as threatening, and the coming of the Ofsted inspector was perceived as even more challenging. Suddenly, teachers were watched, judged and so anxious about their performance. Often those observing were new to the role, unsure of the task, anxious about observing colleagues and making judgements.

Teachers are now under additional scrutiny including threshold assessment, the introduction of performance management for headteachers and teachers with targets being set for all, inspections by the school's LEA to monitor quality in schools and the continuance of the regular Ofsted inspections. Performance management and the imperative for focused targets to be in place may cause anxiety and additional pressure rather than being seen as a positive force for improvement.

There is an obligation on headteachers and senior staff in schools to evaluate how teachers teach, how the curriculum is taught and to appraise the learning environment. Sergiovanni (1995: 215) argues that the issues surrounding evaluation are about a wider conception of the process:

> *Broader conceptions of evaluation include describing what is going on in a particular classroom, discovering learning outcomes actually achieved, and assessing their worth. In broader conceptions, the focus of evaluation is less on measuring and more on describing and illuminating teaching and learning events, as well as on identifying the array of meanings that these events have for different people. Evaluation broadly conceived involves* judgment *more than measurement . . . Using the word* evaluation *in its ordinary, rather than technical, sense will also help dissipate its negative effects among teachers* (original emphases).

The aims and purposes of the process of performance management are to:

- improve the quality of education provided by those who work in the school, through regular professional evaluation and positive, professional discussion about learning and teaching;
- evaluate the teacher's needs in terms of professional development;
- raise the standards of achievement and sustain or improve the progress made by the pupils;
- obtain evidence and information to inform school improvement planning and to monitor the progress of the school's strategic intent;
- gather information about the implementation of Curriculum 2000 and ensure progression through the schemes of work.

All staff need to understand these aims and purposes and to recognise that they encompass whole-school issues as well as personal and professional developmental outcomes.

This chapter will examine the following topics:

- understanding the process and the use of evidence;
- classroom observations – skills and approaches;
- giving and receiving feedback;
- target setting;
- training for observation skills.

Understanding the process and the use of evidence

It is necessary for both those who are to carry out performance management and those who are to be managed to have a shared understanding about the process and the use of evidence collected, not just in the context of recent government legislation about performance management linked to pay but as part of the ongoing evaluation of the whole school and its most valuable resource – the staff. The process needs to be school specific, integral to the school improvement plan, and the development of the process needs to be shared by all stakeholders. Not all senior managers are comfortable with observing, making evaluations and reporting back to other professionals. Nor are teachers used to peer observations and mutual support through coaching. For both groups it can be a threatening process.

Performance management is based on the gathering of evidence to make judgements concerning successes and areas for development within the class-room. Each evaluation needs to have clearly defined foci negotiated for the lesson observations. The type of evidence collected may well focus on:

- teaching and its impact on learning, i.e. each teacher action should have an impact on what the pupils are learning;
- a specified group of pupils, how they learn and what is their preferred learning style;
- monitoring the relationships within a class, not only between teacher and pupils, but also peer relationships;
- monitoring subject specific lesson content, i.e. the head of geography moni-toring teaching and learning within the subject, ensuring breadth and relevance as well as progression across the subject;
- analysing the use of resources, classroom management and effective use of support staff;
- a specific area of the teacher's work that he or she has identified;
- identifying good practice within the school which can be used to help other teachers.

Evidence should be:

- factual and fair;
- in context;
- accurate;
- objective;
- in line with agreed policy.

Classroom observations

Evaluating and monitoring classroom practice ought to be part of the every-day life of the school; it should become a natural, non-threatening activity, that leads to reflective practice by all staff. Pre-observation meetings are very important. These meetings set the tone of the observation or discussion, and should be a time when the focus is agreed and any queries or anxieties are addressed. It is a time to revisit, if necessary, the aims of evaluation and performance management. These may include teaching and learning or may focus on a particular subject area of the curriculum (if the observer is the curriculum co-ordinator evaluating subject content), continuity and the pupils' progress.

Good classroom observation is characterised by:

- *preparation*, i.e. arranging a time with the teacher, knowing what the subjects and age groups are and agreeing the focus;
- *context*, e.g. knowing where the lesson fits into the medium-term planning, or what position it has within a series of lessons (these should be noted on the recording form);
- *time* – staying for a reasonable length of time, at least 40 minutes, although the full period is best so that the introduction and plenary are included;
- *recording* – using an agreed and known format for recording grading;
- *evaluating* the outcome of the observation, i.e. being secure in the records kept and in the judgements, knowing what is acceptable and where there are areas for development.

The observer should use bullet points in the notation, look for evidence and avoid assertions and link what the teacher is actually doing with how it affects the pupils' learning. The observer should look for evidence of the way in which teaching strategies are linked with their effect on the pupils' learning.

It is important to understand what are the indicators of effective teaching and learning as seen in the classroom. Points which can be focused on during observations are, for learning, evidence that the pupils are able to:

- acquire new skills and apply their previously learned skills;
- show an interest in their work and apply effort;
- revisit and demonstrate retention of their knowledge and skills;
- respond at an appropriate level when presented with a task or verbal request;
- explain what they are doing, understand what and how well they have done, and how they can continue to improve.

For teaching, teachers will:

- have clear, shared learning objectives (not aims, but what they want the pupils to learn);
- have high expectations for learning and behaviour;
- show a good understanding of the abilities of the pupils and expect the best from them;
- use the most suitable methods for the learning objectives they are teaching;

- give a suitable time for the task to be achieved;
- match the activities planned for with the needs of the pupils and the learning objectives planned;
- use a variety of methods and resources, depending on the content and context to ensure that pupils understand and learn;
- ensure that the classroom or environment being used is organised for the activity and facilitates learning.

These are elaborated from the *Framework for Inspection* (Ofsted, 1999). I make no apologies for using it as a basis for classroom observations because it is the tool common to all schools, and the benchmark against which we are all judged.

In special schools, particularly where pupils are not attaining at nationally expected levels, it is important that progress against individual education plans (IEPs) is seen as a valid and valuable way of evidencing the progress pupils make over time. During observations of learning and teaching the observer must have access to the information in IEPs in order that the pupils' learning and the teacher's methods are understood. There is also a need to understand in this context that pupils, retention of skills may indicate very good teaching and learning, especially where a child is suffering from a degenerative illness.

The climate for classroom observations needs to be suitable not only for performance management, but a joint learning experience. Watching teachers teach and children learn is one of the greatest privileges of performance management observation and inspection. The issue is not about how the observer would conduct the lesson but how effectively the teacher teaches and creates a good, appropriate learning environment for the pupils. It is quite difficult to begin with when observing, and the great temptation, if it is not a familiar style or method, is to become very critical. Look at the list of effective teaching and learning points and observe in the context of those, not through your own preferred methodology. This can be even harder when the staff are known to the observer. When inspecting or observing it is important to be dispassionate, hopefully without losing compassion.

Feedback

Giving and receiving feedback is a crucial component of the performance management process. It should occur as soon as possible after the observation has taken place, and as soon as time has been taken to reflect on what has been seen.

Effective feedback is:

- a summation of the process to date;
- the basis of effective target setting;

- the key to professional learning;
- a means of enhancing personal and professional relationships.

Giving feedback, even when it is totally positive, is a highly sensitive activity. It requires:

- an appropriate time;
- an appropriate place;
- an appropriate relationship.

Whoever is receiving the feedback will, to a certain extent, feel vulnerable. They know that judgements about their professional skills are being made. For Threshold Assessment, it was very difficult for some teachers to express their strengths, areas for development and indicate evidence available to support their applications, not because they did not meet the requirements, but because as a profession we find it difficult to see what we do in a positive way. The arrival of the external Threshold Assessor often caused more anxiety, especially for those who made up the sample. Therefore, for some teachers regular observations and feedback will be a fraught experience, particularly if it is not part of the culture of the school. Time needs to be set aside and steps need to be taken to ensure that the meeting is undisturbed and that the time and place are agreed before the observations. The place should be as comfortable as possible, with no confrontational seating, i.e. not either side of a desk, and as quiet as possible. The relationship should be appropriate; it is a learning and developmental experience and should be carried out empathetically and professionally. An aggressive, judgemental attitude at this point will create more difficulties than it will solve and make the whole experience negative. It is useful to bear in mind Goleman's (1996: 151) arguement that:

> The emotional vicissitudes at work in marriage also operate in the work-place, here they take similar forms. Criticisms are voiced as personal attacks rather than complaints that can be acted upon; there are ad hominem charges with dollops of disgust, sarcasm, and contempt; both give rise to defensiveness and dodging of responsibility and, finally, to stonewalling or the embittered passive resistance that comes from feeling unfairly treated.

To serve as the basis of target setting and further professional development feedback needs to meet the following criteria:

1 It is derived from clear and shared criteria and a specified focus.
2 The evidence offered is clearly objective and is presented in a factual manner.
3 There is a mutual process of clarification, explanation and confirmation.
4 Conflicting perceptions are negotiated to resolution.
5 There is an emphasis on careful listening, open questioning, clarifying and agreeing conclusions.

One of the most powerful ways to develop professional skills and confidence is through coaching. However, as argued by West-Burnham and O'Sullivan (1998):

> Central to the coaching relationship is the high quality of personal and inter-personal skills and the development of mutual trust, confidence and respect.

(52)

If teachers are to develop professionally and to extend their bank of skills and abilities in the classroom, coaching is a significant process. The needs of the teacher can be discussed at feedback time, ensuring that support is in place for development.

Giving and receiving feedback is an area demanding high emotional intelligence. In his book *Emotional Intelligence*, Goleman (1996: 153) writes about 'The Artful Critique' which 'focuses on what a person has done and can do rather than reading a mark of character into a job poorly done'. He goes on to give advice that comes from Harry Levinson about 'the art of the critique, which is intricately entwined with the art of praise' and makes the points:

1 Be specific.
2 Offer a solution.
3 Be present.
4 Be sensitive.

Operating in this way during feedback needs intrapersonal and interpersonal skills, empathy, social art and understanding of the role of the teacher.

In the final analysis, giving and receiving feedback is a professional interaction which will work if the preparation has been careful and thorough, if there is respect and if the emphasis is on shared understanding to facilitate professional learning and personal effectiveness. Ideally feedback should be in two directions, i.e. mutual and reciprocal.

Target setting

Target setting is the *raison d'être* of performance management. On the basis of observations and feedback it should be possible to agree:

- the current level of performance;
- the desirable level of performance;
- the strategy to move from current level to desired level.

Performance management documentation recommends that targets should be based on professional development, pupils' progress and attainment (i.e. raising standards) and whole-school development. Educational processes do not lend themselves to simplistic reductionist and instrumental outcomes.

Nevertheless, targets are essential to motivation, learning and effective management. Targets therefore need to meet the following criteria. They must be:

- personal to the individual, i.e. specific not generic;
- challenging and demanding but not threatening;
- expressed in terms which are aspirational *and* developmental, i.e. they should refer to specific outcomes;
- set in a realistic timescale and linked, when appropriate, to resources.

For targets to be personal they must be clearly linked to observation and discussion, agreed with the teacher and they must identify what support will be available. For instance, if coaching is to be available to develop aspects of the teacher's practice, it must be clear who will be the coach, when and where they will meet and work together, and what time will be available to them. If teachers are to observe good practitioners in their own or other schools', time needs to be set aside and arrangements need to be made. If teachers are to be exemplars of good practice they need to agree to being observed by others.

Targets that are challenging and demanding also give professional confidence; if they are unrealistic and unsupported they become threatening. Targets that are unrealistic cause teachers to feel threatened and failures; if they have no possibility of achieving the target then what is the purpose of setting it? If the support, resources and time are not going to be made available where appropriate, then the target lacks integrity.

If lessons are taught without specific learning objectives, how can the outcomes be evaluated? If targets are set which are not related to specific outcomes, then what are the success criteria? Targets, while being aspirational and developmental, need to refer to specific outcomes thus enabling an evaluation to be made at the end of the period of time set to achieve them.

Realistic timescales should be set, including time set aside to review the progress of the teachers towards their targets. It would be not only insensitive but also unprofessional to leave a whole year in between discussing the targets and evaluating the outcomes without at least one review. Review is necessary to ensure that:

- the teacher is making progress against the targets;
- there are no problems that are inhibiting progress;
- if the targets have been achieved it maybe necessary to negotiate another target;
- if additional help is needed, i.e. support, time and resources to enable them to continue towards their target, how it can be made available;
- the target is not overwhelming;
- one can celebrate what has been achieved so far.

Target setting in the context of performance management also helps to model good practice in the classroom. Learning and teaching (and improving performance) are enhanced by targets which are **SPECIAL,** i.e. Specific, Personal, Energising, Challenging, Integrative, (in) Alignment and (focused on) Learning.

Training for observation

If teachers are going to be observed as part of performance management, training needs to be given to the observers so that the process is of high quality. One of the criticisms that comes out regularly from inspections is that monitoring and evaluation are not carried out consistently, especially by subject co-ordinators and particularly in primary and special schools. The opportunities for monitoring and evaluating may be limited, but there is also the issue of middle managers having the training and the skills to carry out this role. It may also be an issue for teachers in their first post as a deputy or headteacher. If the skills are not taught, how can they be expected to carry out the role successfully? There are several ways to tackle this problem and develop the skills needed, for example:

- paired observations;
- use of video for training;
- reflective discussion about a lesson observed.

In paired observations it is important that the teacher being observed understands the purpose of the exercise, i.e. for one of the observers to learn how to observe and record the lesson, not to make any specific evaluation about the teacher. As with the whole process of performance management, it needs to be negotiated with the teacher concerned. The pair who are to be observing need to discuss and clarify exactly what is to be looked for and recorded. It is simpler to focus on just one or two aspects of the lesson rather than the Ofsted model of four, and the most appropriate foci in this situation are teaching and learning. The Ofsted *Framework for Inspection* is a useful tool to focus on different aspects of teaching and learning, and it gives a good outline of what should be looked for when observing lessons.

The teacher being observed during observer training should be involved in the process, by asking their permission and making a commitment to them not to use the observational record for any sort of performance management but solely for the use of training an observer. This is very important; it would be unfair to the teacher who is being observed to have the additional pressure of being observed for his or her own performance management through this exercise. Find out from the teacher where to sit whether a lesson plan will be available and, if so, where it comes in the context of longer-term planning. Smile when entering the room – how can any teacher be at their best, focused and relaxed, if the observer is scowling and looking critical? Remember, this teacher is helping the observers as part of a training session for a colleague, and should be made to feel as comfortable as possible.

It makes sense to focus initially on teaching and its impact on learning because they have the biggest influence in the classroom and need practice to be able to evaluate well. During the lesson both observers should make notes separately and then take time to compare their evaluations afterwards. An allocation of time is necessary, preferably straight after the observation. At this time comparisons of what was observed can be discussed, what, if anything, was missed and the criteria which have been used. It is useful to have a professional discussion with the teacher who was observed to gather their view of the lesson and to check the observations.

Videotapes of lessons may be used, although one cannot see the whole classroom or judge the atmosphere, and the camera recording a lesson is also a distraction. However, for initial training prior to actual observation they can be of use.

Reflective discussion about observations between observer and observed can be very helpful in clarifying issues, gaining an additional perspective and in ensuring that the process is inclusive. It also enables the observer to practise discussing the lesson and giving feedback on their perception of the process.

Conclusion

It has always been and will continue to be a privilege to observe teachers, to see the professional way in which they work, the amount of their own time they contribute to their jobs and how much they care about their pupils. The skills of performance management are important to ensure that those taking part are confident in what they are doing. Performance management is about developing professional skills, using agreed criteria and training others, but most of all it is about celebrating and acknowledging what teachers do well – enabling children to learn.

The process of performance management builds on previous appraisal regulations and is the way forward for the foreseeable future. West-Burnham and O'Sullivan (1998: 99) write about starting points to discuss the professional learning of each teacher and how this is contextualised within whole-school planning. This too is significant for performance management:

> Nothing is more important than knowing the starting point of a journey in relation to the destination – it determines both the direction and the pace of travel. Needs analysis provides the crucial information to ensure that professional learning is appropriate, valid and relevant.

References

Goleman, D. (1996) *Emotional Intelligence*. London: Bloomsbury.

Office for Standards in Education (Ofsted) (1999) *Handbook for Inspecting Primary and Nursery Schools*. Norwich: HMSO.

Sergiovanni, T.J. (1995) *The Principalship*. Needham Heights, MA: Allyn and Bacon.

West-Burnham, J. and O'Sullivan, F. (1998) *Leadership and Professional Development in Schools*. London: Financial Times Professional.

6
■ ■ ■

Managing Performance through Investing in People

Gill Bracey and Tony Gelsthorpe

High-performing organisations are about achieving explicit positive out-comes. For schools nationally, outcomes are currently expressed mainly in terms of attainment measured through National Curriculum assessment and GCSE/GCE examination results. The publication of these results in the national press is an indication of the perceived importance attached to them. Their local publication is seen as one key element contributing to parental choice over schools and to public accountability. Indeed, in identifying priorities for the public education service, a chief officer of a local education authority has recently argued in a national education journal (Strong, 2000) that outcomes are more important than processes and processes more important than structures.

While recognising that it is essential for schools to clarify and prioritise learning outcomes and explicit educational goals (hopefully) wider than just academic attainment (Bowring-Carr, Gelsthorpe and West-Burnham, 2000), this chapter challenges Strong's assertion. It proposes that genuine, sustained achievement and progress for all learners are secured through an appropriate interdependence of outcomes, processes and structures. The chapter argues that it is possible to establish this through an exploration of the links between performance management and Investors in People.

Before these links are considered, it is important to clarify the definition of performance management used in this chapter and to summarise what the Investors in People standard is about.

Performance management

The focus here is on the statutory performance management arrangements for teachers that the government required schools to implement from September 2000 (DfEE, 2000a). In practice, the regulations mean that all teachers have an annual review directed towards raising performance and improving effectiveness. During the review teachers agree specific objectives, which are appropriate to their job responsibilities. One of the objectives must be about pupil progress and another relates to teachers' own professional development.

The regulations state that teachers' objectives must be clear and precise to allow progress against them to be measured. This gives rise to the issue of what constitutes 'measurable'. While many aspects of pupil progress clearly can be identified through the use of data, others, such as attitude and presentation of work are less susceptible to the application of mere numbers. Nevertheless, they are observable as having improved. Progress towards meeting professional development or management/leadership objectives is similarly much less easily quantifiable. It is, however, important to endeavour to be clear and precise in formulating and agreeing objectives and reviewing performance. In this way trust and confidence are built resulting in a more positive approach to the whole complex process. Judgements about teachers' performance, therefore, need to take account of both qualitative and quantitative evidence, with 'measurable' understood by all in the wider sense of 'having made a discernible difference', as well as having taken account of relevant data. This means that all participants in the performance management process not only need to be skilled in setting clear and precise objectives; they also must be skilled in identifying relevant, appropriate and clear success criteria and milestones, and recognising the evidence in their practice that demonstrates achievement against these.

There also needs to be clarity about whether judgements are being made about staff performance, pupil performance or both. In fact, the regulations are related to staff performance and its impact on pupil *progress*, rather than performance. What is probably of greatest significance is that they provide a framework which potentially enables teachers to develop more fully the skill of managing and improving their own performance, so that they can better manage and enhance the learning of pupils.

Overall, therefore, performance management in the context of a school community is about individual teachers taking responsibility for their own professional learning, and enabling, encouraging and supporting the learning and development of their team, whether they are leaders/managers or members of that team. At its best, performance management is about much more than this, stimulating a collective and mutual responsibility to promote the learning of all – moving towards the learning school.

Investors in People

Investors in People is a national standard that promotes the development of people in order to improve the performance of the organisation in which they work. In the school context, this means that the purpose of using the standard is to improve the performance of the school, i.e. the achievement of pupils. The Secretary of State for Education and Employment owns the intellectual property of the standard. Investors in People UK is the non-governmental public body responsible for developing the standard and in quality assuring the advice and assessment processes on his behalf.

In April 1999, the government launched a three-year Investors in People Strategy for Schools, to encourage more schools to use the Investors standard to support school improvement and the raising achievement agenda.

In this context, schools are able to approach Investors in People as something to 'use' not 'do'. The standard, appropriately used, helps schools to manage everything they must do and everything they choose to do. It works best when used as an enabling framework to support a school's core business – raising levels of pupil achievement. Ideally, deciding to use the standard involves the community of many different people associated with the school, particularly headteachers, governors, all staff and parents.

The standard:

- links a school's aims and objectives, including pupil outcomes, directly to the development of its people;
- ensures that everyone understands their own role and how they contribute to the school's success;
- ensures that the school evaluates the impact of training and development on the performance of its people and the achievement of its aims and objectives for pupils.

The standard was revised in 1999 and is now written as a series of outcome statements. The language is jargon-free and much more in keeping with school management and development. While the adoption of an external standard could seem mechanistic and instrumental, one of the benefits of Investors is that it describes a coherent series of outcomes but does not attempt to define or require particular processes, procedures or structures to achieve these. It is up to the school to decide what is appropriate.

Revisions to the assessment process have removed the bureaucracy and perceived paper-heavy requirements. Under the new arrangements, the assessor looks for evidence that shows a school is achieving the outcomes the standard requires. As the standard does not prescribe written evidence or processes, there is no need to present lots of paper evidence about policies and procedures, and certainly no need to prepare a portfolio.

Investors and performance management

The DfEE leaflet *Investors in People and Performance Management* (DfEE, 2000b: 2) states:

> *Establishing the links between Performance Management and Investors in People confirms the primacy of raising levels of achievement for all as the key outcome for schools. The links focus on teaching and learning as the core business of schools. Both Performance Management and Investors in People in schools are essentially about enabling the management of learning for all by planning, monitoring and reviewing by all. School self-evaluation is a crucial element of this.*

Essential links between processes and outcomes are the structures that a school sets in place to support the processes needed to achieve its identified outcomes. In this context, 'structures' has a wider meaning than simply organisational arrangements. Staffing structures, meeting arrangements, and monitoring and evaluation processes are all vital, but to work effectively in the interests of promoting and enhancing learning for all they have to be set in a climate of trust, confidence and professional responsibility and integrity. This will be derived from the formulation of the vision, aims and mission of the school. Hence, crucially, structures include the culture and climate engendered through the processes and outcomes themselves and the ways in which they are identified, agreed and enabled to happen.

In the context of both performance management and Investors in People, there are three key linked aspects to the development of a culture and climate that nurture and promote high achievement.

1 The school must provide people with development opportunities that go beyond mere 'training'. The first critical, and what might seem obvious, step is to develop a shared understanding of what constitutes learning, training and development. Schools which have used the standard successfully as part of their improvement agenda have found that widening everyone's concept of training and development has been at the same time one of the most challenging and one of the most liberating barriers to overcome. It requires a paradigm shift that once achieved, can release the most imaginative and creative thinking.

2 The school needs to recognise that individuals, teams and the whole school itself are at different points of readiness and susceptibility to take that responsibility/these opportunities on board. Sometimes, this might relate to a person's experience in the profession, or whether they have a leadership/management role in school, but not always. In planning learning and development opportunities, there is a need to differentiate, but not in a hierarchical way. Critically, the school must be responsive to individual needs, learning styles and approaches, and readiness to take on and learn from different kinds of activities.

3 It is important to remember that weaknesses identified through the annual review and in-year monitoring will not necessarily magically be resolved through the application of training or wider development opportunities. Changes in behaviour, attitudes, skills and performance depend at least as much, and possibly more, on the ways in which a school nurtures and encourages the application of new learning as the quality of the learning opportunity itself (O'Neill, 1994). While performance management provides a structured process that enables development needs to be identified, the Investors in People standard offers a framework for ensuring the application of learning to improve individual and team performance to contribute to improved pupil achievement.

Properly used, the Investors in People standard encourages everyone to see themselves as a learner. Also, because it requires schools to evaluate the impact of people development on their development plan aims for pupil achievement and progress, it actively supports the purposes of performance management and promotes a more rigorous approach to ensuring best value and value for money in relation to learning, training and development.

Another area of congruence and mutual support is that of individual in relation to organisational needs. Both Investors in People and performance management require schools to look at individual development within the context of whole school needs and priorities. Performance management also explicitly promotes consideration of teachers' personal professional development needs. Thus together, performance management and Investors in People can help to alleviate the potential tension between organisational and individual demands.

The emphasis on the core activity of improving the quality of teaching and learning to raise levels of achievement, promoted by both performance management and the Investors in People standard, has considerable implications for school leadership. Key areas for consideration are as follows:

1 The standard enables school leaders to develop and establish a climate and culture throughout the organisation which promote learning, training and development to improve the performance of staff and the progress of pupils.

2 Maintaining the focus on improving the quality of teaching and learning to improve pupil performance, working with the standard provides the people focus which is the route to achieving this through the better management, including self-management, of teacher performance.

3 Use of the standard encourages and supports school leaders to take back responsibility for learning, training and development which meets the school's own agenda and is related to the school development plan for improvement.

4   The standard is holistic in its approach. It is recognised and held in esteem across the wider community. A school's achievement of Investors in People status is thus a mark of quality with which everyone can identify. Investors is about whole communities, whole schools, whole staffs. Hence the concept of leadership is promoted *throughout* the organisation (not just the head/principal or the leadership team). Support staff, paraprofessionals and volunteers can be included in the framework for learning, training and development. For many employees, drawn from the local community, this will open up a new route into lifelong learning and potential qualifications. In this respect, the standard both supports and goes beyond schools' statutory responsibilities for performance management.

This last point brings to the fore the one key difference between the performance management arrangements and Investors in People. Investors requires the involvement of all staff, whereas the requirement to implement perfor-

Performance Management Framework and Policy	Investors in People standard indicators (Indicator numbers in brackets)
Raising standards: looking at the way schools work to provide the best possible education for their pupils and planning the work of individual teachers in that context.	The development of people is in line with the school's aims and objectives. (6)
Continuous professional development: promoting professional growth, identifying and taking account of teachers' individual development needs.	People are encouraged to improve their own and other people's performance. (2) People learn and develop effectively. (9)
Involvement: encouraging teachers to be fully engaged in school planning and to control the development of their own work and to support each other.	People are encouraged to improve their own and other people's performance. (2) The school has a plan with clear aims and objectives which are understood by everyone. (5)
Manageability: so that performance management is regarded as an integral and essential part of how schools operate.	The whole standard contributes to embedding performance management as part of the culture. (all)
Equity: to ensure policies and processes are open and fair, while respecting confidentiality for individuals.	The school is committed to ensuring equality of opportunity in the development of its people. (4)

Figure 6.1: The key elements of effective performance management and Investors in People indicators
(Source: DfEE)

mance management regulations applies only to teachers. A footnote in the Performance Management Framework states that schools may wish to extend the process to cover all staff. The use of the Investors standard would support and promote this. It is also a way of schools demonstrating their commitment to and practice of continuous professional development.

A helpful way of illustrating the congruence between performance management and Investors in People is by showing how performance management processes and practice contribute to the achievement of the Investors in People standard outcomes.

Figure 6.1 is taken from *Investors in People and Performance Management* (DfEE, 2000b).

Conclusion

By considering the detail of both the Performance Management Framework and Policy and the Investors in People standard in practice, it is possible to identify the supportive strategic inter-relationships between outcomes, processes and structures which emerge from their joint implementation. There are strong operational benefits to be gained from the practical links which exist between them. Thereby, the synergy between performance management and the Investors in People standard can be positively and beneficially exploited to raise levels of achievement for all.

References

Bowring-Carr, C., Gelsthorpe, T. and West-Burnham, J. (2000) *Transforming Schools through Community Education*. Coventry: Community Education Development Centre/International Leadership Centre, University of Hull.

Department for Education and Employment (DfEE) (2000a) *Performance Management in Schools*. London: DfEE.

Department for Education and Employment (DfEE) (2000b) *Investors in People and Performance Management*. London: DfEE.

O'Neill, J. (1994) 'Managing professional development', in T. Bush and J. West-Burnham (eds), *The Principles of Educational Management*. Harlow: Longman.

Strong, J. (2000) 'Has the LEA had its day?' *Education Journal*, Issue 48, September. Hove: The Education Publishing Company Limited.

7

■ ■ ■

Ethical Issues in Managing Teacher Performance

John Clark

Introduction

What goes on inside the four walls of the classroom is, on a day-to-day basis, largely a matter for the teacher and students. Their activities and interactions are, in the main, conducted within a context of privacy away from the judgemental eyes of others. This is how it should be. But what goes on in the classroom is not solely the preserve of those in it. Children have friends in other classes (or schools) with whom they discuss their classroom life, moaning about this, being excited about that. Parents often ask their children about what they did at school today, for they are interested in not only their child's welfare but also their learning. Other teachers, especially those in the same workgroup, may talk to one another about resources, programmes, teaching methods and assessment, as well as about performing and disruptive students. Principals and governing bodies have expectations that a teacher in their employ is up to the task of maintaining classroom control and able to provide teaching for effective learning. Beyond the school, educational agencies have a more general responsibility to ensure that the taxpayer's money is being well spent on the best teaching staff possible. So, in their various ways, all these groups have a legitimate interest in knowing a little more about what goes on in any particular classroom.

Although classroom life involves both teacher and student, it is the teacher who is of central concern when the interest shifts to looking more closely at who is responsible for what goes on inside the classroom. What is being sought is a measure of accountability: that the teacher should be able to give an account of what he or she and the students engage in; that the teacher is in some way responsible for his or her performance; and that in some way those to whom the teacher is accountable may either influence or intervene in the conduct of the teacher (Pring, 1978: 252). So, a child may ask 'Why do we have to do this?', a parent may complain about the failure of the teacher to mark her child's work, colleagues may congratulate a teacher on a job well done, the principal may reward a teacher with promotion and an external agency might criticise the extent to which a teacher teaches according to mandated requirements.

Now, if teachers are to be held accountable for what they do, then their teaching (and related activities) must be open to the scrutiny of others, for how else could their work be accounted for? But teachers have some legitimate worries about opening up their teaching practice to the gaze of others: what, exactly, is to be scrutinised? Why this but not that? How is it to be scrutinised? Who is to do the scrutinising? What will be done with the results of the scrutiny? These are key concerns for teachers because their personal self-esteem and professional integrity become the subject of a closer and potentially negative critical examination by those who have power and authority over them.

From the demand for accountability and the scrutiny of what teachers do, it follows that some procedures need to be put in place to ensure that these demands are met. At a national level this may consist of policies being introduced with agencies being directed to implement them. Locally, schools may formulate policies suited to their particular circumstances and engage in administrative action to effect them.

None of this is particularly exceptional because these are the sorts of things teachers have long experienced, and have accepted as part of the job. But, since the early 1980s, countries around the world, which have embraced New Right, libertarian, economic rationalism, have sought to introduce a more tightly defined system of teacher accountability amenable to greater central control.

Accountability

Although the specific details of the various accountability schemes may differ from one country to the next, there are a number of generic features which can be clearly identified:

1 *Top-down*: the demand for a tighter system of accountability comes from the bureaucratic centre rather than from teacher demand, and is an imposition on teachers by central authority rather than a reflection of their professional judgement.

2 *Interests*: the system of accountability is tied to the sectional interests of those who implement it rather than those for whom it is implemented.

In short, it meets the political interests of government officials answerable to government ministers rather than the professional interests of teachers seeking to address the educational needs of students.

3 *Instrumental*: the imposition of a bureaucratic model for extrinsic purposes. That is, it serves as a means for achieving external goals rather than being primarily directed at the improvement of teaching practice.

4 *Performance*: in order to determine whether teachers achieve these external goals, their performance must be monitored, using key performance indicators of a behavioural kind. To be met, these objectives must be clearly specifiable, objectively measurable, and easily evaluated.

5 *Prescriptive*: there is an emphasis on particular outcomes which teachers are required to demonstrate. This, in effect, prescribes behaviours which a teacher must perform if he or she is to be judged a 'good' teacher.

6 *Universality*: a system of accountability should have wide, if not universal, application to all teachers. Accordingly, it emphasises elements thought to be common to all teaching rather than directing attention to those more atypical.

7 *Simplicity*: a simple scheme is preferable to a complex one, for it is easier for the state to establish, introduce, administer and revise if necessary. A simple scheme is one which specifies in advance specific behaviours to be observed.

8 *Sanctions/rewards*: attached to the achievement of key performance indicators are rewards, and to failure, sanctions. The payment of bonuses and the withholding of promotion, for example, are assumed to be significant motivators of 'good' teaching practice.

9 *Monitoring*: there needs to be a process in place for monitoring whether the key performance indicators have been achieved or not, so that rewards and sanctions can be applied. This requires designated staff (curriculum leader, deputy principal, principal) to make such observations and check such lists as are required of them to make recommendation about a teacher's performance. This engenders a hierarchical structure of relationships.

10 *Managerialism*: the whole system of teacher accountability is governed by the underlying assumption that not only should teacher performance be managed, but that for it to be managed effectively and efficiently such management must be in accordance with the principles of managerialism. So, the management of teacher performance must be centrally controlled, empirically based, strictly applied, tightly administered and publicly transparent.

How these assumptions get cashed out in practice will depend on a wide range of factors, some common to countries, others unique to them. As an example of how these accountability assumptions are translated into teacher performance and its management, New Zealand serves our purpose well.

Teacher performance and its management in New Zealand

The more general assumptions of accountability have been translated into practice for New Zealand teachers by two autonomous agencies of the state. The Education Review Office (ERO) has taken the lead in spelling out the performances expected of teachers while the Ministry of Education has made explicit the requirements for the management of teacher performance. Although developed by quite separate government organisations, the approaches of ERO and the ministry dovetail extremely well.

The ERO report, *The Capable Teacher* (ERO, 1998: 3), set out to 'make explicit the characteristics that the Education Review Office expects to see demonstrated by capable teachers in its review of schools'. The ERO sought to operationalise its definition of the 'capable' teacher in terms of teacher competencies, and the capabilities a teacher needs to bring to a teaching position in order to fulfil its functions. Accordingly, definitions of core competencies are linked to established minimum standards for what any teacher should know and be able to do. A distinction was drawn between professional competencies and performance in the job. Core competencies consist of those skills and capabilities which any new or experienced teacher must have, these being sufficiently generic to apply to any teacher in any school. Performance, on the other hand, is defined as the actual results of a teacher as appraised by the teacher's employer. While core competencies may assist in the assessment of a teacher's performance, these in themselves are not considered by ERO to be the most appropriate tool for performance appraisal. These should be measured against performance criteria and expected results.

> *Performance can be defined as the results actually achieved by a particular teacher within the framework of his or her individual performance agreement with the employer, as appraised by the employer . . .*
>
> *The performance of the teacher in the job should be assessed through performance criteria and expected results specified in the performance agreement.*
>
> *Performance appraisal may identify where limited competence in a particular skill is the reason why the teacher is unable to achieve the pre-defined performance requirements.*
>
> (Ibid.: 4)

The ERO went on to specify a generic set of behaviours it expected all capable teachers to demonstrate, identifying exactly 100 behaviours grouped under the headings of 'professional knowledge' (25), 'professional practice' (38), 'professional relationships' (20) and 'professional leadership' (17). While the full specification of all 100 behaviours is unnecessary, their subclassification within each dimension may help to establish their general character. (Examples of behaviours are in roman and within brackets.)

> Professional Knowledge: *A capable teacher demonstrates informed professional knowledge of current curricula, the subject being taught, and current learning theory; the characteristics and progress of students (e.g.* keep useful assessment

records that show the progress of students); *appropriate teaching objectives; appropriate technology and resources; appropriate learning activities, programmes and assessment.*

(Ibid.: 10–11)

Professional Practice: *A capable teacher in professional practice creates an environment of respect and understanding; establishes high expectations that value and promote learning; manages student learning processes effectively; manages student behaviour positively; organises a safe physical and emotional environment; communicates clearly and accurately in either, or both, of the official languages of New Zealand; uses a variety of teaching approaches (e.g.* uses high quality questioning with time for student response); *engages students in learning; provides feedback to students and assesses learning; demonstrates flexibility and responsiveness.*

(Ibid.: 13–17)

Professional Relationships: *A capable teacher, in developing professional relationships, reflects on teaching with a view to improvement; maintains accurate records; communicates with parents and caregivers; contributes actively to the life of school; develops professionally; maintains confidentiality, trust and respect (e.g.* follows agreed school procedures for resolution of complaints).

(Ibid.: 19–20)

Professional Leadership: *A capable teacher, in showing professional leadership, demonstrates flexibility and adaptability; focuses on improving teaching and learning; leads and supports other teachers; displays ethical behaviour and responsibility (e.g.* carries out responsibilities to the satisfaction of the principal); *recognises and supports diversity among groups and individuals; encourages others to participate in professional development; manages resources safely and effectively.*

(Ibid.: 21–2)

This then sets out the ERO's view of teacher performance expected of New Zealand teachers. The management of teacher performance was left for the Ministry of Education to determine.

In February 1997, the Secretary for Education issued a prescription in the *New Zealand Education Gazette* (Secretary for Education, 1997) concerning matters to be taken into account by school boards of trustees when assessing the performance of New Zealand teachers. The notice spelt out three related aspects of teacher appraisal which boards of trustees, as the employers of teachers, must adhere to.

Principles: *Boards of Trustees should ensure that policies and procedures for the appraisal of teacher performance are not only open and transparent, developed in consultation with teachers, are appropriate for individual teachers, have a professional development orientation and maintain confidentiality consistent with the Privacy Act and the Official Information Act but, more importantly for our purposes, are part of an integrated performance management system operating within the school.*

Process: *The Board of Trustees is responsible for ensuring, amongst other things, that a policy for the appraisal of teacher performance is in place which is in accordance with the principles, with responsibility for its implementation formally delegated to a professionally competent person (principal and/or senior teachers). The appraisal process includes:*

(i)   *the development of a written statement of performance expectations;*

(ii) *the identification and written specification of one or more development objectives to be achieved;*

(iii) *observation of teaching;*

(iv) *an opportunity for the teacher to discuss the achievement of the performance expectations and the development objectives with the appraiser;*

(v)   *preparation of an appraisal report.*

Performance: *The Board of Trustees must ensure that the performance expectations for teachers relate to their key professional responsibilities and key performance areas, including:*

(i)   *teaching responsibilities (such as planning and preparation, teaching techniques, classroom management, classroom environment, curriculum knowledge, student assessment);*

(ii) *school-wide responsibilities (such as contribution to curriculum leadership, school-wide planning, school goals, effective operation of the school, pastoral care and student counselling);*

(iii) *management responsibilities (such as planning, decision-making, reporting, professional leadership, and resource management).*

(Adapted from Secretary for Education, 1997. 1–2)

In a subsequent round of collective contract negotiations, primary and secondary teacher unions agreed to the replacement of these key professional responsibilities and performance areas with more elaborate 'professional standards'. These 'standards' are differentiated for beginning, fully registered and experienced teachers. For a teacher to receive his or her annual salary increment the principal must attest that 'satisfactory' 'standards' of 'performance' have been met.

Having dealt with the operational framework for managing teacher performance, I now want to turn to a consideration of ethical issues.

The management of teacher performance: general ethical objections

Although the emphasis in this part of the chapter will be on the ethics of managing teacher performance within a context of accountability rather than with teacher performance per se, it is extremely difficult to avoid considering these when addressing the ethics of management.

Ethical issues in managing teacher performance can be viewed in two rather different ways: the first is internal – just accept the sort of approach outlined, and then get on with ensuring that it is applied in an ethically acceptable sort of way. The second, to be adopted here, is to call the model for managing teacher performance into ethical question, replacing it with a more ethically justifiable framework for enhancing teachers' teaching and learners' learning. In short, it will be argued that the managerial model is, on ethical grounds, unacceptable and ought to be replaced by one built on an educational ideal.

The over-riding ethical question is this: can the management of teacher performance as presented above be justified? If it can be shown that the model of accountability and the conception of teacher performance upon which the management of teacher performance is based is deeply flawed, then there are good grounds for rejecting the whole approach, its management included. The idea that teacher performance ought to be managed in the manner discussed rests on the acceptance of two basic assumptions which are highly questionable. The first is whether the accounts of teacher performance illustrated above adequately represent all that a teacher does; the second is whether teacher performance is something which ought to be managed in the way described.

The ideological thrust

The first principled objection to the management system of teacher performance lies in its ideological thrust. It is abundantly clear that a narrow utilitarian approach to accountability drives the management of teacher performance. It is one governed by economic rationality with an emphasis on prespecified objectives, detailed planning, clear definitions of role expectations and accurate measures of observable performances. Nowhere is this clearer than in the 1984 New Zealand Treasury brief to the incoming Labour government, where advice is given on the management of public service: 'an effective management system . . . requires the following main attributes – clear objectives, appropriate incentives, for performance, clear accountability, delegation of authority and responsibility to the most appropriate level' (Treasury, 1984: 287). As Codd (1990: 21) has noted, this model requires that clearly stated and measurable objectives be established, with a management plan to ensure the objectives are met, and appropriate incentives be introduced to encourage teachers to perform in such a way in order to meet the objectives effectively and efficiently. Accordingly, principals (and senior staff in larger schools) should be managers while teachers should be the providers of specified services, and it is the responsibility of the former to monitor the performance of the latter.

There is something ethically troubling about an approach to management which assumes that no matter the social context or the nature of the task, a single model of management can be applied to all human activity. This was certainly the attitude of those in the 1950s who, following Simon (1957), advocated a general science of administration just as applicable to education as to any other sphere of human endeavour (Griffiths, 1959). It is indeed odd that what was championed half a century ago and then roundly discredited in educational administration (Bates, 1993; Greenfield and Ribbins, 1993) is so slavishly adhered to today. Surely, those who are so deeply committed to managerialism have a moral duty to confront the challenges to their position instead of blissfully ignoring the deep philosophical criticism of it and passing off their unworthy ideology as some newly minted approach supposedly based on the very latest scientific principles of management. There can be few things more ethically objectionable than for those in a position of authority to use their power to impose on those subject to their authority a method of control which is presented to the latter as being in their best interests when clearly this is far from the case at all.

A lack of understanding

A second general ethical objection to the managerialism applied to teacher performance is to be found in the severely impoverished understanding of that which is to be managed – teacher performance. The emphasis on performance as something to be studied via observation of a teacher's teaching reduces the teaching task to that which is behaviourally specifiable, observable and measurable. Clearly, it is assumed that behaviour specified in objectives against which performance can be measured adequately represents the full range and depth of teaching abilities possessed by teachers. But this assumption is fallacious. The relationship between teaching ability and actual behavioural performance is by no means all that simple to establish. Attributes are very general and enduring while behavioural manifestations of these traits are specific, many and fleeting. To illustrate: an attribute required by ERO, 'demonstrating informed professional knowledge of appropriate learning activities, progress and assessment', is expressed behaviourally as six performances including 'allocates time realistically'. The difficulty is that a performance indicator such as 'time management' serves as a most unreliable pointer of the generic ability in question. The reason for this is simple enough. General dispositions can be displayed behaviourally in a vast number of ways on many different occasions under a variety of conditions, generating multiple interpretations depending on who is observing them.

Conversely, one behaviour may be the manifestation of any number of abilities. So, 'allocating time realistically' appears to have very little logical or causal connection to the type of knowledge specified. And, even if it did, this particular activity is a poor behavioural indicator since it needs to be supplemented with a more detailed specification of the actual 'time management' behaviours one could expect to observe. Likewise for the other so-called performances. If the demand for directly observable behaviours is extended to all 100 items in the ERO checklists, then the resultant list of prespecified observable behaviours would result in an outcome not too dissimilar from that obtained by the competency projects of the 1970s where 'people could perform each of the thousands of behaviours, yet somehow still couldn't teach' (Hager and Beckett, 1995: 3).

The sharp swing towards behaviourism is one of the more disturbing features of the ideological stance currently driving the management of teacher performance. The reductionist strategy of defining abilities solely in terms of directly observable behaviours or performances leads to what Leicester (1994: 113) calls an 'instrumentalist perspective' symptomatic of a view of education as 'vocationalism'. The emphasis on observable behaviour from which inferences may be drawn about the abilities a teacher possesses leads to a rather limited conception of teaching since it is easier to infer the possession of technical skills than it is to conclude by reasoning from the evidence that complex, abstract, conceptual thought shapes a teacher's professional practice. The latter may never be observed behaviourally nor inferred from behaviour, yet it is constitutive of all that a teacher engages in professionally. The centrality of teacher theorising and the nexus of the theory–practice relationship is crucial to an adequate account of teaching, yet is largely ignored in behaviourally based performance models of teaching. The primary focus of such a model is on current curricula and learning, classroom planning, objectives and resources, teaching procedures and learning conditions, and school-centred relationships. What is missing is recognition that while these may be important features of teaching, they are not sufficient. What is left out of this overly technicist picture of teaching is an awareness that teaching is a moral, political and educational activity.

An absence of clarity

A third ethical objection is this: reference is often made to the assessment, evaluation and appraisal of teacher performance as part of its management, but the failure to clearly distinguish between them not only conceals important differences but also, and more significantly, masks deeper ethical factors. A good example of this conceptual naivety is to be found in the New Zealand Ministry of Education's stance on the appraisal of teacher performance. In *Performance Managements Systems PMS 1* (Ministry of Education, 1997) the terms 'assessment', 'evaluation' and 'appraisal' are used, the last rather extensively since the focus is on the appraisal of teachers. In answer to the question 'Is there any difference between the terms appraisal, assessment and evaluation?' we are told, 'No, the terms are interchangeable' (ibid.: 5). However, 'interchangeable' they are not, for as Kleinig (1982: 176) has pointed out, conceptually they have very different meanings and they describe quite distinct activities.

1   Assessment is an estimation or a measure of what has been achieved. Assessment of a teacher's teaching will consist of no more that determination of whether or not the teaching reaches or measures up to a particular standard or criterion.

2   Evaluation is a judgement about the value or the worth of the teaching achieved. Evaluation of a teacher's teaching may be couched in such terms as 'good', 'poor', 'excellent', 'weak', etc. Such evaluations may be linked to improvement of practice or to external functions.

3   Appraisal is an evaluation used for external purposes, such as relating a judgement of a teacher's teaching to issues of employment, promotion and teacher registration.

These are clearly distinct processes, with appraisal presupposing the prior completion of assessment and evaluation. Yet, all too often their importance is overshadowed by the weighting given to appraisal. This is particularly evident in the case of the Ministry of Education in New Zealand: little attention is directed to the *assessment* of teachers (mentioned seven times) or to the *evaluation* of teaching (mentioned eight times) in *Performance Management System: PMS 1. Appraisal*, on the other hand, is alluded to a whopping 110 times in 15 pages. To be sure, passing reference is made to 'professional growth, and the provision of appropriate support and assistance to foster that development' (Ministry of Education, 1997: 14) but this appears almost incidental to the more over-riding demand for appraisal to serve instrumental purposes. Indeed, the ministry document refers to performance appraisal systems 'within . . . an accountability framework' linked to the wider performance management system of the school. This includes such personnel management policies as: the recruitment and retention of staff, the selection and appointment of staff, collective and individual employment contracts which relate to performance management, the statutory requirements for teacher registration, the assessment and appraisal of staff, remuneration management (clauses in teachers' collective employment contracts require that appraisal occurs annually for salary progression purposes), and the discipline and dismissal of staff.

What makes this whole system of managing teacher performance so ethically repugnant are, first, the overwhelming emphasis by central agencies on the monitoring of teachers in order to control them and, second, the requirement that school principals enact this on behalf of central agencies. It reflects a deep mistrust of teachers by those who impose such systems on them. Using this model, teachers must not be given autonomy to take professional responsibility for their conduct, rather, the full phalanx of the state must be employed to regulate and curb teachers' work. It is this increasing move by the state towards the deprofessionalisation of the teaching profession which ought to be strenuously resisted.

Managing teacher performance: ethical principles

If we are to proceed with managing teacher performance, and at this point it is by no means ethically self-evident that we ought to, then a number of ethical requirements must be met.

The primacy of education

There is a marked tendency to conceptually separate off a cluster of related matters: education, teaching, performance, appraisal and management are deemed to be relatively discrete activities when closer inspection indicates that they are logically connected in a sequential relationship.

Seemingly, there is a shared stance permeating many educational bureaucracies that schooling must emphasise the knowledge and skills required for economic growth and international competitiveness, be publicly accountable in accordance with measurable performance indicators and not be subject to the 'provider capture' of teachers. The utilitarian agenda is designed to squeeze out educational considerations, replacing them with a narrow functional view of schooling geared to the needs of a global economy and the gainful employment of citizens.

What is missing from this is any comprehension concerning the whole point of being a teacher. It does not seem to be enough to claim that teachers need professional knowledge about the curriculum and that in their professional practice they should promote learning, necessary as these may be. The question must be asked, 'Why do teachers teach and learners learn?' A crude answer might take an instrumental stance along the lines outlined above. But, every teacher needs to lift their sights higher than just being a teacher, for a teacher ought, first and foremost, to be an *educator*. It is educating children that gives teaching its strongest intrinsic rationale.

So, what is it to educate children? Put simply, and without extensive justification, the aim of education is to bring about educated persons who, as rational beings, are able to engage in critical problem-solving. An educated person is one, I submit, who can:

1 *Formulate life plans*: they have an awareness of what they would like their future life to be, even if this is not fully developed in all its details. That is, they can construct future goals. This requires knowledge of various possible forms of life and the ability to make informed judgements about those which are better or worse.

2 *Act upon life plans*: they can make decisions about achieving a desired form of life. That is, they have knowledge that some means are more effective than others in attaining desired ends.

Built into this account of the educated person are a number of quite specific features such as:

- moral knowledge about how to live the good life – what is right and wrong, good and bad, one's rights and duties;
- emotional knowledge required for the removal of psychological constraints such as unwarranted fear or guilt, and the development of appropriate emotional expressions such as control of anger;

- aesthetic knowledge essential for judgements about things to be appreciated, both natural and social;
- a critical attitude that nothing is beyond criticism, best summed up in the Socratic dictum that 'the unexamined life is not worth living';
- emancipation of the individual, especially maximum freedom to hold one's own views and act accordingly, and maximum autonomy from authority, consistent with the rights of others to the same degree of freedom and autonomy.

A teacher who has no conception of what it is to be an educator responsible for educating children to become educated adults falls well short of being a good teacher.

Educating children is the foundation stone upon which all else is built. Any account of teaching must begin with the primacy of this educational ideal; from this, pedagogy, curriculum evaluation and the like all take their shape. Any assessment, evaluation and appraisal of the educative teacher must start with the deep complexities of the task of educating, placing far greater emphasis on the richness of the educative process which extends far beyond the crudities of measurable performances couched in terms of prespecified behavioural objectives. Encouraging a 'love of learning', the 'joy of reading a novel', 'the pleasure of listening to music' and 'perseverance in solving a mathematics problem' are all long-term achievements which cannot be reduced to observable teacher performances. Appraising the work of the educative teacher requires great skill by one who is already educated, and demands much more than the mundane ability to observe teaching performances, for teaching, like educating, is more than merely a technical skill. It is fundamentally a moral activity and moral activities cannot be judged by observations alone.

From this it follows that the accountability of teachers, their appraisal and (if we admit this) their management, must be driven by educational principles of professional practice rather than by performance outcomes, a point well made by Sockett (1980). Anything less is ethically illegitimate.

Respect for persons

A central ethical principle is respect for persons, encapsulated in the Kantian notion that humans ought to be treated as ends, never merely as means to other people's ends. That is, humans are moral agents, so teachers, like the students they teach, ought to be regarded as relatively autonomous and self-determining rather than as objects to be manipulated or controlled.

If used to inform and improve teaching practice, the assessment of teachers' teaching and educational achievement, along with the evaluations made, meets this criterion. The purpose of the description and judgements is to help teachers become better teachers so that students' learning and educational success is enhanced. Both assessment and evaluation are internal to the activities of teaching and education, whereas appraisal is of a different order, aimed as it is at external considerations. The ethical worry lies not with appraisal per se, for teachers have a legitimate interest in securing appointments, achieving promotion and maintaining registration. Rather, the danger is to be found in how this is done. Where appraisals are initiated by teachers for these and other purposes, then teachers are able to exercise their autonomy and act in ways conducive to achieving these goals. But where appraisal is demanded of teachers to meet externally mandated regulatory requirements of accountability, then teachers are no longer being treated as ends in themselves but are being dealt to merely as pawns in a system of political domination over which they have no control.

This criticism should not be taken as a rejection of accountability and appraisal, for it is not. Both are legitimate expectations of teachers provided that accountability has as its central focus an educational concern; and that appraisal is initiated by teachers and engaged in co-operatively, even if this is within a general mandatory framework. What is being objected to is the detailed bureaucratic prescriptions of accountability and appraisal using a top-down management ideology.

Fairness

Any system of accountability, along with any assessment, evaluation and appraisal which support it, must be fair to all concerned. This ethical requirement can be cashed out in a variety of ways, all of which need to be heeded if justice is not only to be done but seen to be done.

First, the actions of those who either design or implement systems of accountability, assessment/evaluation and appraisal must not be unduly biased or excessively ideological. Where such schemes have their origins in the political machinations of libertarian politicians and managerial bureaucrats then the charge of unfairness may reasonably be laid, for ideology drives the programme, not prior educational principles as discussed earlier. The strategy is generated by a myopic commitment to a 'one model fits all' approach rather than starting with the Aristotelian principle of only being as precise as the subject matter, in this case education and teaching, allows. So, start with a clear understanding of education and teaching and then, and only then, ask what is to be accounted for and how may it be assessed/evaluated/appraised.

Second, any system must not discriminate on irrelevant grounds. That is, teachers must be treated equally unless there are relevant and good reasons for not doing so. On their own, the age, sex, ethnicity and social class of teachers do not constitute sufficient grounds for treating teachers differently. Aristotle assists with a further helpful insight: treat equals equally and unequals unequally. So, teachers with ten years of experience should be treated similarly, and teachers in their first year of teaching likewise, but there are relevant differences between the two groups which should lead to them being treated unequally, hence differently for assessment, evaluation and appraisal purposes.

A third point to be made is this: fairness dictates that a person can only be held accountable, hence responsible, for those things which are within his or her control. A teacher cannot be held accountable for those acts of commission or omission beyond their control. The keeping of accurate attendance records, for example, is something within a teacher's control for which he or she can be held responsible. It might plausibly be argued that teachers can be held responsible for employing teaching methods appropriate to the learning abilities of their students. But where teachers do all that can be reasonably expected of them in terms of knowledge of content, understanding their student's abilities, employing motivating pedagogical styles and use stimulating resources, then it is manifestly unfair to hold teachers responsible for the success or failure of students' learning because this success or failure is causally dependent on not just a single factor but rather a complex set of them. Of these, the teacher's efforts are only one (a difficult one at that, accurately to isolate and measure) and probably not even the most significant factor. The ethical impropriety of attaching responsibility to the teacher for student achievement should be obvious enough. Sadly, all too often it is not.

Truth

The legal maxim, 'The truth, the whole truth, and nothing but the truth', applies as much to managing teacher performance as it does to court proceedings. It reminds us that truth is a key element in human affairs and cannot be ignored in relationships between teachers and those who would manage their appraisal.

Talk of 'the truth' reinforces the idea that any accountability undertaken must be accurate and that this facticity must be preserved from assessment through evaluation to appraisal. In other words, what is said of teachers must be true rather than consisting of distortions, untruths or outright lies. There is an onus on those who purport to manage teacher appraisal to ensure that the processes and procedures are authentic.

This leads to the second injunction, 'the whole truth'. A true account of a teacher's teaching is one which embodies both the strengths and the weaknesses of that person's activities. There should be praise when it is deserved and criticism when it is warranted. There is nothing to be gained by extolling the virtues while glossing over the vices. Even less is to be said of the practice of fault-finding at the expense of complimenting good practice. Those who would pass judgement on a teacher owe it to that person to provide an all-encompassing picture of the teacher's teaching.

The final expression, 'nothing but the truth', underlines the ethical point that those who appraise, and manage the appraisal of teachers, must avoid entering into judgements which exceed the evidence of teaching ability. This means personal bias or prejudicial opinions should not intrude, with great care being taken in the choice of words used to convey the assessment, evaluation and appraisal of a teacher's professional conduct.

This reference to evidence is salutary, for as Scriven (1981: 251) has noted:

> Using classroom visits by colleagues (or administrators or 'experts') to evaluate teaching is not just incorrect, it is a disgrace. First, the visit alters the teaching, so that the visitor is not looking at a representative sample . . . Second, the number of visits is too small to be an accurate sample from which to generalise, even if it were a random sample . . . Third, the visitors are typically not devoid of independent personal prejudices in favour of or against the teacher . . . Fourth, nothing that would be observed in the classroom (apart from the most bizarre special cases) can be used as a basis for an inference to any conclusion about the merit of the teaching.

This raises serious ethical problems for those appraisers whose appraisals rest in part or in whole on classroom visits to observe teachers teaching.

Trust

Teaching is built on trust. Parents entrust their children to the care of teachers who are expected to do their best to promote the welfare and wider interests of their students. In the classroom, teachers and students establish and build up relationships of trust and mutual respect. Teachers come to trust the integrity and professional abilities of their colleagues. Trust is essential in the daily interactions of teachers and those who administer schools. Finally, there must be trust between school staff and the agencies of the state responsible for policy and its implementation.

Trust involves having confidence in another person's honesty, veracity, justice and the like. For a classroom teacher, this means any process of accountability incorporating assessment, evaluation and appraisal must be conducted in such a way as to protect the integrity of all those concerned. In particular, there must be trust between the teacher and the school administrator(s) and between teachers and the bureaucrats who moderate such schemes. For teacher and principal, both of whom must work together in the same institution, trust is paramount. The Picot Report (Picot, 1988) which ushered in the 'reforming' of New Zealand's education system in the late 1980s had this to say: 'the collaborative relationship between principal and staff must be protected' (Picot, 1988: 51). This was echoed in the government's policy statement *Tomorrow's Schools* (Lange, 1988: 10–11): The principal 'will be the professional leader of the institution' and that 'principals will be expected to work in a collaborative relationship with their staff'. However, despite this gesture of collaboration, government policy also undermined it, for the principal was also to be responsible for 'the development of performance objectives and measures to assess that performance'. Two years later, responding to central government agency concern that educationalists were reasserting their influence in education, the government established a Committee to Review the Education Reform Implementation Process. It consisted to an ex-Secretary to the Treasury and the Education Manager, a State Services Commission economist, a senior banking officer and the Secretary for Education. *Today's Schools* (Lough, 1990: 18) complained that school principals 'primarily identify as professional leaders rather than managers'. This was clearly out of tune with the tenor of the times. Remedy: educational leadership was to be exercised by 'establishing an educational plan for the school and by communicating it to all staff and students' (ibid.: 23).

This new-found enthusiasm for managerialism was taken up with alacrity by the educational agencies of the state, the Ministry of Education and the Education Review Office in particular. The imposition of a centrally controlled, top-down model of accountability which stripped professional autonomy from teachers eroded any trust that teachers had in the bureaucracy. At the same time, reconceptualisation of the principal as a manager, rather than as an educational leader, led to a sharper role differentiation and a starker awareness of the power relationship between those who managed and those who were managed. The principal as an appraiser of teacher performance now assumed a position quite at odds with that of a collaborating colleague to teachers who, as the appraised, rightly came to distrust the motives and integrity of those who would appraise them. It is here that the whole edifice of managing teacher performance through appraisal falls down, for managing breaks the very trust which is so central to teaching. If teachers can trust neither the system of accountability nor those who introduce and implement it, then this has serious consequences for its long-term success.

If trust is to be restored between teachers and principals and between those in schools and external agencies, such as the ERO and Ofsted (and this may be difficult given the abrasive, populist styles of both the former Chief Review Officer, Dr Judith Aitken, and the former Her Majesty's Chief Inspector of Schools, Mr Chris Woodhead), then the current system of accountability and the management of teacher performance must be replaced by a model which at the very least has the full confidence of teachers and builds on a set of trusting and trustworthy relationships of mutual respect and shared power.

Conclusion

There is little to be said for managing teachers' performance. Ethically, it is a rather bankrupt social practice, employed by those in power to control those whom they do not trust. The language used to describe this social practice, 'performance management in schools', reflects the deep ideological distortions of what education and teaching is all about held by those who dream up such practices and slogans. The whole purpose of managing teacher performance needs to be carefully reconsidered. If language is to be the driver of this redirection, then a new expression may help give effect to this. While it does not fit easily into the taken-for-granted everyday discourse of managerialism now so prevalent in schools and, indeed, jars with it because of its contrary focus, 'conducting teaching verdicts' might serve us better. 'Conducting', because, like an orchestra, where the conductor and the players require each other in a mutual harmony of co-ordination and co-operation, teachers and principals also must work together. 'Teaching' rather than 'teacher', for this serves to remind us that it is the teacher's teaching which is under consideration, not the teacher's persona, thus removing ethically dubious criteria for judging teachers, such as the ERO's criterion for the capable teacher as one who 'participates in community activities and projects' (ERO, 1998: 190). 'Verdicts' because this implies making decisions about teaching which give greater weight to teaching and its improvement than to meeting external bureaucratic demands. This is not to deny that, for teachers, appraisal is important, for it is with respect to their professional careers. But, it is to shift the weighting away from the pre-eminence accorded to 'appraisal' and rightly to reassert the primacy of the assessment and evaluation of teaching directed towards the achievement of educational goals. If this is to happen, then 'managing' teacher 'performance' must go.

References

Bates, R. (1993) 'On knowing: cultural and critical approaches to educational administration', *Educational Management and Administration*, 21 (3), 171–6.

Codd, J. (1990) 'Managerialism: the problem with today's schools', *Delta*, (44), 19–25.

Educational Review Office (ERO) (1998) *The Capable Teacher*. Wellington: ERO.

Greenfield, T and Ribbins, P. (1993) *Greenfield on Educational Administration*. London: Routledge.

Griffiths, D. (1959) *Administrative Theory*. New York: Appleton Century Crofts.

Hager, P. and Beckett, D. (1995) 'Philosophical underpinning of the integrated conception of competence', *Educational Philosophy and Theory*, 27 (1), 1–24.

Kleinig, J. (1982) *Philosophical Issues in Education*. London: Croom Helm.

Lange, D. (1988) *Tomorrow's Schools*. Wellington: Department of Education.

Leicester, M. (1994) 'Competency, knowledge and education: reply to Hyland', *Journal of Philosophy of Education*, 28 (1), 112–18.

Lough, N. (1990) *Today's Schools*. Report of the Committee to Review the Education Reform Implementation Process. Wellington: Government Printer.

Ministry of Education (1997) *Performance Management Systems PMS 1*. Wellington: Ministry of Education.

Picot, B. (1988) *Administering for Excellence*. Report of the Taskforce to Review Educational Administration. Wellington: Government Printer.

Pring, R. (1978) 'Accountability', in D. Lawton, P. Gordon, M. Ing, B. Gibby and R. Pring (eds), *Theory and Practice of Curriculum Studies*. London: Routledge and Kegan Paul.

Scriven, M. (1981) 'Summative teacher evaluation', in J. Millman (ed.) *Handbook of Teacher Evaluation*. London: Sage.

Secretary of Education (1997) 'Prescribing performance appraisal', *New Zealand Education Gazette*, 76 (2), 1–2.

Simon, B. (1957) *Administrative Behavior*. 2nd edn. New York: Macmillan.

Sockett, H. (1980) 'Accountability: the contemporary issues', in H. Sockett (ed.) *Accountability in the English Education System*. London: Hodder and Stoughton.

Treasury (1984) *Economic Management*. Wellington: New Zealand Treasury.

Part Two

■ ■ ■

Performance Management in Practice

8

■ ■ ■

A Passion for Performance Management?

Howard Kennedy

Summary

This case study places passion and conviction at the core of managing the motivation and performance of others. Essential structures and processes of performance management systems are identified but the need for the leader to have a passionate commitment to futures thinking infused by inspirational language is highlighted as critical. The contention is that leadership is about creating futures and the climate in which people perform.

The fulcrum in the emerging story of this case study was the appointment of an executive coach who facilitated our journey to outstanding performance and who, eventually, became the 'critical friend' to the head, senior team and whole staff. Significant elements in this process were 360° appraisals and feedback loops, a demanding focus on improvement and success for all, and a 'no escape' accountability through the coach's regular visits to school to monitor and support implementation and improvements.

Performance management

The working definition for this chapter is all encompassing. The head as leader of the school community is seen as having the challenge of creating with this community the society they wish jointly to become. Performance management in this context covers the performance of both the school as a whole and every part of it.

This case study views the school as a system where all parts are interconnected and influenced by the actions of all other parts. This belief emerged gradually over my 17 years as headteacher. During this time I came increasingly to pursue alignment in all things as the necessary staging post on the journey to excellence and, crucially, as the foundation of a climate in which risk taking, innovation and entrepreneurship flourished.

Context

The school is situated in an urban setting amidst two London overspill housing estates. It was originally viewed as the 'worst school' in the authority. It is a 3–11 school with approximately 450 on roll. Seven years of immense activity had seen the school become popular within the community and viewed by the LEA as a place of excellent practice. But the purpose of this case study is to track and explain our transformation from this point to a higher plane.

Executive coaching

Following a voluntary Ofsted inspection before the launch of the national system of inspection the writer decided that headship was too tough a job to be done alone and in isolation. At this 'low point' that the school decided to appoint an executive coach. It was a leap in the dark but one which proved invaluable in facilitating the process of development first in the leader and, subsequently, in the whole school community.

The external coach ('critical friend', Neville) worked with all staff but especially the headteacher to clarify issues, enable the discovery of solutions which matched our competencies and context, as well as monitoring their implementation and effect on all stakeholders. This process was invaluable and enhanced our individual and collective performances beyond all expectations. The contribution of the deep wisdom of our coach was profound.

A process of 360° appraisal for the headteacher was agreed and initiated by Neville. This involved all stakeholders including all staff, parents, governors and pupils, and the results were published annually. In a sense, this annual appraisal of the headteacher became a 'state of the nation' account for the whole school and was an ideal way of monitoring the 'society' we were in the process of creating. Initially daunting, it led to huge personal and organisational growth. It also established a culture where formative feedback became the norm.

This 360° appraisal process produced numerous creditable mentions which were intrinsically satisfying. But, it also brought forth this memorable conclusion:

> *This means HK changing not just as a professional manager but in terms of basic beliefs, values, attitudes, lifestyle, feelings, thoughts, actions, relationships with self and others.*

I trust that this convinces the reader that there was plenty of room for improvement and change! Neville, our wise 'executive coach' remained connected to support the process of change and development. Like all good consultants, he never delivered answers but worked with us to 'draw out what was within'. In this way solutions and changes in working practices were not imposed from outside but always grew from within.

The process led to fundamental changes:

- a gradual 'paring away' of the noise and distraction of headship to allow maximum time to be spent on its essential purpose: to create a successful learning environment for all;

- the headteacher becoming the 'lead learner' of the school community;

- a significant increase in delegation resulting in people being given true responsibility and accountability and developing their potential to a much higher level than previously;

- introduction of corporate headship;

- development of an agreed decision-making policy, clarification of roles and responsibilities, task forces, flatter organisational structure, emotional and spiritual intelligence both for adults and children and visionary futures thinking.

These issues will be examined later in detail. At this point I wish to explore the emerging 'models of excellence', which are being integrated as the foundation for the national leadership programmes – the National Professional Qualification for Headship (NPQH) and the Leadership Programme for Serving Headteachers (LPSH).

Futures thinking, visions and the models of excellence

These models of excellence have been introduced into the teaching profession as a consequence of Hay McBer's (2000) research into highly effective headteachers (HEFF) and highly effective teachers (TEFF). The model of highly effective headteachers is illustrated in Figure 8.1. At the core of this researched model are the passionate conviction and personal value system of the head. These passions and values lead to the creation of a vision to which highly effective leaders are able to gain the commitment of people. This has a beginning in the mind and passion of the leader but can grow through the

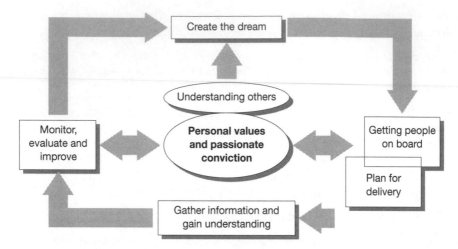

Figure 8.1: Model of highly effective headteachers

contribution and development of others. In this way the vision, always in the process of becoming, is shared in ownership with and through others. The role of the governing body in appointing a headteacher within whom they can work and trust the strategic direction of the school is of critical importance.

Hock (1999) encapsulates the importance of such a concept in his *Birth of the Chaordic Age* where he defines a leader as simply someone who has followers. You cannot be a leader if you do not have followers. Under this definition Hitler and other notable genocidal maniacs were great leaders, which brings into stark relief the importance of the personal value systems of the leader and the aims, values and beliefs of the school community.

In this way headship was a journey of exploration of my own values and beliefs underpinning the concept of 'our' school not 'my'. And 'we' not 'I'. Another, accompanying theme along the 'journey' was a working through of Greenleaf's (1998) concept of servant leadership where the job of the leader is, in the first instance, to provide meaning and at the end to say thank you. In the middle the leader is to be a servant.

I learned that providing meaning in this world of complexity is sometimes a daunting and exhausting process, that saying 'thank you' with integrity needs much practice and that being a servant is often difficult to learn.

Providing meaning ... creating visions

Providing meaning is all about making sense of the pressures which society, government, parents, pupils, community and commerce place and at times even dump on modern schools. It means acting as a sensitive filter for employees and the community to distil and focus on that which is important, rejecting the irrelevant and knowing the difference. It is also about creating visions and dreams which inspire people to commit their effort and test their aspirations to making a difference in individual's lives and in that way contributing without embarrassment or apology to an ennobling vision of making the world a better place.

Back in the 1960s McGregor (1960) introduced his memorable Theory X and Theory Y relating to human motivation. Theory X viewed people as self-interested, not to be trusted, needing to be controlled and made to comply. Theory Y offered a more generous view of human motivation, related to willingness to contribute, integrity, honesty and self-directed learning. In this sense we need to develop Theory Y leadership where Theory X, for example, in relation to the national performance management requirements, appears to be dominant. There has been a tendency, encouraged by government expectations, legislation, and imposed external monitoring systems, for performance management to fulfil external requirements through the erection of a labyrinthine and compliant bureaucracy rather than by transforming and improving through Theory Y the education of our nation's children.

Theory Y leadership is based on a fundamental belief in the value and capacity of people to create and deliver better worlds – worlds posited on an agreed set of shared values. To do so and to regain control of their own destiny, they must be motivated and enthused by exciting visions (dreams) of a preferred future, to which they can aspire while creating cultures in which they have the independence and trust to create and implement their own visions as contributory parts of the overarching and agreed vision. As Hock (1999) enthuses, people have an unbelievable capacity to achieve great things given the right environments, expectations and freedoms. Performance management should be about 'tapping' into this 'unbelievable capacity'.

To engender this commitment the leader must be honest (words matching actions) and act with true integrity (actions matching words). 'Walk the talk', 'live the life', 'become the change you want the world to be', all illustrate the message. This is not a *crie de coeur* for perfection in all leaders but an acceptance that actions of the leader must align with the espoused values and visions of the school. What a leader does and says matter and, as Covey (1992: 192) says, 'It's the little things that count'. In this sense, getting others to enthusiastically give their all is as much about 'noticing' a new hairstyle in one of the pupils/staff as speaking at the annual general meeting. Equally, the leader must also translate into action thoughts about the uniqueness of their organisation. What is our unique contribution to the world?

> *Most don't know the answer. Why then would you want to commit your life to an organisation that can't give something special to the world?*

(Handy, 1999: 127)

But at least one headteacher did know an answer when questioned by Hay McBer for the HEFF research. When asked about the importance of the headteacher's role he replied, 'Headship is of galactic importance. It changes the world'.

In this way leaders deal in hope, and engendering 'followership' in others is dependent on the language and actions of the leader being from the 'spiralling up' domain rather than the 'spiralling down'. Within us all is a tendency to be positive or optimistic. These can be lifetime dispositions or fluctuate according to the climate of the context in which you find yourself. Leaders can influence the climate in which people work by as much as 70 per cent, both positively or negatively (Hay, 2000).

Adults are more difficult to change than infants. They have learned from life and have greater autonomy to make their own decisions. Adults learn with intentionality. They decide whether they are going to join in the process. They decide whether as well as what they want to learn. If we believe in lifelong learning and learning organisations, we need to understand the role of the highly effective leader as facilitator not dictator.

> *At bottom, desire to command and control is a deadly, destructive compulsion to rob self and others of the joy of living.*

> (Hock, 1999: 24)

Adults and children 'downshift' at the first sense of dominant behaviour and control (Caine and Caine, 1991). They need to have the dignity of being responsible for decisions about their life and lifestyles, including those in the workplace. This need enables employees to change from 'mercenaries' to 'citizens' (Handy, 1999: 127) becoming people who have a very strong affiliation with a particular organisation. This has significant implications for leaders at all levels including classroom teachers and how they deal with pupils.

From vision into practice

A recurring thought throughout my career in education had been that children do not fail schools, rather schools fail children. Many years of headship has helped me clarify a conviction that all children could be 'successful' unless they had suffered some sort of brain damage. The notion of some human beings being 'below average' needed challenging. People simply have different aptitudes. Our major task in school is to find ways in which each individual can learn to experience and be a success.

Such beliefs and motivations underlay our school's commitment to a three-year programme of 'success for all'. The criterion was that all children would achieve level 4 in mathematics and English at the end of Key Stage 2 (84 per cent and 69 per cent respectively were the figures for children entering the school at below average levels on the Personal Improvement Plans (PIPs) baseline assessments). This commitment, which took three months to agree, was implemented only after all staff had 'signed up' to total commitment. It became a shared vision even though it was shared more enthusiastically by some than by others. Readers may well react to such a 'narrow' criterion for 'success'. But this was only part of our overall vision and a part driven by the government. In fact we valued flexibility and creativity highly within the school. Meeting external agendas and legal requirements at such high levels of performance was seen as a safeguard against any future interference.

In case some are tempted to conclude that such approaches led to 'cramming', 'hot-housing' and 'teaching to tests' it is important to highlight the multitude of praise heaped on the school, pupils, teachers and parents from Ofsted and other external sources summarised in the quote, 'There was an all pervading sense of joy of learning throughout the entire school' (Ofsted, 1998).

'Success for all' challenges fundamental assumptions about institutionalised failure, the nature of intelligence, the impact of nurture on performance, as well as the beliefs and value systems of a whole group of teachers. It also challenges a community to clarify its stance on positive discrimination and the equitable sharing of resources. Such a vision has also the potency of engaging people in what it means to be human, to become engaged in making a difference in people's lives and in contributing to the burgeoning of a tiny community benefiting from the potential growth of self-esteem resulting from such an inclusive agenda. Fired by this aim, the headteacher analysed all the then current communications, events and educational writings. Then, with the approval of staff, governors and the community, he focused on achieving success for all. The essential commitment was to improve classroom teaching and organisation to ensure a higher standard of learning for all.

The headteacher's role evolved as the provider of every resource, process and learning to make this committed vision a reality. This included the headteacher's total commitment to becoming the 'lead learner' in the process by reading and pursuing examples of good practice from around the globe.

The processes and structures also had to be put rapidly in place to ensure that all could share good practice and themselves becoming 'lead learners' in their own domains. A 'no blame' culture was fostered to encourage all to innovate, 'have a go' and not feel under pressure always to succeed. The price of success is often learning to become good at discarding what does not add value, and this is sometimes painful. We experimented widely to find which worked best in which circumstances. Our inspirations included enabling some staff to travel abroad and experience for themselves the successful practices of others.

The process evolved into creating a culture and a dynamic where the energy of the organisation became totally and effectively directed towards the pursuit of the vision. It entailed creating new structures and processes designed to realise the vision. It involved people and supporting them, providing them with what they needed to keep going, keeping them healthy and fit and enthused. In sum, making sure we really serviced their needs to ensure they could do the best job possible. It was about making sure they had no excuses. Such collaboration involves calculated high risks, but within a culture where failure is acceptable and viewed constructively as a prelude to much deep learning and where a 'no blame' mentality evolves. It was also about creating a high-energy environment which developed a momentum of its own because, people, children and parents actually enjoyed coming to the place because everyone had an identity, and dignity and respect were reciprocal. It was also about doing not 'to' people but 'with' people, especially pupils. In this way everyone's dignity was enhanced and everyone became a researcher into their own and others' success. An unpredicted consequence of this was summarised in the words of Virginie, a child of a French family, which somehow came to send their children to our school for five weeks every summer term,

> 'À Holy personne ne se moque de personne' ('at Holy [Family] nobody makes fun of anybody'). Virginie blurted this out on their journey back to France. When Mum asked her to explain she continued, 'At Holy (her name for our school) you are accepted for what you are. When you fail, nobody laughs at you, they cheer you up. When you succeed, nobody is envious and tries to pull you down, they rejoice with you. You don't have to show off to friends. You feel free to be just you.'

One can imagine a refrain from some elements of the profession that such a picture is some sort of utopia and in a sense they would be right for when it all comes together into simultaneous existence there is a sense of 'flow', which Csikszentmihalyi (1993) has identified as the critical element of the psychology of happiness. Such a climate tends not to just happen. Rather, it is envisioned, led and managed into place.

On this view, performance management develops into a means of not only achieving outstanding levels of performance, but also of creating outstanding communities where the spirit soars, positive self-esteem becomes infectious, bonhomie, endeavour and commitment become the order of each and every day.

Utopia? Perhaps, but experience of such a place is always identifiable. All visitors to schools or any organisation know within moments how it 'feels'. Values, standards, clarity and relationships are all salient from the first point of contact whether communicated charmingly by telephone or environmentally beautifully presented on arrival at a school entry point. Every interaction, piece of information or occurrence observed leads to an understanding of how deeply beliefs and values reflect and affect the culture of a community.

Infrastructure

The above is not a plea for chaotic freedom without structure. In fact the opposite is true. Structures and processes are created and evolve as appropriate, but

Data Management	Continuing Professional Development	Teaching and Learning			
Vision and Inspiration provided by headteacher, leadership group. Agenda and criteria for individual performance agreed in interview	Benchmarked Data, Inspection Reports, Recent Results input from Executive Coaching, Attitude Surveys of Parents and Pupils affect vision, direction and targets of school	Teaching and Learning policy agreed and implemented. New teachers placed with experienced staff. School Improvement Targets are a scaffolding from baseline entry assessment to outcome performance levels at end of Year 6	Detailed analysis of individual pupil performance passed to teacher pre-September academic year start	Detailed analysis of year group and whole-school performance published internally and presented to each member of staff	New targets negotiated and agreed for all pupils, year groups and staff. To involve pupils, leadership group and any members of staff whom targets may effect
All individual staff have a negotiated and agreed Personal Improvement Plan that focuses on achievement of agreed targets in School Improvement Plan as well as own learning needs	School has a negotiated and agreed School Improvement Plan which identifies school targets and areas for improvement	School Improvement Plan is based on trends rather than one year's results. INTERIM REVIEWS of whole school, year groups are held at least termly	Autumn Package and Panda analysis integrated into development and 'fine tuning'	All Lesson Plans are agreed and co-ordinated with parallel class teachers in weekly team meetings	Weekly team meetings Evaluate performance of teachers and pupils
Weekly team meetings Moderate performance of pupils selecting a target group each week and ensuring all 'groups' are dealt with on an equitable basis. Curriculum specialists contribute for VERTICAL COHERENCE	Lesson Plans are compiled on the agreed format implementing the agreed GOOD PRACTICE outlined in the T+L policy. Plans are ANNOTATED weekly following evaluation thereby recording improvements the next time plans are used	All staff receive Support Visits from colleagues/ Leadership group and the Observation Format is in alignment with the agreed good practice of the Lesson Plan format	Lesson Observation should include the teacher's own Self-Evaluation on the agreed format as a step on the way to a culture of Self-Evaluating Professionals	Teacher and leadership group member meet for performance conference at least once a term. This will be more frequent for inductees, new members of staff or those staff requiring extra assistance. One subject area moderated by whole school termly	Unannounced, unplanned visits into the classroom are a normal part of school life and the PM process. Such visits elicit information about day-to-day practice and the performance of students. Any significant issues should be recorded in a teacher's Personal Profile
All staff should undertake the Hay McBer Diagnostic providing a World-Class Benchmark as measured against the national research on Teaching Effectiveness	This diagnostic process should include both Peer and Pupil Evaluations of Performance	The results of this process will form a significant part of the conference with a member of the leadership group and the development of further Personal Improvement Plans. It will also inform the Threshold discussions	All staff should compile their Performance Portfolio to meet all the required areas of discussion for the purposes of Threshold Assessments	All children 'own' their personal Learning Log that facilitates the Learning Conversation between teacher/pupil/parents. This focuses on Formative Feedback	The Learning Log provides the school with an up-to-the-minute Data Management System tracking all pupil and teacher progress. This provides all parents with regular and frequent Reports re pupil performance in the core subjects

Figure 8.2: Success for all: the infrastructure

rigorous quality assurance of the vision helps ensure that only those which add value are maintained. Metaphorically, the infrastructure has the qualities not of tensile steel but of firm rubber. The former are rigid, monitorable and measurable and demand total compliance; the latter are malleable and flexible, its structure provides necessary support, but can 'give' when necessary.

Figure 8.2 illustrates the many systems and processes, which grew out of our journey towards success for all. This infrastructure allowed us to meet confidently any external bureaucratic requirements but, more importantly, assisted in the creation of a climate of demanding challenge *and* support where excellence in every sphere became the desired criteria of an achieving culture.

Decision making

Making decisions is the fundamental lifeblood of any organisation. We worked hard to ensure the process enhanced rather than diminished people. It was agreed that all people had the right to be involved in any decision that impacted on them. This included pupils when appropriate, parents, governors and all staff. It was critical that the concept did not become an end in itself and develop into a structure that was more important than the vision it was helping to create. Therefore, we had an agreed simple commitment that in all things generosity of spirit was to be paramount. Major decisions were taken at executive meetings to which all had an entitlement to attend if the subsequent decision impacted on them personally. An elected member of staff chaired this forum. The head had one vote. Self-esteem was enhanced and the school began to model the democratic processes inherent in our democracy.

At this point a few colleagues expressed incredulous viewpoints and seemed to think the leader has relinquished all control. Such a view forgets the political process. Much politicking went on outside the meeting with various individuals trying to influence the decision-making process. Ultimately, however, the power of argument was critical and the headteacher could easily be defeated and decisions taken that the staff felt to be in the best interest of the school. Experience relates that far from diminishing the role of the head this process enhanced the position considerably.

Roles and responsibilities

All individual roles and responsibilities became part of our matrix management with every aspect of the school visible on three pages of A4 paper.

This was publicly displayed and each year individuals could negotiate a change in role and responsibilities. This created opportunities for people to further their professional growth, enhance their portfolio and to enhance their value in the jobs marketplace. It also improved the school, as motivation was significantly enhanced through these opportunities. Again such a process is as messy as any organisation full of the entire spectrum of humanity. Status and stature arose from contribution, as did pay, reward and recognition.

Task forces

Task forces were groups formed from volunteers to deal with major issues as and when they arose. They elected their own chairperson and agreed a remit with the school leadership. Each task force had a 'timed life'. They would deal with such issues as, future's thinking, new learning technologies, Success for all. These groups would always elicit contributions from the headteacher towards their final reports and would present their findings, as appropriate, to all stakeholders including governors, parents and pupils.

Flat organisational structure

The previous hierarchical structure with the senior management team had caused disquiet for some time. It became appropriate to re create the structure on a much flatter level. Area co-ordinator roles were replaced by revolving chairpersons; curriculum responsibilities remained, although task forces became the significant driving force for change. The senior management team was disbanded and replaced by the decision-making policy group. The role of deputy was enhanced through the introduction of the concept of corporate headship. Leadership began to arise at all levels. Risk taking, entrepreneurship and innovation increased significantly.

Corporate headship

With the agreement of the governing body and overseen by our executive coach our corporate headship was introduced, which saw the two deputies become 'headteachers' in their own domain with the accompanying responsibility and accountability. The executive coach closely monitored the implementation and impact of this development on the individuals concerned and on staff and parents. This structure provided excellent succession training and much needed 'space' for the headteacher to focus on improving learning. The head remained legally responsible for the school, but parents, associated agencies and headteacher colleagues gradually accepted their relationships with someone other than the official 'headteacher'.

This structure was enacted at all levels and had practical implications such as the sharing of one office – an excellent way to monitor each other's performance.

Balance: IQ, EQ, SQ

Our lives, like so many modern-world employees, became dominated by activity. We were dominated by 'doing' and never had any time for 'being'. One of our training days was dedicated to exploring our individual and collective stress levels. This headteacher received a score in the danger zone. Bad enough in itself, but alarming when one considers the impact the leader has on the lives of others. Something had to change. And quickly!

Part of the lead learner experience had been reading a variety of authors (Damasio, 1994; Kushner, 1988; Porter, 1993; Zohar, 1997) who all identified the serious damage continually high levels of stress can have on health, well-being and performance. Siegal (1988) explains the cognitive, emotional and spiritual systems within the body and goes so far as proposing that ill-health, *dis-ease*, comes when one or more of these elements is out of kilter. If one accepts the leap from this, applied to an individual, to an organisational level, then the importance of 'balance' of these three areas within organisations becomes critical; the contention being that 'balanced' leaders create balanced organisations and 'balanced' and healthy employees/pupils.

There appears to be an abundance of cognitive challenge in the complex and rapidly changing world of education. Throughout the last ten years, and for the foreseeable future, change has been and will remain a constant in the lives of every headteacher, teacher and pupil.

Emotional literacy comes through many, interconnected elements of the organisation: relationships, dealing with conflict, understanding and managing self in relation to others, understanding self through others. A variety of structures such as access and contribution to the creation of visions, access to every level of the decision-making process, 360° formative feedback, responsibility and accountability, reward and recognition proved to be of positive value in this area. Perhaps, most significantly, was, the establishment of our Values and Beliefs Charter that underpinned all and every interaction in the school. This became the signpost that emotional intelligence should be encouraged and developed at all levels. As this charter gradually filtered through every aspect and relationship in the school it became the accepted norm for behaviour.

The third element, spiritual intelligence, has only recently come into mainstream thinking as an issue that is central to high-level performance of individuals and organisations. Zohar (1997) claims to have identified 'that which makes us human' (SQ) which she hails as the discovery in the human brain of interconnected brainwaves that produce a basic response mechanism in humans to search for higher meaning their lives. It was interesting that the mission for the school had arisen as, 'Trying to make the world a better place' and Handy (1999) confirms that ennobling visions can have a most positive impact on motivation and performance of individuals.

However, we determined that attention should be given to individuals' spiritual needs in a more systematic way. Conversations were frequent about our frantic, activity led, destructive lifestyles. We had become unwilling addicts to permanent motion, with lifestyles dominated by constant and ever increasing activity. Through the executive's coach's careful nurturing we were able to invent a series of alternative staff meetings that centred on 'being' rather than 'doing'. These were called 'Triads'.

Attendance was voluntary and all meetings were completely confidential. Self-selecting groups met in threes with a stimulus for discussion provided, in the first instance, by myself. The process began by listening, in silence to a piece of music. A small piece of poetry or prose was read and questions supplied to initiate a discussion. These questions tended to centre on 'big issues': the meaning of life, getting old, coping with change, the purpose of education. To an outsider such notions may create interesting responses but for those who participated the increase in intimacy, the 'bonding' that took place between individuals, the contribution to mental and physical health were all major outcomes. The increasing depth within relationships further increased motivation, self-esteem and people's willingness to 'go the extra mile'. This generous contribution of discretionary effort is identified within the models of excellence as the critical factor in outstanding performance. Attendance of staff also rose to an all time high of 99 per cent.

Pupils

It gradually became apparent that most of the elements we created towards our optimal learning/working environments for adults were equally applicable to pupils. Self-science (teaching emotional intelligence) became part of their programme, teachers experimented with triads for pupils, meditation and relaxation became commonplace. Optimal learning environments for pupils became the mission with an accompanying multitude of initiatives. The culture became one of mutual exploration between adults and pupils for what worked best. Pupils took an active role in managing and improving teacher performance through attendance at training days and through participating in teacher appraisal. Children suddenly emerged as teachers of other children, and structures and processes arose to integrate this into our normal activities. If one views the schools as 'wheels within wheels' then gradually all were in motion and all were interconnected. Our pupils had become radical agents of change, interested and motivated about their own brain and learning and participating in the democracy of their classroom and their school. It was a joy.

Results went through the roof. Our 100 per cent was achieved, apart from the lovely Katie with 'brain damage'. What was even more significant was a transformation in our level 5 performance that saw 75 per cent in science, 69 per cent in mathematics and 49 per cent in English. Something was working!

Evolution

Over millions of years our planet has evolved into an ecosystem of unbelievable efficiency and sophistication. Nature is constantly adapting to overcome all problems and issues in relation to its survival and sustaining its future. To do so it has developed a whole series of autopoietic systems (Capra, 1997). These systems are self-selecting organic processes that are all interconnected. All work in equilibrium providing feedback loops to which they adapt and further sustain and guarantee their future existence.

In the same way, performance management cannot be extracted from the 'whole' of the school. It is the whole school. The task for the leader is to create self-selecting groups that work in harmony and are integrated for the greater good of pursuing a vision to which all have assented. Feedback and experience is integrated into the system as each part evolves for the next part of the journey or the creation of new visions. The 'end product' of such concepts is the processes and cultures that emerge. 'Ending' is not the conceptual objective, rather a continuing journey of discovery, evolution and renewal. The journey is, in itself, the endgame.

Conclusion

Performance management is an idea of its time imposed on the profession by a centralist government doing its best to improve the schooling of our nation's children. Like most initiatives it provides an opportunity for the informed leader to maximise and enhance the education provided for the pupils in their care. By definition highly effective leaders will have already been fully immersed in the process. The danger is that bureaucratic procedures are viewed as attractive and sufficient alternatives to fundamentally improving our education system and the performance of each and every individual. In the same way that self-evaluation is only half a story with the other half provided by feedback from others so that individuals and organisations can know self through others, then performance management is, too, only half the picture. Human beings are far too sophisticated to allow any imposition to change their basic ways and motivations; for such a system to 'work' it cannot be imposed and done to all. It must become a choice that mature and committed individuals choose because they see true value in the process as a means to improving self, the education of pupils, and the societies and communities in which they live. It must 'make a difference'.

References

Caine, R. and Caine, G. (1991) *Making Connections*. Alexandria, VA: Association for Supervision and Curriculum Development.

Capra, F. (1997) *The Web of Life*. London: HarperCollins.

Covey, S. (1992) *The Seven Habits of Highly Effective People*. London: Simon and Schuster.

Csikszentmihalyi, M. (1992) *The Psychology of Happiness*. London: Harper and Row.

Damasio, A. (1994) *Descartes' Error*. New York: Putnam and Sons.

Greenleaf, R.K. (1998) *The Power of Servant Leadership*. San Francisco: Berrett-Koehler.

Handy, C. (1999) 'The search for meaning', in F. Hesselbein and P.M. Cohen (eds) *Leader To Leader*. San Francisco: Jossey-Bass.

Hay McBer (2000) *A Model of Teacher Effectiveness*. London: Hay McBer.

Hock, D. (1999) *The Birth of the Chaordic Age*. San Francisco: Berrett-Koehler.

Kushner, H.S. (1988) *When All You've Ever Wanted Isn't Enough*. London: Pan Books.

McGregor, D. (1960) *The Human Side of Enterprise*. New York: McGraw-Hill.

Ofsted (1998) *Report on Holy Family Roman Catholic Primary School, Slough*. www.ofsted.gov.uk

Porter, P. (1993) *Awaken the Genius*. Phoenix, AZ: Purelight.

Siegal, B.S. (1988) *Love, Medicine and Miracles*. London: Arrow Books.

Zohar, D. (1997) *Rewiring The Corporate Brain*. San Francisco: Berrett-Koehler.

9

■ ■ ■

Performance Management and the Church School

Alan Murphy

While this chapter primarily aims to challenge leaders of and within Christian church schools, there are aspects of performance management covered that will also interest forward-thinking leaders in any value-driven school.

It is proposed that schools must:

- take a positive approach to performance management;
- ensure the core values on which the school is built are revisited;
- reflect on leadership and the concept of serving others;
- use performance management as a spur to more focused professional development;
- consider if leadership and management structures are appropriate for this new era and reflect the proclaimed values of the community;
- build performance up from the individual student not down from current league table positions;
- ensure 'soft targets' are given equal priority in our mission to educate in the widest sense;
- develop a school ethos and a classroom climate built upon mutual 'love' and respect.

Performance

After a long time the master of those servants returned and settled accounts with them.

The man who had received the five talents brought the other five. 'Master,' he said, 'you entrusted me with five talents. See, I have gained five more.'

His master replied, 'Well done, good and faithful servant! You have been faithful with a few things; I will put you in charge of many things. Come and share your master's happiness!'

Matthew 25

Performance related pay is not a new concept! However, there are some in education who still consider performance to be a dirty word. The term is associated with cut-throat businesses that put improving performance as the only value to be upheld.

The church school must not aim to be an educational haven, separated from the real world. The state pays the salaries of the church school staff, buys the books for the students and pays the great majority of building costs. We serve the community and in return we must be effective and efficient.

In *Managing in a Time of Great Change*, Drucker (1995: 242) observes that most 'non-profit' organisations never reach their potential: 'The majority still believe that good intentions and a pure heart are all that is needed.' Church schools need to be positive and optimistic about the potential benefits that performance management can bring. Take control of the programme and use it to further the mission of the school.

How do we improve performance – pray harder in assembly?

There is evidence that church schools perform well when measured against most performance criteria. Is this achieved because throughout the land, staff and students in church schools are more effective when it comes to praying for good examination results in assembly? Or perhaps, because they are part of the 'club', their prayers are more likely to be answered! Prayers may help but the school that relies upon them to boost performance is likely to contain more sore knees than A 'stars'!

Schools supported by the churches and other major faith groups are of course, valued by members of those groups. They also have a good record of delivering a high-quality of education to their pupils and many parents welcome the clear ethos of these schools.

(DfEE, 2001: para. 4.19)

Education Secretary, David Blunkett has been quoted as stating that *'he wants to bottle the secret of their [church schools] success'*.

Defining the church school

Just as there is no such thing as a 'bog standard' comprehensive school, there is no definitive church school – they are all very different. Even the two faith traditions, the Roman Catholic Church and the Church of England, which support the great majority of the church schools in England, have in the past taken a different view of the purpose of their schools. Put simply, Catholic schools have usually been set up to primarily serve members of that faith community and this would be very evident in admissions arrangements which will give a high priority to Roman Catholic applicants. Church of England schools, however, were often set up to serve a local community, and allegiance to the church was not necessarily an entry requirement.

At secondary level, both churches responded positively to the movement towards comprehensive schools because of the belief that any gifts we are given by God are given to us not just for our own benefit but also to be shared for the benefit of others.

What is it that makes a church school distinctive? More caring? Better discipline? Good examination results? If the head of a church school was given £1 for every occasion a parent had stated one of these reasons as to why they were opting for a church school for their child, they would have no need for a performance related bonus. These are real perceptions but at best they are myths and at worst are generalisations which slur colleagues working in high-performing, well-disciplined and equally caring 'state' schools.

Any school – church school, foundation school, community school or independent school – should aspire to care for its students, to help them achieve their potential and to thus achieve good examination results. To get beyond the simplistic generalisations, it is important to consider the elements which are likely to be clearly evident in all good church schools. These elements are also likely to be present in all good schools and even in many good and successful businesses. All modern successful enterprises are likely to be built on a foundation of clearly stated, well-understood and wholly accepted values. What differentiates each organisation, and what distinguishes the best church schools from the best state schools may simply be what those values are and where the source of the values is to be found.

Christian church schools have one major advantage in building up their set of core values. They have access to a set of values that has stood the test of time – two millennia. Most church schools proclaim to use 'gospel values' as the foundation upon which the curriculum and ethos of the school is built.

Values, values and values . . .

A set of core values should drive every aspect of the church school as a learning community. They need to be agreed by all – staff, students, parents and other partners – and then stated in such a way that they can be understood and internalised by all. This statement of core values, usually referred to as a 'mission statement', should then be the foundation on which every decision is based.

A major initiative such as the introduction of performance management should be taken as an opportunity to revisit these core values and ensure that any model performance policy is rooted in these.

If performance management is just bolted onto a school's current policies with the simple adoption of a national model it is unlikely to have anything other than a transitory effect. It could even become counterproductive, producing the antagonism that any nationally imposed system tends to generate and actually have an adverse effect on performance!

The introduction of such a significant change should be seen as an opportunity rather than a problem. An opportunity to carry out a stocktake of all the elements which are likely to contribute to the distinctive nature of the church school and to examine how each has an impact on performance. It is a good time to review all current policies and procedures that may impact upon performance and ensure changes and adjustments are made in order to secure further improvements.

Leadership

There is only one role model for leadership in church school. Jesus told his followers that 'The Son of man came not to be served but to serve'. He urged his disciples to serve one another as he served them. By washing the wayside dust from his disciples' feet he carried out an act of hospitality commonly performed by a servant.

How does leadership of the headteacher in the church school you know stand up by comparison to this model? Reserved parking place for the headteacher? The largest office? Head communicating and on good terms mainly with other senior staff? The thoughts of the senior management team more highly valued than the thoughts of the teachers working a full timetable? Servant leader?

Type 'servant + leader' into the Yahoo search engine and you will be pointed to over 30 000 web pages. Some of the top-performing companies in the USA have adopted this leadership model, not just because it promotes a feeling of well-being among employees but also because it is effective in business terms.

How many church schools that claim in their prospectus to be a 'caring community' can honestly claim they have something similar to the following phrase in their staff handbook – as guidance as to how colleagues and students should be treated?

> *People need to be accepted and appreciated and above all recognized for their special and unique spirits. One assumes the good intentions of co-workers and does not reject them as people, even when one is forced to refuse to accept their behavior or performance. The most successful servant-leaders are those who have become skilled empathetic listeners.*

(La Cabana, 2001)

For school leaders to truly harness the potential that lays within the teaching and support staff a supportive leadership model is needed. One that is built upon trust, humility and respect for the team members the leaders serve. Before they judge the performance of others, leaders must first reflect upon their own strengths and weaknesses.

Can one blind man lead another? Surely both will fall into a pit?

Why do you look at the speck of sawdust in your brother's eye and pay no attention to the plank in your own eye?

How can you say to your brother, 'Brother, let me take the speck out of your eye, when you yourself fail to see the plank in your own eye? You hypocrite, first take the plank out of your eye, and then you will see clearly to remove the speck from your brother's eye.

(Luke 6:39 and 41–2)

Writing in *The Message*, Peterson (1995: 513), paraphrases 1 Thessalonians 5:15 with a sentence that should, perhaps, be printed on the cover of every church school performance management policy: 'Look for the best in each other, and always do your best to bring it out.'

Supporting professional development

One key requirement for improving performance and for bringing out the best of colleagues is investment in training and professional development. This is where value needs to be added to the poorly funded nationally imposed model. If the performance management routine boils down to a couple of hours' chat around a single session of classroom observation, it is not going to bring about dramatic changes to the quality of teaching and thus the quality of learning in the church school. Adopting the minimalist approach is the equivalent of burying the 'talent' in the ground and digging it up unchanged one year later!

If the school is truly committed to developing the skills of its people, it must invest in training and coaching. Here are three practical ways of investing in training and coaching – two are virtually cost-free and the third is an expensive but very worthwhile investment:

1 *Abolish meetings – use the time for training.* One English secondary school has gone the whole way and abolished all meetings in the traditional Monday-after-school slot. Instead this precious time is used for in-house training, sharing of good practice, online ICT training etc. Many teachers rightly complain about time wasted in poorly planned, badly structured and unproductive meetings. If a school is to operate collaboratively, meetings are necessary, so perhaps the ideal model is to halve the number of meetings. In the school where I was head, in our Monday 3.30 p.m. to 5.00 p.m. slot we mirrored the school two-week timetable – Monday 'Week A' was for well planned necessary meetings, 'Week B' had a carefully organised training focus.

2 *Set up a truly interactive training intranet.* The typical school handbook is a dusty, rarely consulted list of required routines with little reference to teaching and learning. Who blames colleagues who do not open it from one end of the year to another? It would not be beyond the ability of a sharp ICT co-ordinator to construct pages within a school intranet that allows easy access by all to training ideas and information. There could be links to other top training web sites, and documents such as the Hay McBer report on teaching effectiveness could be accessed. Colleagues could share good practice with a message board. Suggestions as to how best to cope with Wayne Payne in 3C could be added to regularly as inventive colleagues experiment to find the elusive solution!

3 *Invest in a 'super-sub'!* I used this strategy in a school that I was seconded to head when it was placed in 'special measures'. A reliable teacher – a good 'all rounder' who knew the students well – was taken off the traditional timetable and deployed as a full-time cover teacher. He took lessons planned by the subject team to whom he was on loan. A rota, planned a term ahead, ensured every subject team regularly gained his services for a day. Core subjects would gain a day every 11 school days – out of sync with the timetable to ensure the same classes were not regularly affected. The time was used to allow monitoring, evaluating, coaching, team teaching, one-to-one in depth meetings and observing of colleagues in other departments etc. Monitoring and supportive training was now seen by teachers in a positive light. It was not perceived as a burden by the subject leader and his or her team to be added to the many other tasks always on the 'to do' list.

None of the above strategies would be specific to performance management in a church school; the point is that if pronouncements are made by church schools that pupils and staff are highly valued objects of creation one has to invest to ensure the rhetoric is a reality. The cost of the package, including some of the information technology (IT) costs, would be in the order of £30 000 per year. This is only about 1.5 per cent of a typical secondary school budget – a worthwhile investment in performance that will also make the staff feel that their professional development is valued. You cannot get improved performance on the cheap!

Structures and systems

For strategies such as the above to be effective, it will be important that the leadership structure of the school is reviewed to ensure it is compatible with the professed mission and the valuing and empowering of those working closest to the students. There is nothing wrong in paying staff more if they carry greater responsibility – especially if they are truly accountable for the results achieved within their area of responsibility.

The servant leader would, however, wish to ensure that there is equitable distribution of preparation and marking time, access to ICT, availability of teaching assistants and other support staff, reprographic facilities, a good working environment, and a decent space in which to take a break. In any review taking place as part of a performance management, these aspects of the working climate also need to be addressed. It will be counterproductive to produce a raft of measures which are perceived to increase the demands upon colleagues (remember perceptions are as important as the reality) without any measures which alleviate pressure and which ensure teachers are treated as true professionals.

In some large church secondary schools, core subjects will be taught by a team of over 20 teachers. Rank Xerox, despite being a company that employs 40 000 people, never allows any team to consist of more than eight people. How can we ensure the staff in a major subject are well led and work in genuine teams that form the basic performance management unit? One method is to appoint assistant heads of subjects (or 'assistant subject leaders' – a better title) responsible for the work and performance of up to six teachers (Figure 9.1).

This would be a more effective way of structuring for performance than taking the usual approach of appointing people as 'key stage co-ordinators' without responsibility for leading a specific team of teachers. The central subject support team – head of subject with the team of assistant leaders and an administrator – would also take much of the subject planning responsibility off the shoulders of the teachers. They can then concentrate on ensuring that quality teaching and learning is a feature of all the classes for which they are responsible.

All gain. The head of subject knows who is responsible for maximising performance of which groups, and yet the teachers know they have the direct

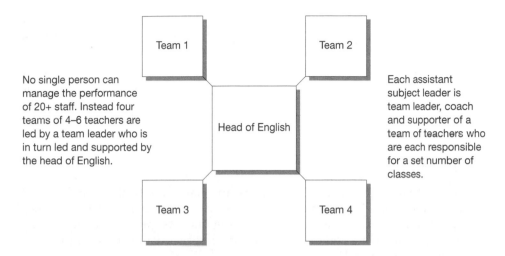

Figure. 9.1: A structure for improving subject performance in the large school

support of a colleague. The mini-team get to know each other well, share good practice, visit each other's groups and support each other with challenging students. If things get really tricky they have further support from the head of subject. A bonus is that the assistant subject leader gains real leadership experience to help their professional and career development.

Hard and soft

Targets

While the church school must, in the interests of developing the God-given talents of its young people, focus on the performance of students in national tests, other targets are equally important. Some of these targets will be so called 'soft targets'. In the current move from the centre to drive up standards there is a danger that anything that cannot be measured is considered to be of little importance. It is very difficult, if not impossible, to measure the growth in self-esteem that can occur if a student spends his or her formative years in a learning community with a strong and positive ethos that works hard to support even the most challenging students.

If in setting performance objectives only 'hard' targets are agreed, there is a danger that church schools will be drawn away for work that should be at the heart of their mission statements. They would then leave themselves open to the critics who see their existence as socially divisive. Challenging students may seriously damage your raw statistics but if these pupils are seen as 'students with problems and not problem students' they may be able to be 'turned around' and given hope. If this is achieved the school will be living out its Christian mission.

> *Christianity is the religion of hope and people in areas of social deprivation might find that a valuable commodity in a dark world. That is a great part of the case for church schools, as I see it.*

> (Lord Dearing, TES, 2000)

Hard targets

In seeking to manage performance against the 'hard targets' the church school must put the individual student first. The study of residuals and all the other paraphernalia of performance monitoring has its place but should be secondary to the work done to ensure every single student is making progress appropriate to their ability.

The form tutor in the secondary school should be the students' 'guardian angel' – watching over them, talking to them about progress with their learning, helping them set and understand the targets they have to achieve, challenging them. The tutor must always approve of each student as precious individuals, even if not always approving of his or her behaviours.

In challenging the students to reach targets, it is critical that the tutor has access to the data on which targets are based and the data which measures how close to or far from these targets each student is.

In Figure 9.2, students (1 to 26) in one Year 11 form group are ranked by Key Stage 3 SATs average score – the line joining the solid dots. Other data displayed for each student is:

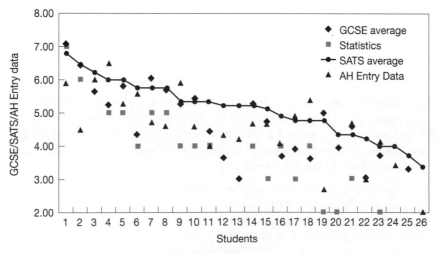

Figure 9.2: Understanding student performance

- diamond – GCSE 'mocks' average; numeric equivalent;
- triangle – potential as measured by standardised tests on entry to the school;
- square – GCSE grade when entered for statistics at the end of Year 10.

The student number code on the X axis protects the identity of the other students when the chart is shared in a 'one to one' with student and/or parent.

In this form group, the chart suggests:

1   student 1 is on course to achieve above the potential indicated in standardised tests at age 11, achieving just below a mean of level 7 at Key Stage 3, has already gained a GCSE grade A (7.00) for statistics in Year 10 and is averaging A grades following GCSE mocks. Little intervention needed! Just praise!

2   student 6 is on course to underachieve. He performed well at Key Stage 3 – just below an average of level 6, in line with potential. But, he only managed a D (4.00) in statistics in Year 10 and mocks suggest he is on line to average D grades with only a couple of Cs at GCSE. Key Stage 3 performance suggests he should be aiming for Bs and Cs. A typical male? Serious intervention needed!

3   student 19-standardised tests on entry suggested she was one of the academically 'weakest' students joining this all-ability school. She performed well above this indication of potential in her Key Stage 3 SATs, coming close to averaging level 5, and is on course for five+ A–C grades in her GCSEs. She did not do well in her Year 10 GCSE so should be given lots of encouragement to ensure this does not affect her confidence. This case also reminds us not to put too much weight on standardised entry tests. 'The stone the builders rejected has become the cornerstone' (1 Peter 2). The church school must be wary of adopting rigid streaming or banding systems based on entry data as teachers may lower expectations on the basis of data that is far from perfect.

Soft targets

Mike Tomlinson, England's Chief Inspector of Schools, told delegates to a National Association of Headteachers conference in February 2001 that schools should be given credit for boosting achievement in ways that are not currently measured: 'Let us not value only that which we can measure. Education is about a great deal more than that.' Soft targets are those that are more difficult to measure in the traditional way but it does not mean they should not be set. They do allow important elements that contribute directly or indirectly to performance to be kept under review.

Although progress towards the achieving of a soft target such as 'improving mutual respect between all members of the school community' cannot be measured by hard statistics, qualitative data can be obtained from a variety of sources which will provide indications if progress is being made. These sources include: questionnaires to parents, students and staff, focus groups – made up of parent representatives and perhaps school council members – feedback boxes on school web sites.

Parents regularly have to spend a lot of time hanging around at the traditional school parents' evening. This is an ideal time to issue a survey form or a questionnaire – or just to talk to the parents – and do some serious listening!

To maximise performance, it is also important to analyse attendance at such meetings. What percentage of parents regularly attends? If it is low, is this an indicator that the school is not very welcoming or that the timing is wrong? Which parents are attending – only the parents of those achieving well? If so, how do we harness the support of the parents of the under-achieving students?

Ethos and climate

Prospectuses of most schools of all types claim that the school being promoted has a strong ethos. The 'quality' of the ethos is referred to in most Ofsted inspection reports on schools – church schools or state schools. Many believe they can sense the ethos of a school as they walk around in the school. Church schools are *expected* to have a strong and positive ethos. Easy to sense, difficult to define, impossible to quantify? The 'characteristic spirit or attitudes of a community' is one dictionary definition.

Headteachers of church schools must have the confidence to prioritise resources in support of those activities that build a positive ethos in the school. The climate within the school and in the classroom does have an impact upon performance, although it is difficult to quantify how significant that link is. The nature of the day-to-day interactions between teachers and teachers, between teachers and students, and teachers and parents, all contribute to the building up of a community underpinned by mutual respect. It is also hard to measure respect but it must be valued as a significant contributor to building self-esteem and, therefore, performance.

In their *Research into Teacher Effectiveness* Hay McBer (DfEE, 2000: 45) refer to an ethos of 'mutual trust' and 'mutual respect'. The report stresses how important it is that all involved in the life of the school help to create this.

In their research report they give a great deal of attention to the term 'class-room climate'. This is defined as the collective perceptions by pupils of what it feels like to be a pupil in any particular teacher's classroom, where those perceptions influence every student's motivation to learn and perform to the best of his or her ability.

The ethos of the school, or the climate within the classroom, does impact on learning and, therefore, contributes to high performance of individuals and of the school. An attempt must therefore be made to 'assess' the quality of the ethos in any performance review.

Every staff member – teaching and support staff – of a church community must actively contribute to building that all-important ethos. This must not be left to chance in the high-performing church school. One performance objective in each teacher's set should be related to furthering the school's mission in general and to any specific element of this mission being prioritised for improvement in the school improvement plan.

The most significant behaviour that can contribute to the quality of ethos in a school is the way all individuals demonstrate 'respect' or 'love' for each other. Hay Mcber reminds us of the impact that a climate of mutual respect can have on motivation: 'Teachers, when they explicitly value others, shape pupils' and colleagues' perceptions of themselves. This helps them to recognise their unique talents, to feel special, and to have the confidence to succeed. It increases the motivation in all to achieve more than they ever thought they could' (DfEE, 2000) and, writing in the New Testament, St John actually commands us to behave this way!

This is my commandment; that you love one another as I have loved you
(John 15:12)

Summary

1 If church schools are to justify their existence in an increasingly secular society they must be distinctive.

2 In Christian denominational schools, this distinctiveness must be rooted in the values of the gospels – 'love one another as I love you'.

3 Revisiting the core values of the school should be the starting point for the development on any performance management policy.

4 The servant leader will always support the person even if he or she does not approve of a behaviour or an action, but will first look at their own behaviours.

5 There must be significant investment in professional development.

6 Structures should be built to enable teachers to ensure teachers are well led and supported in the work they do for their students. No team should consist of more than six teachers.

7 Performance improvements should be built up from the support given to individual students. The pastoral leader has a key role to play in maximising the performance of individual students.

8 Ethos is hard to define and measure but must be founded on mutual respect.

References

Department for Education and Employment (DfEE) (2000) *Research into Teacher Effectiveness*. London: DfEE.

Department for Education and Employment (DfEE) (2001) *Building on Success*. Green Paper. London: DfEE.

Drucker, P.F. (1995) *Managing in a Time of Great Change*. Butterworth-Heinemann.

La Cabana (2001) 'Our value: committed to a caring attitude', La Cabana – Beach Resort and Casino! www.lacabana.com/qualityjourney/leadership.shtml (26 April).

Peterson, E.H. (1995) *The Message*. Colorado Springs: NavPress.

10

■ ■ ■

Performance Management and the Giant Teddy Bear

Mike Wintle

It was Thursday, 8 February, and all the 320 primary children filed into the Upper Hall for their normal morning assembly. Children between 4 and 11 years of age, all immaculate in their blue school uniforms, filed into the large hall ready to listen and take part in their assembly on 'Festivals', which was the theme of their week.

All came in quietly and somewhat nervously because there in the middle of the floor sat a 5-foot high teddy bear, called Trevor, sporting a royal blue Birmingham City shirt and a blue and white scarf. The bear sat motionless (as only a teddy could!) watching and waiting for the assembly to finish. Nobody batted an eyelid. No member of staff said a word and no child asked the obvious!

The assembly went its course; the children had time to reflect, pray, sing and then the notices were read out. Another assembly bit the dust and the children went off to their lessons and the teddy bear sat outside the school office for a further week, being kidnapped twice by four parents and held to ransom. That night, the governors agreed the performance management structure for the school, but all the talk was of the teddy bear!

All that term and most of the previous one, the staff had made performance management their main thrust of professional development within the school, alongside ICT, and all teaching staff had just acquired their European

113

Computer Driving Licence. This had proven more of a challenge than perfor-mance management ever would, mainly because ICT meant more work and new structures.

The policy for performance management had been introduced over two staff meetings and had been agreed in early spring at a full governing body meet-ing. The whole school had agreed the bog standard (pardon the pun!) policy and this was adapted at the same time that three governors had agreed to be performance management governors. Interestingly, those chosen were the same governors that already looked after the old appraisal system and were confident with this type of monitoring.

Nothing had had to change; or at least no member of staff or governor had noticed.

Work and staff moderation simply continued as before. These were:

1 *Termly headteacher worksifts.* A number is chosen from the register and every child with that number comes to the headteacher with all his or her work. No warning is given and there is always a set focus that the staff are aware of. For example, the focus could be making sure that the school's marking policy is being adhered to, or that writing is being targeted through regular teacher written targets.

2 *Weekly handwriting reviews* by the headteacher. The head views all 320 chil-dren's handwriting every Friday. A 'winner of the class' is chosen and 'a winning class' every week. Handwriting certificates are given out in Mentions Assembly and the names are placed on the handwriting board. The effect on writing over the last three years has been dramatic.

3 *Lesson observations.* Every member of staff has at least one lesson observa-tion by the head or deputy headteacher every academic year and probably more. These are formulised into the same structure that was adopted for the performance management structure.

4 *Yearly staff interviews.* These are with the head and deputy headteacher and consist of quite informal discussions that follow a set format. They include questions relating to their position in school, their role in the future devel-opment of the school and their opinions of where the school is going in terms of the School Development Plan.

5 *Informal lesson observations* made on a weekly basis by the headteacher.

All the staff quickly picked up the jewel in the new performance management structure and that our current way of self-assessment could and would con-tinue and the new performance management initiative would give better access to increased resources for staff development. It meant greater time for staff to focus on staff development. The school had recently obtained Investors in People from the Training and Enterprise Council so we already were very confident about our training and levels of staff development. Indeed, the Staff Development Policy was one of our most secure policies in school.

Performance management just increased the focus a little and at the same time significantly increased the resources to undertake it. That seemed like a good deal to me. For example the policy states:

It is the intention of this school to develop all staff and governors both profession- ally and personally. Essential in this is the notion of every member of staff having personal and corporate training needs which when taken together will develop the whole performance of the school, this can be encapsulated in the notion of the Learning School.

The Senior Management Team in conjunction with the governing body needs will determine corporate training. These needs will be ascertained by looking at current strengths and weaknesses as highlighted through Ofsted reports, PANDAs, school targets, classroom observations, monitoring of planning and children's work, dis- cussions with the whole staff, current national initiatives and questionnaire.

Training

As with all new and important initiatives, the training of staff was seen as all- important and one that we approached seriously and systematically. The format was as follows:

Head and deputy headteacher

Both the head and deputy headteacher undertook six full days of training at various locations and in line with most schools. However, we both spent the intervening time reporting back to senior management, staff and governors at the respective meetings. We worked really hard at keeping regular staff brief- ings on a Friday morning to update and advise staff, and wrote these out for all staff. This again is part of the school's plan for professional development and not only kept staff up to date, but also involved no extra work.

It was seen by both the head and deputy headteacher that they should have undertaken not only their training before the process of staff performance management started, but also that they had both completed their first target- setting initiatives that took them onto the Leadership Scale. Very early on in the new process (October 1999) both were set targets and a time frame drawn up by the governors.

The headteacher was asked for ideas from the governing body and these were produced to governors at a September 1999 meeting. All targets were heavily connected to the current School Development Plan. It was important for all staff to have confidence in the head, especially as he was seen as being the organiser of performance management. It was, therefore, very important that I was seen 'leading from the front' and not only being appraised by another headteacher and adviser, but also that my new targets were seen as 'big targets'. This is a very personal belief but, as all my targets are linked to a whole school development plan, I have no problems with all the staff knowing what my own personal targets are. After all, it is through the work of the staff that my targets would be reached. It makes sense that the staff know what they are! For the record, my first targets were deemed to have been obtained very early in January 2000 and were:

1 Increase SAT results in Key Stage 1 and especially in writing.

2 Be appraised.

3 Write new job descriptions for all staff in the school.

My present key targets are ones that have been agreed by both myself and the governors involved with performance management and are as follows.

1 To increase the percentage of children obtaining level 2 in writing to 88 per cent by May 2001.

2 To improve the mathematics Key Stage 1 SAT levels in May 2001.

3 To implement a whole school Performance Management Policy and to have it highlighted in the School Development Plan. This should include individual targets for governor perusal.

4 To formulate a new School Development Plan.

5 To improve the overall school punctuality particularly at the start of the day.

Threshold

The threshold part of performance management was split away from the whole process mainly because we felt that threshold was urgent and all six teachers applying needed the information, guidance and resources to undertake the completion of the form quickly. Again, like many schools, we involved all teaching staff in the familiarisation of the processes and this was very successful in convincing the staff that the threshold was a seven-year (and in some cases more!) culmination of teaching experience, professional development and recording pupil progress. The advice given at our whole-school training days was very detailed and broke down the main eight standards into manageable one-page advice sheets. It was intended to be a crib sheet and an example from the Teaching and Assessment part is given below:

Assessment
- *The words consistently and effectively are important. The school's assessment practices are very important in this section and should be used.*
- *Refer to policy and practice 'In the light of the school policy I do . . . and have demonstrated . . . '*

- 'When talking to parents at parents' evening I drew upon the targets set in the reports to parents and . . . '
- 'I follow the school's marking policy and give regular written feedback in handwriting that has dramatically raised standards and has meant 84% of Year 6 obtaining a Level 4 or above in last year's Key Stage 2 Standard Attainment Tasks or 89% were at Level 2A or above from the last Year 1/2 teacher assessments.'

However, because of the headteacher interviews with all staff that has been mentioned earlier, we already had identified not only which staff had shown a desire to go for the threshold assessment, but also we already knew the one real concern they all had for the process. It became very clear that Pupil Progress would be the main target for development as this caused the greatest amount of anxiety amongst the staff. This is probably true in nearly all schools and will be the main cause of grief over the next five or six years in many, in other words, however long the process runs for in the present format. There is no doubt, therefore, that the schools that ease their way into the threshold process most easily are those that have in place an effective and workable assessment policy and practice in place and use these initiatives as routine practice. More of this later.

All the information given for threshold was bullet-pointed and filed for future threshold teachers to use. Again this is proof of how PM can be simple and effective practice.

Whole-school training on performance management

All staff were also involved in two full days of in-service training (INSET) and three staff training evenings. This establishes whole school awareness and growing confidence mainly because staff were fully prepared for the initiative. Most schools did the same sort of thing.

Team leader training

The performance management material makes no mention of the importance of choosing the right team leaders for PM. In fact it assumes that the head-teacher will simply pick various teachers to undertake the process. We felt that it was professional for the staff to choose the two team leaders who would be involved and feel strongly that this was the way forward. With this in mind, the staff expressed a desire that they should come from the senior manage-ment team at that time. Their reasons were twofold. First, they felt experienced and senior teachers should be the people to undertake all staff PM. Second, not many of them were prepared to do it themselves for a number of uncon-nected reasons. Furthermore, the Senior Management Team felt that, if possible, the three stages of the National Curriculum should be represented. Therefore, we chose a team leader from Reception and Year 3 to undertake the team leaders' role and took that to the staff.

The two team leaders undertook two full days of training and then spent two hours feeding back to the staff. It was here that the whole process, mentioned at a later point, was thrashed out and debated. The major points of consent were:

1 An eight-month first cycle was agreed.
2 The autumn term was viewed as the sensible place to begin and end each Performance Management Cycle. Furthermore, this fitted into the existing professional development framework.
3 No team leader would have more than two teachers in their PM team, except the head who would have no more than three.
4 A paper recording structure would be drawn up.
5 A maximum of one hour would be allocated for the initial planning meeting and the setting of personal targets.
6 All meetings would be in school time and not during lunch breaks or after school finished. In other words, school Standards Fund would pay for the initiative and not teachers in their free time.
7 All staff would link the School Development Plan into their PM and also link our ongoing curriculum targets to each other. Therefore, all staff would have the setting of literacy targets as one of their personal targets for performance management.

As already mentioned, assessment of Pupil Progress (or payment by results as the daily tabloids call it!) was identified very early on as being the big obstacle for both threshold and evaluating all staff's ongoing performance management. However, as a school, we realised a number of years ago that all schools that have an effective assessment and target-setting policy and practice in place are winning the race for higher standards at an alarming rate. Anyone with a teacher with SAT marking experience will be able to confirm this. Any marker would be able to endorse my theory that you can look at a school that you have no knowledge about, mark their work for Key Stage 2 SATs and after five scripts in English know if they have an assessment policy and target-setting practice in place. Alarming, but true!

Teachers regularly view our assessment practice, coming from across the country to view us and seeing the practice in action. If this assessment practice is in place and in the words of my Assessment Coordinator 'running itself', then schools have no problem dealing with this aspect of showing pupil progress.

Our policy follows on from what Sir Ron Dearing famously wrote in 1993 with the introduction of the last National Curriculum review: 'Records should be *useful, manageable* to keep and *easy to interpret* . . . It is not possible for teachers to record all their knowledge and they should not be tempted to try . . . If record systems do not provide a significant contribution to teaching and learning there is little point in maintaining them' (emphasis added).

Our assessment model consists of:

Assessment Policy	This provides a structure.
Portfolio	Helps teacher judgements and supports staff.
	Provides evidence and ensures consistency.
	Becomes a reference point.
	Monitors the Assessment Policy.
	Provides assessment opportunities.
Record of Achievement	Helps celebrate children's achievements.
	Helps set targets.
	Helps children be self critical.
Assessment File	Provides a systematic structure.
	Helps with regular ongoing teacher assessment recording.
	Records evidence.
	Shows progression.

With all the above in place, we were well set to meet this new challenge. An example of how well can be seen in the teacher's written record of the Pupil Progress sheet taken directly from a 'live' threshold application form:

Comparisons of last term's teacher assessment and entry levels in September show a progression through levels for many pupils, e.g. out of 38 children, 20 children have gained a level 3 in English, 6 of them moving from level 3 to 4. Gregory Brown's levels in English have increased for level 2 to 3. See assessment file.

I have compared the results of N.F.E.R. taken by my Year 4 children in English, mathematics and reading in May 2000 to the results of the same tests in May 1999, and apart from one child, all have gained positive progress in English with scores ranging from +1 to Jane Green's score of +29.

A further 4 out of the 16 Year 4 children have gained progress scores of +10 or more.

In mathematics all progress scores were above +7 with 5 exceeding +15.

In reading, the only children who have a 'no change' reading age, are those who achieved a Reading Age of 12:03 last year. Susan Grey's Reading Age has risen from 7:01 in 1999 to 11:00 this year.

Again, all the school had to do was to rely upon an existing practice to help complete the threshold data. Furthermore, the same process is also useful in the annual performance management target-setting process for all teachers.

This was never a big deal because we already had, and used, the pupil data. It is important to note that all staff, whatever incremental point they are on, were involved in the establishment of the threshold training.

The staff had no faith in the old-style appraisal training, mainly because resources had dried up and because it bore no resemblance to their everyday working practices. I think that it is true to say that over the last four to five years not one child benefited from staff appraisal and the teachers knew it. Money had dried up for staff development and the old system was seen as unmanageable and not relevant to them as professionals.

The introduction of performance management quickly led to awareness that this new model could be used in conjunction with the new School Development Plan. Like other school improvement plans, ours had a number of key areas for action over the next two years and clearly showed where we wanted to go as a school. However, the staff believed, as in the case of limited learning objectives in their teaching, the value of limited core areas for action. We had the new school improvement plan in which only four areas would be resourced and targeted. These four areas are:

- target setting;
- religious education;
- the foundation stage;
- performance management.

All staff and governors saw this as important in producing an improvement plan that could be effective over the next two years. It was also a clever way of linking performance management with the School Development Plan. The National Literacy Strategy, Autumn 2000 Package, given to headteachers as part of their training for improving Key Stage 1 and 2 literacy results, believes that this idea of layering of targets across the planning and delivery of the curriculum is sound practice: 'Just as a school numerical targets need to be broken down into curriculum targets, so curriculum targets need to be broken down into key stage, class/cohort and pupil learning targets . . . It is this layering of targets which connects to school targets to lessons and individual children.'

Furthermore, and crucially, the School Development Plan includes literacy targets for every child in the school. Planning for every teacher to set important long-term literacy targets for their children is not only linking the development plan to real curriculum issues and pupil improvement, but also makes the process of performance management that much easier. This is because each teacher can put as one of their first personal/learning objectives the fact that every child in their class has a literacy target. This is something that they were doing in their strategic planning anyway. Very clever and effective!

Structure of performance management

The structure of our performance management practice came about through all those many hours of training and consultation with the staff. Behind it lies a number of fundamental issues. Performance management should:

- link into existing practice;
- *be manageable.* This is the key issue to our staff;
- be resourced by the Standards Fund so that it has an impact on individual professional development;
- be resourced by the Standards Fund so that it has an impact on school performance.

Staff at the school were already well used to having people coming into their classes, and saw monitoring of lessons as simply good practice. Indeed, it is also practice in the school for classroom assistants to view other lessons.

We adopted the exemplar given in the performance management booklet issued by the DfEE, mainly because the staff felt that it was simple to understand and to use. As a staff, we agreed that it would be sensible to stay in line with the existing practice of limited objectives and to date no member of staff has set more than four personal and professional objectives. As a staff we are already very familiar with setting SMART targets (specific, measurable, achievable, relevant and time related) and used this to set our new performance management targets.

An example of these is given below:

1 Whole-School Objective: to set individual literacy targets for every child in the class.
2 Professional Development Objective: to explore ways in which expressive arts – music, art and drama can be delivered through the literacy hour.
3 Pupil Progress Objective: to develop drama skills through the literacy hour – with a view to raising children's confidence levels and encouraging the use of a wider vocabulary in written work.

The immediate effect on staff development within the school was excellent, and for a number of reasons:

1 Staff were confident that we had a systematic structure in place that they knew and trusted.
2 Staff were comfortable with the fact that the system was seen to be manageable and that they were all involved in the same structure.
3 Because PM was seen as one of the top school priorities, the staff felt that it was important to overlap certain initiatives, e.g. the literacy targets.
4 The funding from the Standards Fund was seen as important, especially in

terms of staff development in areas that they felt were their weaknesses, e.g. awareness of foundation stage issues that could only be solved by attending focused training events.

So why the giant teddy bear mentioned at the start of the chapter? Well, all schools should be about being fun places to go. It is important that the core skills are bashed pretty hard all day and every day. But if you had asked me at age 11 why I went to grammar school, it was to play football – why else does anyone go to school! The important message here is that children learn when there are lots of things of real interest going on. Some people call this a broad curriculum, but we call it school being a good place to be. The vision of any headteacher should be exactly that, and performance management should under no circumstances get in the way of this idea.

All good schools have adopted performance management in a style that backs up already existing structures. We simply used the introduction of welcome new finance to back up an existing quality staff development programme. It was planned to be manageable and to fit in with the ethos of the school. Performance management worked around our existing systems, and not the other way around.

To conclude, we see performance management as backing up the existing culture in the school. All good schools were already doing performance management anyway, but they called it by a different name. Performance management provides us with a structure for staff development and a career path through which our staff can travel. In this respect it is long overdue. There is no doubt that talking to colleagues involved in the setting of targets also has the uncanny ability to underline the strengths *and* the weaknesses in the school. That's the nature of the beast.

And where is the teddy bear now? Well he went to Cardiff to see the Worthington Cup Final and he had a good day out. And yes we were robbed! But setting up a performance management structure in school was a picnic compared with supporting Birmingham City FC!

References

Dearing, R. (1993) *The National Curriculum and its Assessment: Final Report*. London: SCAA.

11

■ ■ ■

School Self-Review and Performance Management

Mike Mayers

Many papers, articles and books have been written by very eminent educationalists in an attempt to define the factors that contribute to the development of a successful school. Schools are complex communities and there is a great danger of either being overwhelmed by their complexity, or taking such a simplistic view that any resultant analysis is meaningless. After 28 years of teaching and ten years as a headteacher in two contrasting comprehensive schools, I take the view that the most successful schools are those that focus their developmental work upon the quality of teaching and learning, developing techniques that allow continual self-review, in what can become a supportive performance management system.

In those 28 years I can remember only a handful of teachers whom I considered to be incompetent. I have met many hundreds of teachers whom I admired, and in whose classes I would have been delighted for my children to be placed. For me this is the ultimate test of a teachers' performance. Would my son learn effectively in that classroom? Could the teacher keep appropriate discipline and care for my child? Would my son gain the examination grade that he should? Well, in all schools there will be some teachers who will cause concern, some major, some minor, and some that will only appear at certain times of the term, year or as a result of external factors. These 5, 10, 15 or 20 per cent of teachers can make the real difference to a school, and because they are not incompetent the easiest course is to do nothing to turn a blind eye to understand their problems, but not to consider the effects upon their pupils. Too often teachers are able to say, 'I have been teaching this way for over 20 years, and nobody else has ever complained'.

The real problem created by this group of staff is that they cause inconsistencies to occur which confuse pupils, encouraging some to exploit weaknesses in policy implementation. This in turn makes the job of those who are effective, and who are following agreed policies, much more difficult. The dedicated classroom teacher can receive challenges such as 'nobody else makes us take out our earrings', or 'Mr X doesn't set us as much homework as you'. Any fool can write a policy, but it takes dogged determination to ensure that it is implemented and monitored effectively.

Improving the quality of teaching and learning

As head of The Pingle School in Swadlincote from 1991 to 1999 and Chaucer Technology School from September 1999 to the present day, I inherited schools where much good work had already been carried out. In both I was delighted with around 80 per cent of what was happening in the classroom, but I had real concerns about the lack of consistency in some areas and procedures. A good Ofsted report in 1996 noted that there had been considerable improvement in academic achievement, but there was still a need to ensure greater consistency in the quality of teaching and learning. In effect what the school needed was for all the teachers to do what was being done well in 80 per cent of classrooms.

A voluntary working party was established, made up predominately of heads of department, and they were given the task of creating policies to ensure that the quality of teaching and learning was improved further by creating clear expectations and the consistent operation of those policies. The first task was to determine what the school considered to be the characteristics of an effective lesson and, as I was particularly concerned about the quality of some sixth form teaching, this was defined separately for the 11–16 and 16–19 age groups. It was important that all teachers had an opportunity to contribute to what I considered to be a vital task, and initial drafts were amended extensively in an attempt to produce a model that all were prepared to accept. It was also vital to create a framework that allowed individuality to be preserved, for all agreed that individual flair enriched pupils' experiences.

The framework, which resulted from much debate, is noted below, and needs little further explanation. Points 9 and 10 were particularly important at the time as the school was moving to gender setting in a number of subjects.

Characteristics of an effective lesson

While individualism in teaching is important, so is consistency. The following models are accepted as good practice, and all teachers should strive to follow them. They will form the basis for all future lesson observation, support and monitoring.

Characteristics of an effective lesson (11–16)

1 Discipline is established clearly and effectively at the start of the lesson, possibly by lining up in silence outside the room, standing behind chairs in silence, or making the class sit in silence. The end of the lesson is equally orderly.

2 Discipline is strict and very consistent. Threats are not made unless they will be carried out. Only one warning is given before action is taken.

3 Praise is used extensively and openly, and a positive/purposeful atmosphere created. Students feel valued.

4 Seating arrangements are dictated by the teacher.

5 The purpose/objective of the lesson is briefly but clearly stated at the beginning, and what has been achieved summarised briefly at the end.

6 The teacher does not talk excessively, and this includes question/answer sessions where almost all the class are passive for almost all the time. As a guide, do not expect a mixed class to listen to a teacher talk, or a question/answer session, for more than five minutes maximum. Girls are able to listen for longer, but no more than ten minutes. There is no point sending a message if all the receivers have switched off!

7 Teachers give clear instructions, have high expectations, and demand high standards.

8 A wide range of activities is used, and alternative strategies planned in case problems arise.

9 When boys are bored they become disruptive, and they have no respect for teachers they consider to have weak discipline. With boys:

(a) Strict but fair discipline is employed.

(b) It is clear whether a class should be working as individuals or groups, if individuals work in silence, if as a group, there are clear guidelines. Groups of more than three are not used unless there are clear rules/tasks for each member (boys quickly get bored in inactive group work and time in group work should be limited).

(c) There are a variety of activities within a lesson, the more active the better.

(d) There are strategies to help boys to have a clear structure to their work by
  (i) very clear instructions about setting out work;
  (ii) providing templates for written work (models or plans of answers);
  (iii) being clear about homework – what and how much is required;
  (iv) having equipment checks, and follow through with those who forget.

10 Girls often underestimate their abilities and when bored they talk:

  (a) In some classes, individual work in silence may be beneficial, but in others it could be that girls will gain confidence by a period of small group work to discuss and plan a piece of work.

  (b) Confidence is built and individual reassurance given.

  (c) There are fewer activities within a lesson than for boys, and it is noted that in general girls are better organised.

  (d) Girls are challenged to aim high, and not to play safe in their answers.

  (e) There is a mix of individual and group work, but groups of more than three are avoided unless each member has a clear task that will employ them fully.

11 Rote learning is used to learn basic facts, and there are frequent short tests to reinforce basic knowledge/terms.

12 Exercise books are not marked by the teacher in a lesson, and when students are working the teacher goes around the class assisting individuals, reinforcing comments made in marking, and *praising*!

13 Work is marked promptly and the individual feels that the teacher cares about how they are doing, and feeds back information, through marking, about whether the targets set are being achieved.

14 The lesson contains content that is challenging, and appropriate for all individuals in the class.

15 School policies on setting homework, marking, discipline and uniform are supported.

Characteristics of an effective lesson (16–19)

1 There is a clear statement of the objectives of the lesson at the start.

2 At the end of the lesson a brief summary is given of what has been achieved.

3 The content is *appropriate* and *differentiated*. (Some A-level groups are of very mixed ability.)

4 The content is set in context, e.g. what part of syllabus is the lesson, is it a 'stand alone' or a contribution/follow up of previous lessons.

5 The content and activities are challenging for all students, and there are high expectations.

6 The content and activities are inclusive, e.g. every student is involved at all parts of the lesson – 'no hiding place'.

7 Teaching strategies are varied and appropriate for the topic and students. Lecturing is limited to no more than 15 minutes. There is a mix of group work, pair work, individual note taking, problem solving, discussion, question and answer, student presentation and teacher input.

8 Assessments are carried out and feedback given on a frequent basis. For individuals, progression needs to be identified (what do I need to do now . . .). Work is marked promptly.

9 Enthusiasm is evident from the teacher, and praise is used extensively.

10 There is clear and specific guidance on work to be done out of the lesson which amounts to a minimum of five hours per subject per week; 'read around the subject' is never given as a task.

11 The lesson makes reference to any prior learning where applicable and is built upon the knowledge/skills acquired.

12 The lesson develops a range of student skills – not just listening. Teachers do not talk at length, certainly not for more than 15 minutes within a lesson.

13 Lessons start promptly, students are ready for action with books, equipment and folders, and lessons finish on time, certainly not before.

14 There is a disciplined, supportive attitude.

The observation sheet Figure 11.1 was designed and used for all observations in the school.

This work proved invaluable, and it is interesting that in the DfEE's work to introduce their performance management scheme, guidance for lesson observation has been designed. The staff at Chaucer Technology School used that guidance, but felt that an individual school-based standard of the characteristics of a good lesson was essential. A similar voluntary working group produced an original statement that was again used as the basis for all lesson observations.

Having agreed a standard, supportive quality control methods were designed and introduced. In both schools it was felt that heads of department should encourage an open-door policy, to permit the free exchange and transfer of good practice. However, it was felt that there should be a minimum of one formal lesson observation per year by the head of department, while others could take place for developmental purposes.

In both schools heads of department were supported and monitored by a designated member of the senior management team. They assisted the heads of department in their lesson observation programme within the department, aiming to observe each departmental member, including the head of department at least once every two years.

STAFF:_____ CLASS:_____ DATE:_____

1. Beginning of Lesson   Orderly ☐   Disorganised ☐
    Comment: _____

2. Introduction – Expectations/objectives put into context   Clear ☐   Unclear ☐
    Comment: _____

3. Appropriateness of content   Yes ☐   No ☐
    Comment: _____

4. Appropriateness of activities/teaching style
    Appropriateness for content   Yes ☐   No ☐
    Appropriateness for ability   Yes ☐   No ☐
    Comment:_____

5. Motivation comes from   Teacher ☐   Work ☐   Pupil/self motivation ☐
    Comment: _____

6. Pupil behaviour   Excellent ☐   Good ☐   Satisfactory ☐   Unsatisfactory ☐
    Comment (include specific pupils if needed): _____

    _____

7. Teacher's classroom management of pupils
    Comment: _____

8. Were all pupils on task?   All lesson ☐   Most of the lesson ☐   Part of the lesson ☐
    Comment: _____

9. Homework set (if appropriate)
    Comment: _____

10. Lesson ending   Orderly ☐   Disorganised ☐

11. Quality of learning – were the objectives achieved?   Yes ☐   Partially ☐   No ☐
    Comment: _____

12. Quality of teaching   Good ☐   Satisfactory ☐   Unsatisfactory ☐
    Comment: _____

    _____

    _____

Signature of teacher: _____ Signature of observer: _____

Figure 11.1: Lesson observation sheet

In both schools I invited my working group of heads of department to suggest a schedule for observations by the headteacher. The two groups produced individual, but largely similar, procedures, the Chaucer model being noted below.

The headteacher should observe

(a) Heads of Department formally at least once a year.

(b) newly appointed staff formally at least once a year, and

(c) others as part of a rolling cycle, so that all staff were observed at least once every two years.

This programme had an immensely positive effect at The Pingle School, and I have no doubt that once it is embedded, it will have similar effects at Chaucer. Perhaps the most beneficial effect has been to congratulate the vast majority of teachers on how well they taught their pupils. I rarely fail to learn something when I observe a colleague, and frequently feel privileged to be associated with an outstanding professional.

There are, of course, observations where quite important areas of concern need to be raised, but as long as the positive is also stressed, and the agreed statement of the characteristics of a good lesson is used as a benchmark, positive development points can be made and programmes of support designed. It is also important to acknowledge the benefits of two professionals sitting down to discuss their practice, and the way in which they can learn from each other.

There are a number of different views as to how observation feedback can be most beneficial. I consider that it is vital to provide a very accurate timed description of what the teacher and pupils actually did. Teachers tend to talk far too much, and believe that they talked for a much shorter time than is often the case. Teachers often overestimate the involvement of individual pupils in so-called question and answer sessions, and I attempt to record just how many pupils are involved, as well as the number who simply listened. Very often I will ask the teacher to complete the observation sheet himself or herself before I show them mine. This can be extremely valuable in clarifying where there are differences in expectations. Whatever the situation, I always endeavour to give a few words of verbal feedback when I leave, and if I am unable to discuss the lesson immediately, I do so within 24 hours.

Consistency

Another key part of attempting to create consistency is to be clear about what we expect staff to record, and to monitor that all colleagues then follow the agreed procedures. Most schools issue staff with planners, and at Chaucer we have agreed that they should be used to record:

- pupil attendance at all lessons;

- all marks for written/practical work including classroom, homework, assessment scores, exam results, predicted grades etc.;
- details of prior attainment, including content attainment target (CAT) scores, SAT levels, effort and attainment in the previous academic year;
- effort grades;
- all homework tasks set;
- details of any special needs, IEP targets etc.;
- day by day simple statement of lesson plan, i.e. textbook, page reference, outline of activity etc.

Planners are checked by heads of department once a term, allowing them to both identify development needs and to check that agreed procedures are being followed.

Most schools have excellent homework and marking policies, but relatively few monitor that the procedures which have been designed, are being followed. To create consistency it is vital that quality control is maintained, with responsibility being very closely defined. The following sections appear in the policies of Chaucer Technology School.

Monitoring homework

(a) *It is the responsibility of the subject teacher to monitor the recording of homework in the pupils' planners, and check that homework has been completed.*

(b) *It is the responsibility of the form tutor to check that pupils are using their planners effectively.*

(c) *It is the responsibility of heads of year to monitor the work of their team in checking diaries. The headteacher and deputy headteacher will also undertake a comprehensive programme of monitoring.*

(d) *It is the responsibility of Heads of Department to ensure that the quality and frequency of homework is checked on an ongoing basis, with a formal review of a sample of books at least once a term.*

(e) *It is the responsibility of the headteacher, assisted by heads of year, to undertake a survey of homework of each teaching set at least once a term.*

Monitoring marking

(a) *It is the responsibility of the head of department to monitor the marking of work on an ongoing basis, and formally at least once a term.*

(b) *It is the responsibility of the appropriate member of the Leadership Team to monitor the marking of departments on an ongoing basis, and formally, at least once a term.*

(c) *It is the responsibility of the headteacher to undertake surveys of marking at least once a term.*

These key measures to ensure consistency need to be embedded in job descriptions, but it must also be recognised that those in positions of responsibility must also support their junior colleagues, and that maintaining the correct balance is essential. Of vital importance are heads of department, who should be the engine room of any school. At Chaucer the following balance between support and monitoring has been agreed.

Heads of department – support

Timetable

There should be departmental consultation and negotiation with regard to each teacher's timetable to ensure fair distribution of classes, however, the head of department will be responsible for the final decision, subject to any reference to the headteacher.

Rooming

There should be departmental consultation and discussion with regard to rooming to ensure fairness in room allocation. Particular consideration should be given to part-timers, however, the head of department will be responsible for the final decision, subject to any reference to the headteacher.

Schemes of work

The development of schemes of work may be allocated to different members of a department but the head of department will have overall responsibility for monitoring and reviewing.

Discipline

There should be a formalised disciplinary procedure and policy within a department, which is developed from the school Discipline Policy, and procedure. Departmental policy and procedure should be laid out in the Departmental Handbook with step-by-step disciplinary stages and action clearly defined. Examples of support, which may be requested from head of department include:

- lesson observation;
- advice;
- classroom support;

- pupil withdrawal;
- inset for training in classroom management;
- departmental detention.

Motivation

The head of department should take reasonable measures to motivate individual department members and pursue means of raising morale and building team commitment within the department.

Professional development

It is the responsibility of the head of department to oversee the professional development of the members of his or her department to ensure provision is fair and equitable for all, including part-timers.

Pastoral information

It is the responsibility of the head of department to implement the mechanism employed within the department to make use of pastoral information held by year heads, which may inform department decisions, i.e. disciplinary action.

Absence

If a colleague is absent and unable to set work in the usual manner, it is the responsibility of the head of department to ensure work is provided for cover or supply teachers.

Heads of department – monitoring

Lesson planning

Heads of department should monitor lesson planning. This should be carried out through termly checks of Teacher Planners with an agreed checklist and a simple signature to indicate the check has taken place.

Lesson content

Heads of department should monitor lesson content, continuity and progression. This should be carried out through termly checks of Teacher Planners with an agreed checklist and a simple signature to indicate that the check has taken place.

Homework

Heads of department should monitor homework is set when required by school policy and that it is of value. This should be done through termly checks of Teacher Planners with an agreed checklist and a simple signature to indicate that a check has taken place.

Marking and assessment

Heads of department should monitor marking of pupils' work, ensuring it is marked regularly, consistent with the school's Marking Policy, and that details of prior attainment such as SATs, CATs, Year 11 Information Service (YELLIS), targets (including those from IEPs) etc. are recorded in the Staff Planner. Monitoring should be carried out through termly checks of Teacher Planners with an agreed checklist and a simple signature to indicate that a check has taken place.

Attendance

Heads of department should monitor attendance registers, ensuring they are kept in accordance with school policy, through checking Teachers Planners on a termly basis.

Punctuality

Heads of department should monitor teacher punctuality to lessons, speaking to departmental members as appropriate.

Lesson observations

It is hoped that heads of department will encourage an open-door policy within departments with regard to observation so that free exchange and transfer of good practice may take place, benefiting teachers and pupils. There should be a minimum of one formal lesson observation per year by heads of department; others may take place for developmental purposes. No formal lesson observation should take place without one week's notice; there should be consultation and negotiation as part of the process.

Discipline

Heads of department should monitor pupil discipline within lessons in accordance with school policy.

In both The Pingle and Chaucer, I believe that it was important to gain a consensus on the supported monitoring role of the headteacher, and I asked my working groups to design proposals that were considered by all teachers.

Role of the headteacher

The headteacher has overall responsibility to maintain and monitor high standards of achievement and behaviour in the school, and to promote the school in the wider community as a centre of excellence.

Observation

The headteacher should observe:

- Heads of department formally at least once a year;
- newly appointed staff formally at least once a year;
- others, as appropriate, to support heads of department and year head as part of their observation programme on a rolling cycle, observing all staff at least once every two years.

Around the school

The headteacher should aim to be a visible presence in the school as often as possible, walking corridors and playgrounds and visiting classrooms on an informal basis. Class teachers may indicate to the headteacher if they would prefer him or her not to enter the classroom at a particular time.

Teaching

It is important for the headteacher to maintain an involvement with pupils, and classroom teaching is a way of ensuring this takes place. Therefore the headteacher should, wherever possible, be:

- a classroom teacher;
- available to demonstrate good classroom practice and management.

Meetings

The headteacher should meet at least once a term with heads of department and their senior staff mentor to discuss:

- examination results;
- development plan;
- budget and staffing.

Pupils' work

The headteacher should monitor pupils' class work and homework by collecting in exercise books/folders on a regular basis, e.g. two pupils at random per year group per term.

Discipline

The headteacher should be the ultimate sanction with regard to pupil discipline, when all other disciplinary measures/stages have been used.

Praise

The headteacher should be available at agreed times to offer congratulations and praise for excellent work, conduct or contribution.

Assemblies

The headteacher should present an assembly to each year group once every half-term.

I have had many discussions with headteachers with regard to the workload that this programme of monitoring produces. However, I believe that with perhaps the exception of staff appointments, it is the most beneficial work that I do. I note below my monitoring programme for the autumn term 2000.

Headteacher's monitoring programme – autumn 2000

1 *Observations* – I would be grateful if the following could provide for me a list of four possible lessons from which I might select one to observe this term:

Jacqueline Bray	Dominique Micheloud
Daphne Candler	Marissa Perkins

Mark Cheeseman	Caroline Pestell
Lesley Evans	Tony Phillpott
Peter Goodey	Malcolm Rogers
Victoria Hale	Andrew Shears
Sharon Johnstone	Giles Tarver
Abigail Kent	Michael Walton
Peter Lansley	Rachel Weeks

2 *Pupil books* – I will be viewing all of the work of two students at the time noted below and ask colleagues to co-operate with heads of year, who will be provided with further information later:

19 October	Year 7
3 November	Year 8
9 November	Year 9
16 November	Year 10
24 November	Year 12
6 December	Year 11
15 December	Year 13

3 *Homework* – I will liase with heads of year to record the homework set and completed for every teaching set in each of the following weeks:

9–13 October

16–20 October

4 *Departmental reviews* – as notified I will meet with all heads of department and their mentors, with the following agenda:

(a) review of examination results;

(b) review of programme of departmental development plans;

(c) other issues raised by any party.

At The Pingle School the systems outlines were a major constructive force as the school increased the number of pupils gaining five A–C grades from 19 per cent in 1991 to 50 per cent in 2000, with a new school record in every year but one. It helped create a thinking school, where self-review was continual, and where increasing numbers of teachers were developing so effectively that they were successful in gaining promotions elsewhere. It is a system of performance management that works, and in both The Pingle School and Chaucer Technology School it will form the foundation of the scheme now imposed by the government.

Note

I wish to acknowledge the outstanding contributions of many colleagues in both The Pingle School and Chaucer Technology School to the material contained above.

12

∎ ∎ ∎

Training for the Implementation of Performance Management in New Zealand Schools

Graham Collins

Introduction

This case study focuses on skills training for performance management imple-mentation. In the last decade of the twentieth century 'performance management' implementation became a significant issue for most New Zealand schools. In 1997 and 1998 the New Zealand government introduced successive performance management initiatives, which required all schools to review existing practice, and in most cases, to introduce 'more robust' provi-sions in line with modified national specifications (Ministry of Education, 1997; Ministry of Education, 1998). Massey University College of Education, based in Palmerston North and for which I work, was contracted in both these years by the Ministry of Education to provide support to schools in its region as they went about getting to grips with the new requirements. In both years I directed the team of facilitators hired by the college to provide the support needed on the ground.

In this chapter I will focus on the training programme provided by the college of education in the second of the two years, 1998. This training programme was known as the 'Skills for Appraisal' programme. There were three key skills covered in the programme – appraisal interviewing, classroom observation and providing/receiving feedback. The chapter will discuss (1) the context within which the programme was conceived, (2) the nature of the initial programme that was delivered, (3) the additions to the programme that resulted from modified requirements in the middle of 1998 and (4) the outcomes that resulted.

The context, 1989-97

Massey University College of Education is located in the Central North Island of New Zealand; and is one of six colleges of education throughout the country that, in the early 1990s, had responsibility for pre-service teacher education. The Central North Island region has about 450 schools; 40 secondary schools and 410 primary schools. In comparison with other parts of New Zealand, many of the primary schools are small, with almost 70 per cent having a roll of under 150 students.

All schools and colleges in New Zealand were affected by a major restructuring in educational administration that took place in 1989, known as the 'Tomorrow's Schools' reforms. At the school level this restructuring meant schools taking on a range of self-managing responsibilities (previously undertaken by regional or district administration offices). Amongst the new responsibilities devolved to schools in 1989 were employment of staff and management of staff performance. For the colleges of education the main change from 1989 was the assumption of new responsibilities for providing professional development advice and support for schools in their region. Much of this work has been initiated centrally in the form of competitive contracts. The Ministry of Education in Wellington was given responsibility for drawing up tender specifications for each contract and monitoring contract delivery, within policy guidelines set by the government of the day.

From 1989 to the end of 1996 schools were free to develop their own appraisal and performance management processes, to suit their particular local circumstances. However, to ensure greater uniformity in professional accountability the national government moved in 1995 and 1996 to introduce new 'performance management' requirements, applicable to all schools. In 1996 the Ministry of Education produced *Draft National Guidelines for Performance Management in Schools* (Ministry of Education, 1995) for trial and consultation. In February 1997 the new requirements were gazetted, with schools having 12 months to develop the necessary policy and process (Collins, 1997).

In 1997 Massey University College of Education had a contract with the Ministry of Education to support school management staff with the initial implementation work for the new performance management requirements.

The six facilitators in this contract were either management advisers, seconded principals or ex-principals who worked with the principal and board members in each school to draft the necessary policy and plan the required process. About half the schools in the region were involved in the Massey University College of Education performance management in schools (PMS) contract. Schools were free to choose whether or not they participated.

In October 1997 the college was contracted by the Ministry of Education for a further professional development programme to be run over 1998, this time focusing on the 'skills for appraisal'. The target group for the 1998 contract programme were 'lead teachers', that is those who would be responsible for making the planned system work in each school.

The initial 1998 'Skills for Appraisal' programme

The contract negotiations for the 1998 programme concluded in November 1997. As programme director there were a number of tasks that I had to complete before the 1998 school year started. The first of these jobs was preparing the necessary resources. In late 1997 we filmed a video that covered the typical mistakes made in an appraisal interview (a John Cleese type sequence), and what should happen in an effective interview (focusing on the setting of the annual 'development objectives' relating to the teacher's personal-professional goals). We also put together a folder called the 'Appraisal Implementation Handbook'. There were four main sections in the handbook – an explanation of the National Appraisal Requirements, a summary of the various appraisal process skills, an outline of the various action-training exercises which would allow the practice and development of key skills, and a section called 'Making Appraisal More Effective' which looked briefly at the research findings on appraisal and what these might mean for schools wishing to review their existing process. All schools involved in the programme received a copy of the video and handbook. My second task was to advertise for schools to participate in the programme. One hundred and seventy schools responded, 143 primary and 27 secondary. My third task was to put together the team of facilitators to deliver the programme. Half the facilitators I chose had been involved in the previous PMS training programme in 1997. The other half were seconded from schools that already had quite advanced appraisal processes. The latter were deputy principals from schools that had already begun to plan what the new appraisal requirements might mean in practice for their particular type of school. The facilitators seconded from schools covered the range of types of schools we were scheduled to work with – large secondary school, middle sized primary school and smaller primary school. My final task was the facilitator training. In the last week of January 1998 all facilitators met together for three days in Palmerston North to plan the work for the first part of the programme and to familiarise themselves with the materials to be used.

In the first part of February, facilitators visited each school in the programme to make an initial needs assessment. This needs assessment resulted in a decision being made about which particular 'strand' of the programme the school should be involved in:

Strand One, Skills-based training: a programme for the teaching staff of schools with an 'average' level of starting implementation. This training was delivered initially in a lead-teacher workshop; with moderate level of follow up in each school.

Strand Two, Needs-based training: a programme for the specific school-by-school requirements of schools with *either* an 'above average' level of starting implementation (and therefore having one or two specific needs), *or* 'below average' level of starting implementation (and therefore requiring a more intensive level of support than would be available in the Strand One programme).

To assist in the needs assessment we developed a four-point scale to rate the degree of current implementation. The four levels on this scale were:

Level 1: not yet complying on paper with the national requirements;

Level 2: have necessary paperwork to comply but no real commitment or meaningfulness to process;

Level 3: complying on paper, and making a commitment, but not yet fully implemented;

Level 4: balanced compliance fully implemented.

Level 2 schools were placed in 'Strand One'; levels 1 and 3 were placed in 'Strand Two'.

In early March, a series of two-day lead-teacher workshops were held around the college's region, with 'Strand One' schools sending nominated 'lead teachers' (at least two from every school; up to six from the largest school). This workshop covered the four areas in the Appraisal Implementation Handbook (Day 1), and also the specific issue of classroom observation (Day 2). The Day 2 programme was based on videotaped excerpts of classroom teaching; with the workshop participants drafting comments and practising giving feedback in constructive ways. In late March, these same aspects were covered in a school based workshop for the staff of 'Strand Two', level 1 schools. For the rest of the school year facilitators worked in individual schools, with one day per term being allocated to each 'Strand One' school, two days per term to each 'Strand Two' level 1 school and a half-day per term to the 'Strand Two' level 3 schools. Visits were tailored to cater for each school's emerging needs.

Additions to the initial programme

Early in March 1998 the Ministry of Education Industrial Relations Unit began negotiations with the primary teachers union, NZEI, to put in place the details of 'pay parity' (that is, a framework within which all teachers with equivalent qualifications and experience would get the same pay, no matter whether they taught in a primary or a secondary school. This was to be achieved by lifting existing primary school salaries to the secondary school level). By the end of March the negotiations had concluded with an agreement to implement pay parity, backdated to the start of 1998. However, as part of the agreement new clauses were included in primary teachers' conditions of service which established a national framework of 'professional standards'. These were formulated at five levels – 'beginning teacher', 'fully registered teacher', 'experienced teacher', 'deputy/assistant principal' and 'principal'. In future, all primary teachers were to be assessed each year against the appropriate set of national standards. Teachers were to be assessed by the principal or his or her nominee and the principal by their board of trustees. New salary provisions, for example discretionary increments or an annual bonus payment, were to be dependent on the outcomes of the assessment.

Following this employment contract settlement, all 'Skills for Appraisal' contractors were asked by the Ministry to agree to an extension to their original contract, covering the modified requirements. After consideration of the issues involved, Massey University agreed to the proffered extension. The extension involved the preparation of material to be sent out to all primary schools in the region (whether or not they were in the 'Skills for Appraisal' programme) on the changes to policy and process that were now required. In addition, information meetings (two hours after school) were held around the region where interested teachers, principals and board members might hear more about what the new salary requirements meant in practice. There was also provision for each of the primary schools in the initial programme to receive one further facilitator visit focusing on the amended requirements.

As a result of the extension to its contract, the college made contact with the other 240 primary schools in the region not in the initial programme and provided them with samples of the new policies required and suggestions for implementing the new processes. The extension was clearly based on a different training philosophy from the initial programme. The initial programme tried to model the well-known Joyce and Showers (1982) principles of:

- give them some theory first to base it all on;
- demonstrate to them what they should do;
- give them the opportunity to practise in a 'safe' situation (through simulation/training exercises);
- coach and support them as they apply the new skills/knowledge in the real world.

The extension was based much more on the training philosophy of an earlier era:

- tell them what they are meant to do;
- give them a model which they can copy/adapt.

Schools participating only in the extension also did so from a rather different motivation base than those that had volunteered for the initial programme. As part of the requirements for the salary increase to principals that was part of the employment contract settlement, all schools were to have their performance management system vetted by the Education Review Office (ERO, the New Zealand equivalent of Ofsted) before the start of 1999. Only those schools with an ERO 'seal of approval' would receive the funding to pay for the principal's salary increment.

Outcomes from the programme

Ministry of Education contracts typically require careful programme evaluation. As far as the *initial programme* was concerned, from the beginning there was a clear set of expected outcomes. At the end of the programme each participating school was intended to:

- have a positive understanding of the national appraisal requirements amongst all staff;
- have all staff (both appraisers and appraisees) skilled in the process;
- have conducted a school based self-review of the effectiveness of their process in action;
- have the capacity to maintain the process in 1999 and beyond.

The formal evaluation (Table 12.1) conducted at the end of the programme clearly indicated that most participating schools believed they had achieved most of these outcomes.

		Primary (N = 132)	Secondary (N = 24)
1.	Schools with an ERO approved policy and process	127	22
2.	Schools with all appraisers suitably trained	112	22
3.	Schools with all appraisees suitably trained	106	21
4.	Schools which have successfully completed one full cycle	116	17
5.	Schools which have self-reviewed and refined process at end of cycle	115	16

Table 12.1: Participant evaluations, end of 1998

When asked to identify the factors that contributed to this, some clear patterns emerged (Tables 12.2, 12.3 and 12.4).

Each school was asked to name up to three key factors:

Factor	Number of mentions
Facilitator visits	121
Sample documents provided	81
On-site staff meetings	57
Workshop training activities	55
The provided handbook	25
The provided video	9

Table 12.2: Factors that contributed to primary school implementation (N = 132)

Factor	Number of mentions
Principals lack of time to do job properly	30
Negative impact of 'professional standards'	29
Changing requirements midway through implementation	26
Additions to teaching workload	16
Lack of board understanding	6
Change of principal	5
New staff	4

Table 12.3: Factors that inhibited primary school implementation (Factors self-identified by schools)

Factor	Number of mentions
Further facilitation to review process-in-action	2
Support with whole school consolidation	15
Working with professional standards	14
Upskilling new staff	14
Board training	9
Principal training	6

Table 12.4: Further training needs identified by primary schools

Secondary schools, whose employment contract had been settled in 1996 to run till the end of 1998, did not have to deal with changing national requirements midway through the programme. In secondary school evaluations there were a similar pattern of positive factors, and fewer negative factors/further training needs.

While the data that was reported to the Ministry of Education generally painted a positive picture of the outcomes, our in-house evaluation conducted by the facilitators at the end of the contract painted a rather more complex picture. Because of their specialisations, facilitators reported separately on three main types of school in our region. Some of the major points they made included the following.

Small primary schools

At the start of the year most of these schools were committed to the appraisal process and had shared goals (that is, level 3). The smaller size of these schools meant the appraisal process was generally less formal than in larger schools (teachers in these schools usually have a good knowledge of everyone's teaching style and give each other a good deal of informal professional support). Facilitators felt professional standards were unlikely to alter this.

In 80 per cent of these schools all teaching staff in the school attended the initial workshop. Because of the smaller range of needs within any individual school the support/assistance from the facilitator could be accurately targeted to readily evident needs.

With the introduction of professional standards the appraisal of the teaching principal in these schools became particularly complex, because of the two distinct aspects to be assessed – teaching and management. By the end of the contract most smaller schools were still struggling with this.

Larger primary schools

Workshop participants (typically about a quarter of the school staff) developed excellent knowledge of the national requirements, and did a good job in 'cascading' their knowledge and understanding amongst other staff over the rest of the year.

Facilitator visits supported the lead team in the 'cascading' process and provided the mix of ongoing support plus pressure needed to move some of the reluctant few amongst other staff to a more positive outlook by midyear. However, the introduction of the professional standards in the middle of the year increased levels of scepticism and cynicism. Facilitators generally found it hard to counter the feeling of threat that resulted amongst the few in these larger staffs.

Secondary schools

At the start of the year about half the schools had a policy and a process based on peer appraisal within departments. However, developments in the primary sector sparked many secondary schools to reconsideration of this midway through. By the end of the year all but one school had switched to a system of hierarchical appraisal based on line-management responsibilities.

In a number of schools this switch was regarded by most staff as a positive move, giving some teeth and meaning to a process which was viewed earlier as soft and wishy-washy. However, in two schools in particular the switch was regarded by a sizeable proportion of the staff as a sell-out by school management to prevailing pressures of managerialism in the wider environment.

As far as the *extension* programme was concerned, there was no formal evaluation of its outcomes carried out by Massey University College of Education. However, ERO data on PMS compliance by mid-1999 showed that the Central Districts region (that is, the region covered in this training programme) had the highest level of compliance in the country, with over 99 per cent of its schools being compliant by that stage.

Overall, then, the following trends were noted in my final report to the Ministry at the end of 1998:

1 The very high degree of compliance-implementation (over 95 per cent of both primary and secondary schools had a working system by the end of 1998; approximately 90 per cent of staff felt they had been suitably trained).

2 The positive response and high value placed on facilitator visits to schools as an aid to implementation.

3 The workload/time strains the requirements had created.

4 The negative response in many primary schools to what they saw as the Ministry's imposition of 'professional standards' and performance related pay.

5 The relatively low demand for further training.

Conclusions

Looking back on this experience with the benefit of three or four years hindsight, it would seem to me that the case highlights at least three aspects which might be applicable to other settings and contexts:

1 The speed with which schools can create at least the appearance of compliance with statutory requirements, which they may regard as of doubtful educational value, where money is involved. For most teachers the salary increase offered in April 1998 was in the region of $5000–$8000 (a 10–15 per cent

increase). Schools often took most of 1996 and 1997 to 'consider', 'consult' and 'conceptualise' their original appraisal policy and process. Within the space of several weeks in the middle of 1998 most of these same schools 'adopted' new policies and implemented various aspects of performance related pay, even though their earlier policy deliberately excluded such elements.

2   The utility of a training model based on the Joyce and Showers (1982) principles, where discreet skills are to be disseminated. Based on our experience, a key factor here would seem to be the credibility of the facilitators who provide the in-school coaching or support. Other factors would appear to be the accuracy of the initial needs assessment, and flexibility in follow-up provision to cover the full spectrum of needs identified.

3   The moral and ethical dilemma created by the contracting system for a university that, on the one hand, has a statutory responsibility to act as the 'critic and conscience of society' and, on the other hand, needs to maximize the amount of entrepreneurial income to assure its financial viability. This dilemma also had a personal element. At the time I held a national level position in an educational union that was opposed to performance related pay, yet I was the director of a Ministry of Education funded programme that, in part, showed schools how to implement this. As a result, I have a few more grey hairs now than I did at the start of 1998!

References

Collins, G. (1997) 'Performance management: development and implementation issues', in J. O'Neill (ed.), *Teacher Appraisal in New Zealand: Beyond the Impossible Triangle*. Palmerston North: ERDC Press.

Joyce B, and Showers, B. (1982) 'The coaching of teaching', *Educational Leadership*. 40 (1), 4–10.

Ministry of Education (1995) *Draft National Guidelines for Performance Management in Schools*. Wellington: The Ministry, December.

Ministry of Education (1997) *Performance Management Systems: PMS One: Performance Appraisal*. Wellington: The Ministry, February.

Ministry of Education (1998) *Interim Professional Standards: Primary School Teachers, Primary School Deputy/Assistant Principals*. Wellington: The Ministry, April.

13

■ ■ ■

Headteacher Development and Performance Management

Maureen Doyle

Our LEA has been judging the performance of its headteachers since 1990 when it introduced performance related pay (PRP) for new and existing headteachers and deputy headteachers. Existing headteachers had the option of joining the scheme. New headteachers did not. The LEA was formed after the break up of the Inner London Education Authority (ILEA). It was new to education and it wanted to succeed. The PRP incentives it offered to headteachers joining the scheme were very generous. What it expected in return was both demanding and challenging.

The LEA scheme was more rigorous than the current DfEE initiative. In that sense, it prepared us well for what was to come. The LEA also introduced its own five-day inspection programme, which Ofsted were later to refine and adopt. One can imagine the subsequent pressure brought to bear on headteachers.

At its introduction, many of our headteachers rose to the challenge of PRP and appreciated being rewarded for something they would naturally do in the course of their work. Others experienced undue pressure, particularly those in difficult schools with high mobility rates, high percentages of English as an additional language (EAL) children, and high numbers of children classed as being socially deprived. Some felt that targets were *forced* upon them because of national and local initiatives. There was always, too, a hint of cynicism when things became a bit too challenging. 'She'll have that as a target, I'll bet' became a bit of a catchphrase, be it in the context of staff and headteachers, or headteachers and LEA officers.

The LEA inspection and the subsequent Ofsted inspection also judged one's performance. With Ofsted, schools are judged to be excellent, very good, good, weak or failing. These judgements are summed up in a statement that declares whether or not the school gives value for money. This brings a tremendous pressure to bear on the headteacher. Weak schools are perceived to be led by weak headteachers. The message, therefore, is that headteachers must be strong if they are to succeed. This must surely impact on one's chosen style of leadership.

My performance to date has always 'exceeded the expected targets' and for that I am grateful. However, not too long ago, I found myself asking, 'Is this judgement enough to sustain me and the children for whom I am responsible? Whose opinion really matters? What motivates me? Why do I want to stay in this job? What do I still have to offer these children?'

Having completed ten years of headship, seven of which were in my current school, I felt the end of a successful Ofsted inspection was the ideal time to move on. It was now appropriate to allow someone else to move the school forward into a new phase of its development. Personal circumstances, however, prevented me from doing this.

I was, therefore, faced with the task of keeping both the school and myself fresh in our approach to learning and achievement. I needed help with this. Performance related pay was not enough.

The Leadership Programme for Serving Headteachers (LPSH) emerged at this time, and I was interested in what it had to offer. I remember reading a press release, which suggested that the programme was designed for headteachers who were somehow perceived to be failing, either by Ofsted or by the LEA. If this was, indeed, its purpose I did not wish to be associated with the programme. To 'sign up' would be an admission of failure. However, after some discussion with the principal of our professional development centre, I was persuaded to give the programme a chance. This was to prove to be the best programme of professional development that I had, to date, undertaken.

The programme operates on the premise that it is the quality of leadership that determines the success or failure of a school, and that the leadership qualities of the headteacher in particular are of paramount importance. The purpose of the programme, therefore, is to improve the quality of leadership in headteachers and, thus, improve the quality of standards in education and achievement in their schools. I felt I could go along with this. Having had two good inspection reports (LEA and Ofsted), our school was in danger of coasting or, indeed, declining without fresh impetus. The LPSH focuses on the link between the personal effectiveness of headteachers and school improvement. This programme, therefore, seemed to be the answer to the burning question currently facing me: 'How can I, after seven years in the same school, continue to make a difference to the education and lives of these children?'

Before the programme began members of the school community and myself were asked to complete a diagnostic questionnaire. This would identify my predominant leadership style and characteristics as headteacher. It was important that those completing the questionnaire varied in their tasks and responsibilities within the school and were honest in their answers. The outcome of the questionnaire, therefore, would provide a baseline, or personal starting point, from which improvement in leadership could be made.

The next stage of the programme involved participation in a four-day workshop. During the first half of the workshop I received feedback from the questionnaire. This assessed my personal performance as perceived by my colleagues and me. We considered this information and used it to explore the links between leadership styles, the context for school improvement and the school's performance. We then worked on producing an appropriate action plan, which not only addressed goals for personal development but also set targets for whole school improvement. The one-to-one consultancy session was crucial to helping me understand the context and reasons for the outcomes of the questionnaire.

We were given a portfolio of our results with a summary of outcomes for the 15 competencies of headteacher characteristics as described by Hay McBer (2000). These competencies were clustered into six groups. I was delighted to see that I succeeded in five out of the six groups. I missed succeeding in all six groups by just 0.1 point within the category labelled 'Impact and Influence'. I felt quite pleased with myself.

Closer scrutiny of the data within two other categories, however, left me feeling puzzled. These related to the characteristics, 'Hold People Accountable' and 'Develop Potential'. During the four-day workshop, and beyond, my understanding of these two characteristics of leadership was to change.

I had been of the opinion that I *did* hold people accountable. I checked to see if work had been done. I monitored the teachers' planning. I carried out lesson observations, albeit only once a year. I met with the site manager to discuss issues relating to the premises. I overheard a member of staff saying, 'I wouldn't dare *not* hand in my planning'. Another was overheard saying, 'I wouldn't like to cross her' (referring to me). In developing potential, I ensured that every member of staff had opportunities to attend courses relating to their areas of responsibility or relating to areas where they needed additional support. Professional development received high priority in the planning of the school's budget and in the school development plan. I was now faced with reflecting carefully on my practice, and rethinking my understanding of these concepts.

The data revealed that my perception of my headteacher characteristics, and those of my colleagues, were in tandem. For that I was grateful. Two assessors did not respond to two questions in the section 'Hold People Accountable'. These questions dealt with contracts for performance, adherence to a principle, policy or change, allowing latitude within clear boundaries and setting limits for what is and is not acceptable. I have to admit to feeling tempted to dismiss the suggestion that I was weak in this area because not all assessors had submitted an opinion. I chose, instead, to be brave and to look at where there was most discrepancy. It was in these areas that I could focus on improving my leadership style.

Two areas presented themselves within the category of holding people accountable. First, I had to allow latitude within clear boundaries and set limits for what is and is not acceptable. Second, I had to publicly monitor, and follow up, if there was deviation from agreed goals. Similarly, two areas presented themselves within the category of developing the potential of others. It seems I could do more to provide reasons and support to help others understand a situation and act accordingly. Also, there was scope for me to improve on giving feedback in a way that would encourage and help others to develop, thus building their confidence to take on challenges. It seemed that the key words for me to focus on when reflecting on these areas were, *clarify, follow up* and *challenge*. Words I had to lose from my thinking were *presumption, avoidance* and *threat*.

The programme gives some useful suggestions for developing areas of weakness. A useful tool for me was keeping a log. In holding people accountable, I kept a log of specific interactions I had with others, be they formal or informal. I focused on the feedback I gave relating to performance. I analysed how well I communicated the purpose of any meetings that were held, and whether or not I had clarified its objectives. I also looked at how I clarified the consequences of succeeding or failing in the work at hand, and whether or not I gave a clear target for follow-up action.

The entries in the log told me more about myself than I realised. I presumed that people understood the task in hand. I often failed to check for clarity. I would set dates for follow-up and inevitably something would happen which prevented the follow-up meeting from taking place. I would, reluctantly, accept excuses for deadlines not being met because I was aware of the pressures people were under or, indeed, the limitations of those carrying out the tasks. My log indicated that I needed to change my practice and soon.

The programme suggested observing a colleague who was particularly good at communicating their performance expectations. Those colleagues that I spoke to did not feel confident enough in this area. Indeed, they could empathise with my own perceived weakness. The link with a business partner could possibly address this need to observe good practice. I set this as my goal for our link. We focused on performance management and how it could be utilised to promote even greater achievement. We shared our appraisal systems and learned from each other. We visited each other's workplace and shared our values and beliefs in its purpose. It was a rewarding and challenging time and has had a very positive influence on how I implemented the DfEE's performance management structure in our school.

There are still times when circumstances prevent me from following up on tasks. However, I am becoming better at rescheduling meetings or, better still, delegating to other senior colleagues to follow up on my behalf.

Our School Development Plan now focuses specifically on raising achievement with the emphasis on teaching and learning. Each part of the plan has a clear strategic intention. It identifies those responsible for carrying out specific tasks, those responsible for monitoring its success, what resources will be made available, and it sets dates for completion. Agreed expectations of the quality of planning, teaching, marking, assessing, reporting, dress code and behaviour are all made explicit within school policies and are monitored for success.

My own accountability towards the governing body and towards staff is greater. Reports are clear and concise, and more informative. Staff members are given more information about the day-to-day running of the school as well as the rationale behind decisions that are made. The formation of a school council has enabled staff and children to be accountable to each other in matters relating specifically to the children. Working within this framework has had a positive impact on the morale and ethos of the school. There are good working relationships with a focus on raising achievement and celebrating success.

With regard to 'Develop People' I, if I am honest, understood this characteristic mainly as providing training to enable staff to carry out their jobs effectively. I really value training opportunities for staff and delegate a considerable part of the budget to ensure all staff have training opportunities. I was puzzled, and quite disappointed, that my score for this characteristic did not reach the suggested target level. This challenged me to rethink and to broaden my previously narrow perception of this concept.

My thinking led me to believe that holding one accountable and developing one's potential dovetailed together very easily. To hold someone accountable presumes that 'someone' has been given responsibility. This in turn assumes that person has the potential to succeed in the task they have been given. Sending people on courses will not necessarily enable them to carry out the task effectively. There is a much deeper level of understanding required when choosing to delegate responsibility. Being taught how to play a violin does not make one a maestro. For that, one needs a natural talent, a love of the instrument and what it can do, and a discipline and desire to continually improve. One cannot, necessarily, turn a school keeper into a site manager. However, given the right opportunities, a school keeper might reveal a natural business sense, which could be used to the advantage of the school and free up valuable 'learning time' on the part of the headteacher. I was challenged to look at my staff with new eyes.

I kept a log for a week of all the meetings I attended within the school and externally, and noted where my time was spent. I discovered a lot about myself that week. While I was happy to delegate some tasks, I was reluctant to give full control. I suppose this goes back to the longheld belief that 'the buck stops here'. I truly believed, and probably still do, that the success or failure of the school is down to me as headteacher. This attitude made me reluctant to hand the reins over to someone else. I found myself sitting in meetings that did not require my attendance, e.g. with the special needs co-ordinator at annual reviews, at the Key Stage team meetings, at difficult meetings between parents and teachers. I found myself photocopying, mounting displays, writing and collating documents. Why? Because I wanted them done 'my way'. Frank Sinatra sang my theme tune.

The programme suggests that we identify some tasks that could be delegated to others. It also suggests that we ensure that we are creating a real development opportunity and not simply getting rid of things that we would rather not do!

I now leave the special needs co-ordinator (SENCO) to manage special needs, and attend special needs meetings only when I am invited. I did, however, intervene at the end of one meeting when a colleague suggested that a bit of 'clout' was necessary in persuading the educational psychologist to change her view about the perceived needs of a particular child. I used that as an opportunity to demonstrate to, and discuss with, the SENCO appropriate strategies for persuasion. We succeeded in initiating a statutory assessment of the child's needs. The SENCO now conducts all meetings with parents, staff and other agencies and keeps me informed as appropriate. We agree deadlines for the completion of paperwork. She organises cover arrangements for staff to attend relevant meetings and takes responsibility for ensuring IEP's are regularly reviewed and implemented. She is now a regular member of the team that audits special needs provision in the borough. She is highly skilled and very competent in her job.

I have a site manager, but I am no longer his line manager. I have delegated that responsibility to the administration officer. They liase over contracts, draw up estimates for work, request invoices and ensure that contractors meet all their requirements. I attend meetings that they consider to be relevant. The administration officer has drawn up procedures to ensure that work requested of the site manager by other members of staff is carried out efficiently and effectively.

The two senior teachers meet with their team of teachers every two weeks. We meet as a senior management team the following week. Issues are discussed, strategies planned, implemented and evaluated. Neither the deputy nor myself attend the Key Stage meeting unless invited. As a result, the status of these teachers has been raised. They are mentors to their colleagues, loyal to me and capable of running the school when the deputy headteacher and I are off the premises at the same time. Gone are the days when the deputy headteacher could not be out of school at the same time as the headteacher. Teachers refer difficult parents to their team leader. The problem only comes to my attention if either party makes a request.

Photocopying is now delegated to classroom assistants. I have only one administration officer, who is already overloaded in her work. The school purchased a machine that collates documents. This speeds up the process and avoids pages being placed in the wrong order. A rota is now in place for displays around the school. Classroom assistants back the walls, staple in borders and make appropriate labels. The class teachers ensure the display is bright, attractive and interactive. Classroom assistants are also engaged actively in teaching and learning activities. Some have received intensive training at their request. They have been invited to put themselves forward for a review of their performance, which, if successful, will result in a rise in salary.

Class teachers are now observed teaching three times a year: once by myself, once by the deputy head and once by their team leader. This will offer them different perceptions of their teaching style, which, we hope, will affirm good practice, give suggestions for further improvement and provide evidence to support their professional portfolio of achievement. Subject leaders have been invited to arrange lesson observations with colleagues to enable them to grasp the quality of teaching and learning within their subject area.

I have still so much to learn. As a natural progression to the LPSH I have begun to read for an International MBA in School Leadership. This course has lifted the weight of DfEE management directives and put in its place time to think, reflect, practise, refine and develop.

Developing people is about providing opportunities for their potential to be realised. It is about empowering them to seize opportunities and to discover strengths in themselves that they were previously unaware of. I know that if I had not been given such opportunities throughout my career, I would not be where I am now, leading a school of malleable, receptive young children into a future that is uncertain but full of hope.

Reference

Hay McBer (2000) *A Model of Teacher Effectiveness.* London: Hay McBer.

Part Three

■ ■ ■

International Perspectives

14

■ ■ ■

Performance Management in Victoria, Australia

Ken Thompson

Australia has six states and two territories. The Commonwealth has some overview in education funding and promotion of national goals, but the states and territories run their government school systems. In 1996 3145015 students were attending schools in Australia.

This chapter focuses on the Victorian state government school system. In Victoria, school is compulsory for young people aged 6 to 15. Seventy per cent of students attend government schools.

The Victorian government school system had been evolving towards a form of school-based management for some years. For example in the early 1970s, the Whitlam Labour federal government introduced funding for disadvantaged schools, with a structure where funding decisions were devolved to the area and school level. In the late 1970s, the Fraser Conservative federal government provided funds to assist students in the transition from school to work. In Victoria a substantial proportion of these funds were provided to schools to generate 'bottom up' reform.

In 1986 the then Victoria state Labour Minister, The Honourable Ian Cathie, introduced a document titled 'Schools Into the 1990s' which was a blueprint for school self-management. The reaction to these ideas was quite negative. The government did not proceed any further with them. However, it is likely that the debate surrounding the Cathie proposal did get many educators thinking about the possibility of devolving decision-making power to schools. Also around 1986 to 1987 Caldwell and Spinks won a contract to introduce programme budgeting to all Victorian government schools. The development of these processes has proved to be foundational in the building of schools' capacity to embrace self-management successfully.

Near the end of the 1980s local management of schools was introduced in England and soon after in New Zealand. Around this time, the early 1990s, the John Cain led Labour government in Victoria was in financial, then political, trouble. A radical conservative government came to power in late 1992, with a strong mandate to get the finances of the state into order. The Cain government had been locked into formal agreements with the teachers' unions. The new government was keen to cut unions out of the equation and communicate directly with school staff through the principal.

The new government reined in expenditure by privatisation of utilities and cost cutting in areas such as health and education. Approximately 8000 (of 40 000) teaching posts were abolished, 300 schools were closed. Budgets were tightened.

Victoria's version of site-based management was introduced, called 'Schools of the Future'. Schools volunteered to be a part of several initiatives. The new model was focused on meeting community expectations, making resource allocation decisions at the school level based on a knowledge of local needs, strengthening the role of the principal, providing a statewide curriculum framework with outcomes-based assessment, the school charter as an agreement between the school and Department of Education (DoE), an accountability framework based on the school charter, the strengthening role of the local representative governing body, significant devolution of finances (prior to 1992, 6 per cent of the state education budget was devolved to schools, by 1998 it was 90 per cent and this proportion has since increased further) and finally staff selection, workforce planning and staff appraisal was to be devolved to schools.

Unions were hostile to the new government and school staff members were somewhat angry about all the funding cuts. It was in the 1970s and early to mid-1980s that an unpopular system of inspecting teachers to assess their readiness for promotion was abolished.

This, then, is the broad context for the introduction of the Performance Recognition Programme (PRP), the performance-related pay framework introduced by the government for staff employed in government schools in Victoria.

Performance related pay has been a controversial issue in government schools in Victoria for half a decade. Apparently intended to reward those making a significant contribution to their schools and students, it has been rejected by those it was supposed to motivate.

It is interesting to note, in this globalised world, that a new Labour government in Victoria has abolished an individual reward system for Victoria, just as the Blair Labour government has introduced a performance related pay system in England.

This chapter aims to give a brief overview of how the Victoria government school system version of performance related pay (the Professional Recognition Programme) worked and whom it involved. Some of the problems with the PRP as perceived from an educator's point of view and the fatal flaws that, in the end, maintained the resistance to this approach to remuneration are outlined.

The chapter does not examine closely at the government's intentions other than to quote official Department of Education sources.

Performance management for teachers

Performance management for teachers was introduced in Victorian government schools in 1995. The rationale for the programme was that:

> A high-quality teaching service is a vital element in the creation of a better future for all young Victorians. The Professional Recognition Program recognises the expertise and professionalism of teachers, provides ongoing support and feedback and recognises and rewards teachers who, through their ability and commitment, have a direct impact on standards of student achievement.
>
> (DoE, 1996: Foreword)

The Department of Education view was

> The Professional Recognition Program (PRP) is part of an integrated approach to staff management incorporating performance management processes and enhanced opportunities for planned teacher professional development.
>
> The Professional Recognition Program aims to provide a working environment that encourages and rewards skilled and dedicated teachers and formal feedback on a teacher's performance so that appropriate career development may occur through professional development.
>
> (DoE, 1996: 1)

The approach included local merit-based selection of teachers, a probationary period for teachers appointed on an ongoing basis, and three levels of classification. The base level, level 1, was classified into 'beginning teacher' and 'experienced teacher'. Progress through a 12-point incremental scale was based on an annual review against set professional standards with outstanding performance being recognised by acceleration through the scale.

There were two levels of 'leading teacher'. Once appointed to these classifications, incumbents were eligible for full accreditation, gained through an assessment process, after 12 months. Successful accreditation gained the access to the possibility of performance payments of up to 10 per cent of salary subject to the successful completion of an agreed annual performance plan.

Performance review, special payments for base-level teachers for particular positions of responsibility, performance payments for leading teachers, and a self-funded sabbatical leave scheme were introduced.

Annual reviews for teachers

An annual review followed the well-known performance cycle where a cycle commenced with either discussion or provision of information about the standards and evidence required, provision was made for a mid-review cycle and a principal's assessment and decision at the end. Assessment was against the professional standards (see Figure 14.1 and 14.2).

The principal or appropriate delegate made decisions regarding the assessment in most instances. In cases where acceleration or deferral of a decision was likely, the principal formed a panel to assess the teacher's performance against the standard using the evidence provided by the teachers.

The outcome of the teacher reviews could be progressions of one point on the incremental scale, accelerated progression or deferment of the increment. In the case of the acceleration, the teacher was awarded the incremental point, with the next review, and opportunity for the next incremental progression, scheduled for six months or nine months rather than the standard 12 months. Where an increment was deferred, the teacher would have three months to remedy any problems with a further review at that time. If the teacher's performance was still a problem, a decision could be deferred and a further review could be taken in three months.

The guidelines made provision for dealing with a range of different circumstances such as teachers on leave, teachers on secondment or international fellowships and those transferred during a review cycle.

The principal had room to comment on the review proforma, including recommendations for further professional development. It was expected that these matters would be included in the teacher's Professional Development Plan.

Performance management for leading teachers

Leading-teacher positions are fixed-term promotion positions., Typically leading teachers would hold the roles of faculty head, head of year, professional development co-ordinator, timetabler or daily organiser for example. It was envisioned that:

> *Performance management for leading teachers at Level 2 and Level 3 supports the professional growth and career development of each teacher through a review of performance, provision of feedback, recognition of achievements and encouragement of continued development.*
>
> (DoE, 1996: 18)

The aim was to link the performance plans of leading teachers to school charter goals and Department of Education priorities.

Dimensions of teaching	Professional standards
Content of teaching and learning	• Demonstrate basic knowledge of areas of the Curriculum and Standards Framework and/or the Victoria Certificate of Education and school charter goals applicable to their teaching • Know and apply materials, teaching methods and programmes associated with the curriculum area being taught • Know the characteristics of learners and current educational trends and strategies
Teaching practice	• Plan activities and present curriculum content in accordance with Course Advice relevant to their classes • Identify individual learning needs, and teach in a way that enables all students to achieve success • Apply teaching methodology and resources to meet the range of abilities and diversity in their classrooms • Develop constructive relationships with students and maintain a positive working atmosphere in the classroom • Implement and maintain an appropriate student management plan within the context of the school's discipline and welfare policy and charter goals • Set clear, challenging and achievable goals for students
Assessment and reporting	• Use appropriate assessment and reporting methods to monitor and record student learning progress • Provide parents or guardians and students with positive and appropriate feedback on performance through informative written and verbal reports
Interaction with the school community	• Demonstrate effective communication skills with teachers, parents or guardians and others • Work effectively in a range of school activities as a member of a school team
Professional requirements	• Carry out responsibilities in a conscientious and diligent manner • Strive to improve their own performance and skills • Act in a professional manner with colleagues, students and parents or guardians • Ensure a safe and supportive classroom environment • Act in accordance with the school charter code of practice • Understand the employer's requirements and act in accordance with school policy and procedures as set out in the school charter

Figure 14.1: Beginning teacher professional standards

Dimensions of teaching	Professional standards
Content of teaching and learning	• Demonstrate a high level of knowledge of relevant curriculum areas, student learning processes and resources and can apply it in implementing programmes that enhance student learning
Teaching practice	• Demonstrate high-quality classroom teaching skills and successfully employ flexible and adaptive approaches and constructive strategies to allow students to reach their full potential
Assessment and reporting	• Successfully employ assessment and reporting strategies that take account of relationships between teaching, learning and assessment
Interaction with the school community	• Demonstrate high-level communication skills and professional behaviour when interacting with parents or guardians, students and colleagues
Professional requirements	• Respond effectively to emerging educational initiatives and priorities • Successfully organise and manage aspects of the wider school programme • Demonstrate improved teaching and performance skills through critically evaluating professional practice • Provide high-level professional assistance to other teachers in classroom related areas

Figure 14.2: Dimension of teaching and professional standards for experienced teachers

The main characteristics of performance management for teaching teachers are:

- an induction period of 12 months followed by an assessment of key competencies resulting in accreditation;
- a performance planning process that defines the key outcomes required of each leading teacher over the school year and provides the basis of evaluation of performance;
- a salary structure with ranges to provide for recognition incentives of up to an additional 10 per cent above the appointment salary to be determined on the basis of performance.

Following appointment, 12 months was spent in an induction phase. This period would see professional development, on the job training and support. At the end of this period, the Leading Teacher could seek endorsement from the principal to seek full accreditation as a Leading Teacher. The teacher could be required to provide evidence that may have included a sample work program, student progress records, student reports and there was also an observation of lessons, usually by the principal.

The accreditation process involved the principal's endorsement followed by a day at an assessment centre undertaking a range of activities aimed at assessing the competencies of; Professional excellence, Educational Leadership, Team facilitation, Interpersonal effectiveness, Problem solving and Program management.

(DoE, 1996: 20)

Accreditation if gained was valid for five years. Leading teachers unsuccessful in gaining accreditation could present again at a later time. Once accredited, leading teachers became eligible for performance payments and performance related pay.

The performance review for both levels of leading teacher was based on an agreed performance plan. The stages of the planning process included the development of the plan itself between the principal and leading teacher, the option of a mid-year review, end of year evaluation and the principal's decision.

According to the guidelines the plan must:

- be consistent with school charter goals and priorities;
- determine a suitable combination of specific result areas, selected in agreement with the principal;
- contain a strategic focus that is clearly defined and rigorous for each specific result area;
- have agreed targets that define the major improvements the leading teacher is expected to implement;
- identify appropriate evidence that will demonstrate the achievement of each target.

(DoE, 1996)

The specific result areas included in the plan were: curriculum leadership, staff management and development, student management, school improvement initiatives, school accountability responsibilities and a category simply entitled 'other'. This latter category provided local flexibility.

It was intended that performance plans should be integrated, first, across the school and also with the individual teachers' professional development plans.

The mid-year review and end of year assessment provided the principal and leading teacher with the opportunity to discuss performance, progress and especially what assistance the leading teacher may need. At the end of the year, the principal would assess the performance of the leading teacher with respect to the level of achievement of each target (outstanding, excellent, fully effective, partial, no achievement, no demonstrated effort to achieve the target). The level of performance would be factored against the weighting of the target previously agreed. The opportunity for further

163

discussion of the assessment was provided to the teacher before the signing off of the plan. A performance salary outcome was then calculated and paid from the school's budget.

Annual reviews and performance management for School Support Officers

The School Support Officers (SSOs) category takes in all administrative staff, laboratory, library technicians and aides, integration aides, some canteen staff in some schools and some professional workers such as youth workers and school counsellors where they are employed directly by schools.

The school support staffing structure has seven levels, 1 to 7. Each level has subdivisions. Officers appointed at levels 1 to 6 gained access the next subdivision within their level by way of an annual review. Officers at level 7 have access to performance related pay, based on the achievement of agreed (with the principal) targets. Very few schools employ support staff at level 7.

The principal in consultation with the school council (governing body) determined the support staffing structure for their particular school. The number of students multiplied by a per capita amount determined the amount of funds available. It is then up to the principal to plan the support staff structure. It is up to the principal whether this area of the budget is under or over spent and therefore subsidises or is subsidised by other areas of the budget.

Probationary process for School Service Officers

School support officers may be appointed to a fixed-term or ongoing position. Principals are required to ensure that a probationary process takes place for all appointed to an ongoing position.

At the beginning of the employment the principal explains the process, sets priorities, establishes measures and establishes support processes. For a period of up to three months regular feedback, work observation and peer support is available. At the end of the three-month period the principal may determine that employment be continued, the probationary period continued or employment discontinued (DoE, 1997).

Annual reviews for School Support Officers

Annual reviews apply to all SSOs at levels 1 to 6, whether they be ongoing (following their probationary period) or fixed term.

Annual reviews support professional growth and career development through review of performance, provision of feedback, recognition of achievements and encouragement of continued development.

The review process defines what is expected of an employee during the review period and the support and guidance that is available. It aligns the employee's professional needs with the priorities of the school as defined in the school charter and their own career ambitions.

(DoE, 1997: 19)

Progression within the level to the top increment is dependent on the outcome of the annual reviews.

The process operates as a cycle with the key elements of discussion of standards, mid-cycle review, an assessment and the completion of the cycle. The review can conclude with incremental review being granted, accelerated progression within the particular level or deferment of the progression. If deferment is likely, support to the officer needs to be provided by the principal, and a panel must be formed to provide advice to the principal. Various arrangements are applicable to staff on various forms of leave.

Performance management for school service officers level 7, including performance plans leading to a performance related salary component, is similar to the process followed for leading teachers.

Performance management for principals

With the advent of the radically conservative government in 1992, principals were appointed on fixed-term contracts of five years after many years of being appointed to tenured positions. In return they were to receive increased remuneration, and access to salary packaging.

Official processes originally mapped out for performance management of teachers, leading teachers and school support staff have remained the same since the publication of the original guidelines. The processes for principals have changed a good deal, almost each year since the introduction of performance related pay.

In outline, the process has always involved initial appointment, then an opportunity to be accredited after 12 months in the position. Accreditation is

165

carried out on a day when a variety of activities are conducted (for example, in-basket exercises, interviews). Subsequent to successful accreditation, access to performance payments became available.

Principals were also to be subject to a performance management system. Initially this was meant to put up to 15 per cent of a principal's salary at risk if performance was not up to expectations. Principals by and large seemed comfortable with this and signed up to these arrangements, on the advice of their industrial federation, while the details were being worked out.

Subsequently the system was changed so that instead of 15 per cent of salary being at risk, the last 15 per cent of salary had to be earned via the completion of requirements outlined in an agreed plan. The plan was to be agreed with the regional general manager or delegate.

The plans were to be based on specific agreed outcomes on specific result areas. Considerable variations developed across schools. The degree of difficulty of targets seemed to vary greatly. Of course, some of this was due to the individual circumstances of schools. (A particular project in one school might be more significant and difficult to implement than in another school.) In some schools the members of principal teams shared goals, that is, the same goals were in more than one of their plans. In other cases, each member of the principal team had different goals from those of their colleagues.

The evidence required to prove that the goals had been achieved was specified at the time of writing the plan. At the end of the year or beginning of the subsequent year a folder of evidence was forwarded to two trained peer reviewers who checked to see if the evidence demonstrated that the goals had been achieved. The principal or assistant principal would also submit a self-assessment of performance for each of the goals. The trained peer reviewers were permitted no communication with the principals and assistant principals they were reviewing. Recommendations were then forwarded to the general manager for endorsement and payment.

The first year saw levels of payment differ from region to region across the state. One region granted an average 12.5 per cent of salary, others less. It was revealed that the government was unhappy about the high levels of payments. Subsequently regions were provided with only 8 per cent of principal salaries in the performance budget pool.

What evolved was a system that, over time, involved personal visits to principals by regional delegates for both plan development and approvals. This meant the evidence on paper could be discussed with the regional colleague, which was welcomed. The assistant principals' plans were originally assessed by the regional general manager or delegate, but in later years were assessed by the principal of their own school. The assessment for principals was to become not an absolute amount (e.g. 6 per cent of salary) but a proportion of an available regional pool and relative to the assessment of colleagues in the same region.

Other changes to the system included the level of assessment. In 1996 agreed plans included agreed criteria to judge outstanding performance. This made clear what evidence was needed to prove the outstanding level of achievement, and therefore, higher levels of performance remuneration. By 1998 the evidence for an outstanding levels of achievement was not specified and left to the discretion of the general manager.

Union views on principal performance related pay

Both government sector principal unions held strong views on performance related pay for principals as developed in Victoria. It is reasonable to say that their views would be similar with regard to leading teacher performance related pay.

The view of the Victoria Principals' Federation (VPF), was that the performance system Victorian-style was that it was incompatible with the nature and purpose of education, it wasted time and money, it took away from the real task of the principal, it never seemed to be sufficiently objective or transparent to have any credibility, and the 8 per cent budget made a mockery of genuine access to a 15 per cent reward. The VPF argued for an 8 per cent increase in superable salary together with a non-pay related appraisal plan.

The Australian Education Union (which covers teacher, principal and support staff) had the view that performance plans linked to pay were divisive, that superable salary should be increased, that performance plans should relate to the school charter (School Development Plan), and that a non-pay related appraisal system would be supported. Despite much opposition and dissatisfaction, the conservative government maintained a commitment to performance related pay.

In September 1999, the Labour Party unexpectedly won office. The new minister agreed to abolish performance related pay as soon as practicable. In effect, the year 2000 was the final year of performance related pay. At the time of writing this chapter, new arrangements for performance appraisal are yet to be announced.

The following statement from an Australian Education Union Official of the time, Terry Danckert, sums up the views of many principal class officers (PCOs).

PCA (Principal Class Association) members are well aware that the new certified agreement will abolish the current unsatisfactory performance management system. However, members have consistently agreed that they ought to be subject to an appropriate accountability process. The argument is not whether PCOs should be accountable, but the process by which such accountability occurs.

(AEU, 2000)

It is likely that any new system will be standards based, relate directly to the school charter and government priorities but will not be related to remuneration.

Strengths

Despite the judgement being made by many that, overall, the performance related pay system was too problematic; it did have some positive features. It can be argued that these features should be considered for inclusion in the next version of performance management.

Linking individual plans to school plans

There was considerable potential to bring about high levels of congruence in the work of staff where school goals in the school charter became the goals in individual plans. Heads of year and heads of faculty plans can be aligned with each other and those of assistant principal and principals. All staff holding formal leadership positions would be contributing directly to an agreed direction.

Generating discussion between the principals and staff

In Victoria, apart from a handful of schools, there was no existing format of periodic discussion or information exchange between the principal and other staff regarding their professional performance and development. The PRP provided that opportunity.

Development of a portfolio, useful when seeking promotion

It was typical of the process that staff of all levels prepared a portfolio of evidence for endorsement of accreditation. This could be both an onerous task and a rewarding one: onerous in getting the material, remembering to take copies of student work during the year; rewarding in reflecting on one's work over the year and receiving feedback on it.

The portfolios prepared for the PRP may have a benefit in assisting the staff member in preparing applications for promotion. If kept, each folder brought together a wide range of documents (rolls, students work, references, evaluations, and examples of exemplary curriculum materials prepared) that may provide useful material for a selection process.

Encouraged reflection on and celebration of achievement

Prior to the PRP very rarely did a principal have the opportunity to look at material indicative of a staff member's work. Some found the time to discuss the material and work it represented with the staff member. Most often the work was very good and well worth celebrating.

Simple pro formas for recording the process

The pro formas used to record goals and assessments were very simple and useful. They comprised just four A4 pages and were more than adequate for the purpose. It is always important that any system in a school does not bury the participants in needless paperwork, and this process did not do that.

Problems

The workload seemed to be great. The system for teachers, school support officers and leading teachers, and in later years assistant principals, implied that principals needed to interview each staff member at the beginning of the performance or annual review period, halfway through the period and at the end to make the assessment. Especially for large schools this was not possible without substantial delegation. Some principals, in the end, ran the process with provision of information at the beginning of the process, the option of a discussion at the midpoint and the provision of written evidence at the end with the option of a discussion. Some principals delegated the process to assistant principals and/or, in the case of teachers and school support officers, heads of department. For implementation processes, there was wide variation from school to school.

In the early years, the burden of proof weighed heavily on principals and lots of paperwork was generated.

Underfunded

For schools with a full leadership structure (i.e. full entitlements of leading teachers and assistant principals) the available funding was insufficient to pay all commitments if all were assessed at a high level such as 'outstanding'. The school budget was, however, somewhat protected from this situation by the scaling of the assessment scale. The scale rewarded the teacher and assistant principal with a 50 per cent rating if a target was fully achieved. It took an 'outstanding' rating for a target to be fully weighted. The higher rating was difficult to achieve.

Budget planning difficulties

Not all leading teachers were prepared to negotiate performance plans each year. Some found the task onerous, sometimes the goals expected by principals were seen to be too demanding and sometimes the teacher was philosophically opposed to a performance related pay system. Also the actual performance rating of each teacher and assistant principal was difficult to predict. These factors made budgeting difficult.

A range of strategies was possible. For example, like the regions, schools could limit the amount available and then share the available funds across each leading teacher and assistant principal in proportion to the performance of all other leading teachers and assistant principals. Another strategy was where a principal would in part negotiate goals that were important but required modest effort, on the understanding that there would be a modest gain in return for the achievement of the modest goals.

Performance payments not superable salary

A further disadvantage was that the performance related pay component of income was not superable. This saved the government money but was seen as less desirable than the funds being part of superable salary.

Pressure to assess positively

As with most local processes where a principal has to make a judgement about a teacher colleague, there is pressure to assess positively. The process placed a heavy onus on the principal to justify a negative judgement or anything less than outstanding.

Teachers at the top of the incremental scale

There did not appear to be much objection by teachers to their annual reviews when still working up the incremental scale. Once they had reached the top of the incremental scale, however, they were often reluctant to go to the trouble of preparing a portfolio of material for assessment. The Australian Education Union supported teachers in this position who did not want to prepare material. However, the union did support a process of discussion between the teacher and principal.

The fatal flaws

While there were problems with the system, there were broader philosophical issues that seemed to be perceived as the fatal flaws of the PRP. Much of the approach seemed to borrow from business and the public service. While some ideas that emanate beyond schools can translate well into school settings, for example total quality management, the PRP incarnation of performance management was not perceived to be helpful in schools, at least at this time and in this form.

Individual rewards in school for what is often a group achievement

Much of what is done in a school may be initiated by individuals. However, little can be achieved on a schoolwide or facultywide basis without co-operation and effort from a team. The PRP rewarded individuals.

It is believed that a few schools tried to reward teams, however, there is nothing in the literature to indicate how these experiments occurred.

Potentially divisive

This writer is not aware of any thorough study into the impact of performance related pay in schools in Victoria. However, anecdotes shared between principals indicates that the initiative was potentially very divisive. Some principals kept their own, assistant principals' and leading teachers' performance plans confidential. This meant there was the potential for other staff to be cynical about any initiatives being taken as being linked to the initiator's receipt of performance related pay. The reaction could be one of non-co-operation given the initiator might be getting extra pay for the project. When some principals made the performance plans public, some staff members were certain they would leave the work to the one(s) who was getting paid for it.

Organisation opposition

The Australian Education Union and the Victoria Principals Federation both opposed the performance related pay. They faced the dilemma of wanting access to higher pay for members, but not related to performance, especially individual performance.

Volatility of a school environment

The system was found at times to be too inflexible. This was particularly the case for principal plans agreed at the beginning of the year with a regional officer. During the year some new initiatives may be imposed on the school by the department or government. This new work may take up a lot of time and distract the principal from the agreed goals, but the principal's performance would be judged on the achievement of the originally agreed goals.

This seemed to be less of a problem within schools where principals seemed to exercise a sensible amount of flexibility in changing circumstances.

Epilogue

There is a clear logic in the intent of the former government in the introduction of performance related pay for school-based leaders. They intended to reward contribution and the improvement outcomes. The approach has not won acceptance of the teaching profession. The basis of a system offering individual reward seems to fit uneasily into the school environment. The system tended to generate a lot of additional work that was unwelcome. There seems no opposition to educators being accountable. It is desirable that school leaders speak with team members about their progress, and principals discuss their progress with a senior manager. The profession has deemed it not desirable to have remuneration outcomes as part of the discussion.

It is interesting for school leaders in Victoria to see the UK education system under a Labour government move to performance related pay, just as a Labour government in Victoria is taking the profession away from performance for money. Developments in both places, and others around the world, will be worth watching over the coming years.

References

Australian Education Union (AEU) (2000) *Principal Class Newsletter*, 5 September.

Department of Education (DoE) (1986) *Schools into the 1990s*. Australia: Melbourne, Victoria: DoE.

Department of Education (DoE) (1996) *Professional Recognition Program for Teachers: Guidelines*. Australia: Melbourne, Victoria: DoE.

Department of Education (DoE) (1997) *School Services Officers Handbook*. Australia: Melbourne, Victoria: DoE.

15
■ ■ ■

Performance Management in New Zealand

John O'Neill

Introduction

In March 2001 the Chief Executive of the New Zealand Ministry of Education, Secretary for Education Howard Fancy, told a parliamentary select committee that 'there was no specific work going on in the ministry linking teachers' pay to the educational achievement of students', that the ministry's 'focus has been on developing the professional standards and focusing on good professional practice' and that changes to schools' reporting requirements would provide further accountability for teachers' performance (*NZER*, 2001: 4).

The regulatory framework for 'Performance management in schools' (Fancy, 1996) in New Zealand is simple in conception and design. Appraisal regulations and professional standards for teachers, those in positions of responsibility, senior staff and principals were implemented between 1996 and 1999. The larger panoply of monitoring and surveillance systems for boards of trustees (governing bodies), schools and teachers originates from the Education Act 1989 and now bears close comparison with teacher and senior management appraisal structures, and school reporting, development planning and inspection requirements that have been developed since the mid-1980s in England and Wales. Nonetheless, the key point to be made at the outset is that it is only since the introduction of 'performance management' and 'professional standards' in the mid-1990s that specific regulatory procedures have been in place to require the appraisal and development of all teachers and senior management staff in New Zealand's version of the 'self-managing school'.

The shape and principal components of performance management at both school and classroom levels in New Zealand are summarised in the first part of the chapter. The more interesting analysis to my mind, however, lies in the examination of the historical and educational tensions that have led over time to the situation in which these particular formulations are seen to be both necessary and desirable policy solutions to the 'problem' of performance management in schools. This will form the major part of the discussion, focusing by way of illustration on the shifting politics of teacher development and accountability in the secondary school sector since the 1940s.

Performance management in schools

In New Zealand, performance management frameworks operate at both school and classroom levels. Thus individual teacher appraisal is nested within an increasingly pervasive and homogenising set of accountabilities that are legislated for by government, regulated by the Ministry of Education and inspected by the Education Review Office (ERO). In this part of the chapter, I describe the basic framework of accountability for the 'self-managing' school and then locate specific developments in the area of 'performance management' for teachers within this. (The introduction of performance management for primary and secondary school principals, a proportion of whom were until recently employed on individual contracts, has been more complex and is beyond the scope of this chapter.)

School performance management

Overnight the landmark Education Act of 1989 made the approximately 2800 New Zealand schools autonomous, self-managing units. Legislation in 1989 and 1990 disestablished most of the administration, curriculum and professional development and inspectorate functions of the old Department of Education in Wellington and its regional outposts. These were replaced with elected boards of trustees at school level, a Ministry of Education reduced largely to a policy function and a number of educational quangos with statutory inspection (ERO), registration (Teacher Registration Board [TRB]) and validation (New Zealand Qualifications Authority) roles. Boards of trustees became the employer of staff in the school, with the school principal as their 'chief executive', and were required to act in accordance with the 'good employer' responsibilities set out in the State Sector Act 1988. Initially, it was envisaged that both operational and salaries funds would be devolved to each school as bulk grants and that boards would develop their role as employer through performance management systems, with the opportunity to vire funds between operations and salaries grants in order to gain some local flexibility. In practice, classroom teachers' salaries remained centrally resourced in most schools during the 1990s.

The political rhetoric that preceded the 1989 Act suggested that self-management would provide a 'partnership' between the Crown, individual schools and their local communities, articulated through each school's charter. Each charter had to contain both the National Guidelines (legal obligations in the areas of curriculum, personnel, property, finance and equity) and local goals and statements of purpose. Over time, the more ephemeral 'partnership' component of the charter has waned in importance; the quantifiable 'accountability' component, waxed. By 1991, the charter was seen as 'the foundation-stone of accountability' for the school (NZEG, 1991: 2). In 1993, the Secretary for Education (O'Rourke, 1993) gazetted revised National Administration Guidelines (NAGs), covering governance and management, and National Education Goals (NEGs), covering curriculum, to be included in the school charter. The ERO inspects all schools periodically against their charter obligations and, specifically, the extent to which they are delivering the NAGs and NEGs. The reports of each school review are publicly available.

In 1999, the Labour government revised the NAGs (NZEG, 1999: 25) to include a specific focus on government priority areas (Maori students, literacy and numeracy, and students with special needs) and the more detailed use of national curriculum statements and assessment information for school review and planning purposes. In addition, schools were required for the first time to develop a strategic plan and engage in self-review, and to report to parents on the achievement of students as a whole. At the time of writing the Education Amendment Bill (No. 2) proposes to replace the charter with a school plan that has both long-term and annual planning sections and to require the school board to prepare an annual report after the end of each financial year. The bill also gives the Minister of Education a wider range of powers to intervene in 'poorly performing schools' (ibid.: 3–5).

Teacher performance management

One of the original principles of the *Tomorrow's Schools* reforms (Lange, 1988) was that boards of trustees would act like any other public sector employer, introducing performance management for staff and exercising some local discretion over staffing levels and teacher salaries on appointment (ibid.: 11–13). This agenda was, for a number of reasons, slow in coming to fruition (see below). By 1995, the ERO was publicly expressing exasperation at the delay in providing school boards with the performance management systems that were deemed necessary to guide their work (O'Neill, 1998). In 1996, the Ministry of Education circulated *Draft National Guidelines for Performance Management in*

Schools (MoE, 1995) for consultation during the school year and in December 1996 gazetted a skeletal framework for the annual appraisal of teachers and principals (Fancy, 1996). The model adopted is a standard managerial cycle of appraisal requiring classroom observation, self-review, the setting of development objectives and a statement by the appraiser regarding performance against a number of areas of classroom and management activity. The system introduced by each school requires the verification and approval of the ERO.

In their respective collective contract negotiations in 1998 and 1999, primary and secondary teachers agreed to the incorporation of more specific 'professional standards' (differentiated for beginning, fully registered and experienced teachers) against which individual performance would be measured (*NZEG*, 1998; MoE, 1999). The standards were developed from various taxonomies in circulation including the TRB criteria for teacher registration. Progression through the salary scale was made subject to annual attestation by the principal that satisfactory levels of individual performance had been achieved. The modified arrangements provide for competency procedures to be instituted against any teacher who is considered to have failed to meet the professional standards in a subsequent assessment. There are now provisions to allow principals and boards to address more quickly 'teachers causing concern'. Moreover, schools have also been allocated a number of 'remuneration units' that may be awarded to individual staff on a temporary basis for particular purposes.

Finally, the Education Amendment Bill (No. 2) (2000) proposes to replace the TRB with a New Zealand Education Council responsible for teacher registration and disciplinary matters. The council membership would include teachers. However, at the time of writing some concern has been expressed by teacher unions at the extension of council powers to include enquiry into lay complaints of teacher misconduct, and the emphasis on discipline rather than the promotion of teaching as a valued profession.

In the remainder of this chapter, I want to examine the historical developments that have 'produced' these contemporary performance management systems.

The model teacher

Hargreaves (1994: 248) argues that governments face a basic choice in their approach to educational reform, between, on the one hand, 'bureaucratic control' that emphasises the regulation and management of teachers to ensure that they implement centrally mandated change and, on the other hand, 'professional empowerment' that emphasises the provision of support, encouragement and structured opportunities to teachers 'to make improvements of their own'. As well as being fundamentally different conceptions of the management of teachers' work, and what that 'work' is, these competing views also reflect different assumptions about how teachers learn to develop and improve their practice. At one level we may discern in New Zealand a stark transformation from 'professional empowerment' (pre-1989) to 'bureaucratic control' (post-1990). At another level, these 'before' and 'after' cameos are too crude.

Rather than a bipolar division, there is an identifiable trend in teacher–state relationships in New Zealand. This might be summarised as a gradual shift: from naive trust in the 1940s and 1950s, to benevolent centralism in the 1960s, to corporatist partnership in the 1970s, to professional accountability in the 1980s and, finally, to contractual accountability in the 1990s. These phases subsume distinct yet related conceptions of the teacher and his or her development, with each new version evolving from the perceived 'shortcomings' of previous conceptions.

Models of performance management in schools are also based on particular conceptions of teaching, teacher development and teacher accountability. These conceptions are neither objective nor static, but derive from broader social and economic concerns. They reflect prevailing societal views of 'social efficiency' at any particular time and how teaching should contribute to this (Hamilton, 1989). In this part of the chapter, three broad conceptions of postwar teaching in New Zealand are discussed: those of the 'ideal' teacher, the 'professional' teacher, and of the 'accountable' teacher. In the following part of the chapter, we consider briefly the development and management strategies put in place to accompany these models of the teacher.

The ideal teacher for 'every person'

The development of 'comprehensive' secondary schooling to suit the needs of 'every person' in New Zealand dates from the *Post-Primary School Curriculum* report to the Minister of Education in 1942. Although the committee's terms of reference excluded 'problems of teaching method, of corporate life, and of internal school organisation' (*The Post-Primary School Curriculum* (Thomas Report), 1959: 1) their proposals for a core post-primary curriculum in the 1940s were based on a normative image of teaching, both individual and collective. As Whitehead (1974: 57) aptly put it:

> In brief, the Committee was anxious to see an end to the formality, narrowness and authoritarianism that was then characteristic of the teaching methods in the schools. Instead, they wished to see classroom work conducted in a freer, democratic and more humane setting, with greater emphasis placed on flexibility, diversity and increased pupil participation.

The committee noted, for example, that in the past 'the nature of the education a pupil has been given has frequently been determined less by what his teachers have believed he actually requires, even for vocational purposes, than by the demand for attainments that can readily be marketed' (ibid.: 5). It was argued, also, that a 'fairly general change in approach' was needed from teachers to 'cater for pupils of widely differing abilities and interests' and that in order to meet these diverse needs, 'differentiation should often be considered not so much as a problem of curricular content as one of method – i.e., of adapting the approach to the abilities of pupils' (ibid.: 7). Equally, in calling for each school to openly and thoroughly review its current practice and act on the findings, the committee was making considerable assumptions about the capability of schools to do precisely that. It commented that the development of a curriculum geared to meeting the needs of each student:

> *involves very close co-operation among teachers, who must themselves, under the leadership of their principal, achieve unity of purpose and work as a team. There are schools in which staff collaboration is well developed, but more of it is needed if what we have in mind is to be accomplished.*

(Ibid.: 18)

What the committee did not predict was the rapid post-war expansion of the economy and the schooling system (and the attendant 'crisis' in teacher numbers and quality), the influence of the School Certificate examination on the entire curriculum, and changes in student composition and retention rates. All these militated strongly against the successful development of classroom teaching and staff collaboration along the normative lines envisaged in the report.

In attempting to explain why the implementation of the proposed curricular and pedagogical changes largely failed, Whitehead provides a useful synthesis of the practical problems faced by schools. In addition to the difficulties of even obtaining a copy of the Thomas Report until 1959 when it was reprinted by the Department of Education:

> *Third- and fourth-form classes were large and often housed in temporary buildings, and there was a shortage of suitable source material in subjects like social studies and general science. These circumstances, of necessity, forced many teachers to employ traditional teaching methods characterized by 'chalk and talk', and to continue using existing and often out-of-date textbooks. Teaching aids were also in short supply, and this fact prevented teachers from innovating with new techniques and classroom methods. Staffing shortages also forced teachers to teach subjects, especially in the common core, for which they had no qualifications or interest.*

(Whitehead, 1974: 62)

In a sense, discourses of teaching, teacher development and, most recently, performance management since that time may all be seen as attempts to remedy the national failure fully to realise the Thomas Committee's liberal-progressive vision of curriculum and methods differentiated to meet the real needs of each student, developed at school level by teams of energetic and appropriately qualified teachers. Indeed, from the 1960s to the late 1980s, politicians, the Department and the New Zealand Post-Primary Teachers' Association (NZPPTA) together participated in exhaustive efforts to develop training, employment, in-service and accountability structures to attempt to ensure that teacher supply and quality would not again be the major impediments to secondary schooling reform that they proved to be from the mid-1940s to the mid-1960s.

The professional teacher

If, in 1961, Phoebe Meikle's pamphlet *School and Nation. Post-Primary Education since the War* and the NZPPTA's *The Critical Situation in Post-Primary Schools* captured the 'desperate' mood of educationists in the 1950s, the NZPPTA's *Education in Change*, published in 1969 represented a forward-looking attempt by teachers and teacher educators to redefine the objectives of secondary education, and teachers' envisaged role in securing those objectives. While the NZPPTA has since the 1960s attempted to secure regular *industrial* improvements in teachers' pay and conditions of service, it has also taken an active and collaborative *professional* role in defining 'the teacher' and promoting the participation of teachers in curriculum development and decision making at both national and school levels (Webster, 1981).

In a series of three publications between 1969 and 1974 (*Education in Change* [NZPPTA, 1969], *Secondary Schools in Change* [Shallcrass, 1973], *Teachers in Change* [NZPPTA, 1974]) NZPPTA made a major contribution to the development of another model of the preferred teacher (Smyth and Shacklock, 1998) to supersede that articulated by the Thomas Committee in the 1940s. The NZPPTA's conception of individual and collective teachers' practice was of autonomous, educated, thoughtful and creative professionals working on the basis of 'mutual respect' in a humanistic partnership with students:

> *If mutual respect is a desirable basis for classroom activity, the implications are clear: in order to allow children the freedom necessary to develop initiative and self-respect teachers must be prepared to do things* with *children rather than* to *them or* for *them. Moreover, the teacher who wishes to release this independent drive in his pupils must know a great deal about them so that he can organise their learning activities and set appropriate goals. He must know about their interests, skills knowledge, attitudes and values before he can lead them to contribute fully to classwork and thus to participate in their own education. Much of this understanding can be obtained more readily outside the classroom in informal discussions with pupils and during other school activities. Many more opportunities should be provided for teachers to learn more about their pupils by mixing with them in small groups.*
>
> (NZPPTA, 1969: 11–12, original emphases)

This image stood in direct contrast to that of the *Report of the Commission on Education in New Zealand* (Currie Report) in 1962, which had emphasised teachers' lack of training and competence to deliver the core curriculum. In addition, the commission reported that the possibility of school-based curriculum development was hampered by 'young and less experienced teachers who have had, in the explosive expansion of the schools, not only to take most of the rank and file positions but also to assume positions of responsibility and guidance beyond their seniority and experience' (ibid.: 267).

Between the report of the Currie Commission and the end of the 1970s a raft of policy and procedural changes were instituted in order to transform secondary teachers from an inadequately qualified, poorly paid labour force into a modern profession. Central to this was the creation of an image of the secondary teacher as guide or facilitator of enquiry-based learning. Notwithstanding the apparent consensus on the vision, there was recognition of the difficulties involved in moving towards it, of the problems of classroom control that many teachers faced and of the need to provide more time for teachers outside the classroom in order to undertake the necessary curriculum and assessment work that was required under a school-based curriculum development approach.

In 1978, a survey of secondary schools undertaken by Dr E.M. Campbell on behalf of the Department of Education found discrepancies between the official or intended curriculum in schools (as evidenced in policy and discussion documents in the early 1970s), and what teachers were able to realise in practice. Campbell noted that, despite teacher support for liberalisation, the curriculum and its assessment were still dominated by tests and external examinations, that memorisation of facts received greater emphasis than higher levels of learning, most talking was done by teacher, there was little integration of studies in a subject-focused curriculum, schools were more discipline than guidance oriented, with sanctions outweighing rewards, and that pupils had little say in rules, curriculum content, methods or reporting.

From the mid-1960s, the professionalisation of *subject* teaching also became more organised. The NZPPTA established its own subject committees, the Department of Education instituted a round of major subject revisions by syllabus committees on behalf of the secondary schools and there was a growth in the numbers of regional and then national associations established in the principal secondary school subject areas. Together with the piloting of internal assessment for School Certificate in the mid-1970s, these changes firmly established teachers and their representatives at the heart of curriculum and subject development in New Zealand secondary schools. Teachers were to enjoy this 'partnership' role until the early 1990s when official curriculum development was undertaken by consultants through contracts let by the Ministry of Education and responsibility for course approval, validation and credentials was transferred to a new quango, the New Zealand Qualifications Authority.

The accountable teacher

Running parallel with these professionalising trends were issues regarding the training, registration and discipline of teachers. Although the 1964 Education Act required teachers to be registered prior to employment it was not until 1974 that secondary teachers were required to hold a trained teachers' certificate. In 1978, the statutory provisions for teacher registration and discipline were reviewed and amended. Just as attempted curriculum and assessment reform in the 1980s reflected a conflict between various 'progressivist' and 'restorationist' lobbies, so too did arguments about teaching and the accountability of teachers (Openshaw, 1980). In 1983, the conservative Minister of Education announced his intention to introduce, within the year, a personal grading or assessment scheme for all teachers (previously only beginning teachers and those seeking promotion had formally been assessed). The proposal was unanimously rejected by the NZPPTA at its annual conference and had only qualified support from secondary school boards. It was not, then, until 1986 that the first concerted ideological attempt was made to link teachers' claims to professional status to the requirement that they be held specifically accountable for their and their students' performance. Using an explicitly managerial language of 'quality', 'standards', 'outcomes' and 'accountability to consumers', the *Report of the Inquiry into the Quality of Teaching* in 1986 (ESSC, 1986) argued that as professionals, all teachers should be held accountable for learner outcomes. According to the Education and Science Select Committee, 'professionalism must emphasise learners' rights. Professionalism must not become protectionism ... [Thus] professional standards must not be determined or assessed solely by the profession. Both consumers and providers must have an equal say in what is acceptable as quality teaching' (ibid.: 6).

The report went on to define what it saw as the attributes and characteristics of 'quality teachers' and recommended the development of schemes against which individual teachers' performance could be 'assessed' in order to both 'monitor standards', 'recognise good teaching' and identify teachers for promotion, further assistance or removal from the workforce (ibid.: 39). The report contained as an attachment, the NZPPTA's proposed revisions to the criteria for the classification of teachers which would 'apply to all practising secondary schoolteachers in permanent positions and cover skills needed to be a classroom teacher'. The NZPPTA's proposals listed a number of 'demonstrable abilities' under the headings: Planning and Preparation, Subject Competence, Teaching Techniques and Management, Relationships with Students and Relationships with the School (ibid.: 67–8). Subsequently, in 1990, and following the *Tomorrow's Schools* (Lange, 1988) and *Today's Schools* (1990) reforms of school management, the *Tomorrow's Standards* (1990) report on assessment made a sharp distinction between the 'formal assessment of teachers and their ongoing appraisal for professional development' and recommended that guidelines and resources for the latter be developed for use in schools (ibid.: 60–1). This twin agenda was pursued in a number of guises under the auspices of the Ministry of Education, the ERO and the State Services Commission (SSC) in the 1990s (Collins, 1997).

Controlling teachers in the 1990s

To reach an understanding of these developments it is essential to realise that the 'self-managing school' reforms of educational administration instituted through the *Tomorrow's Schools* and *Today's Schools* reports were part of a larger New Right structural adjustment project in economic and social policy. The success of this project depended on introducing private sector management controls and 'labour market flexibility' to public sector collective employment practices through deregulation, enterprise bargaining, bulk funding of salaries and productivity gains (Jesson, 1989). Many of these principles were embodied in major employment and industrial relations law changes between 1987 and 1991 and were applied by the SSC in its role as bargaining agent for the Ministry of Education. Between 1989 and 1991, the SSC was unable to secure the introduction in secondary schools of individual contracts for senior staff, flexible pay scales and formal teacher assessment schemes in its negotiations with the NZPPTA (Rae, 1991). Equally, the national government was encountering strong opposition from the NZPPTA in its policy to devolve bulk funding of teachers' salaries to schools in 1990–91 (Simkin, 1995).

In 1992, the industrial climate worsened and, under pressure from the School Trustees' Association (STA) and the NZPPTA, the government modified its attempt to secure direct changes to teachers' work and conditions and established consultative groups, initially to negotiate over bulk funding, and later to review the staffing formulae for schools. As a result, in secondary schools, the government was able to (a) implement bulk funding of salaries for senior staff and most (in some cases all) teachers in positions of responsibility, and (b) replace historical patterns of discretionary funding of additional teachers to (small, rural and/or socially disadvantaged) schools with capped contestable funds in government priority areas for which all schools could apply in direct competition with each other (Simkin, 1995).

The other part of the 'flexibility' agenda, performance-based assessment for teachers, was also proceeding slowly. Progress was hampered by the reality that government control agencies (SSC, ERO, Treasury) and libertarian lobby groups (e.g. the Education Forum) clearly saw a direct link between teacher performance, assessment, in-service training, management and remuneration. Appraisal, to these groups, was not simply a cyclical form of planned professional development for teachers (Education Forum, 1992; O'Neill, 1998). The ambiguous status of appraisal was reflected in the fact that while SSC was pursuing teacher assessment as an industrial issue in contract negotiations in the 1990s, the Ministry of Education was in the same period developing its own teacher appraisal initiative, one in which teachers' performance was linked to professional development and better outcomes for students (Collins, 1997). Thus, at the end of 1995, when the Ministry's discussion document *Draft National Guidelines for Performance Management in Schools* was released for consultation during the following year, it attempted to unite accountability and development agendas in the one bureaucratic concept of 'performance management'.

Supporting and managing teachers' work

In this part of the chapter we consider the state's response to a crisis in teacher quality in the 1960s, the 'partnership' approach to teacher development in the 1970s and 1980s, and the shift to performance management in the 1990s.

Crisis and response

In 1942, the Thomas Committee had urged each school to 're-examine its whole theory and practice, make up its mind about the real needs of its pupils and the means by which they can best be met, and then act courageously in accordance with its findings' (*The Post-Primary School Curriculum*, 1959: 3–4). However, other than encouragement, it could suggest little by way of tangible support for schools and teachers that might be provided by the Department of Education.

By 1960, a combination of (a) rapid growth in the student population, (b) a parallel increase in the size and number of schools, (c) severe teacher recruitment and retention problems and (d) a shortage of good quality, well-qualified, experienced teachers to take up positions of responsibility, prepare schemes of work and support less experienced colleagues, had created what most contemporary commentators called a 'crisis' of teacher quality, but which might equally well be labelled a crisis of government legitimation (Habermas, 1975) in as much as the anticipated innovations in universal secondary schooling from 1942 had clearly failed to eventuate. This crisis provoked a particular kind of state response.

In 1962, the Currie Commission recommended the centralised development of curriculum, resources, teacher handbooks and the provision of in-service training in content and method organised by Department of Education staff, together with explicit differentiation of the curriculum into three ability bands and the use of national standardised testing as checkpoints at various stages of primary and secondary schooling. As a result, in the 1960s subject syllabus revision for forms I–IV (upper primary, intermediate and lower secondary school years) and the development of guidelines and teaching materials proceeded rapidly under the auspices of the Curriculum Development Unit (established in 1963) and the School Publications Branch of the Department of Education. Thus, in 1974, McLaren (1974: 112) could claim that:

> The Curriculum Development Unit has, in its few years of existence, gone some distance towards developing a national curriculum as distinct from a set of syllabuses. Each subject area is being developed on the basis of a common pattern involving the statement of precise objectives in terms of intended changes in pupils' cognitive and affective behaviour, the drafting of learning materials designed to achieve these objectives, the trial and appraisal of these materials in schools and then revision in light of the trials prior to publication and dissemination.

These developments created, inter alia, pressures for more in-service training for teachers. From modest beginnings as summer vacation courses arranged for their members by the teacher unions in 1944, the years following the report of the Currie Commission saw the establishment of a national advisory committee for in-service training, two permanent residential in-service centres, and accredited distance learning courses for the Correspondence School's Diploma in Teaching, and by Massey University.

A professional partnership for teacher development

In the 1970s, the relational and 'classroom manager' aspects of the ideal teacher's role were consistently advanced by the NZPPTA and the Department of Education as solutions to rapid societal changes and an older secondary school student population that, in the 'liberal milieu' (Jesson, 1989) of the 1960s and 1970s, was less accepting of authoritarian and conformist forms of control. Onto this was grafted the text of 'teacher education [as] a process which must continue throughout the professional life of a teacher' (ACEP, 1973: 2). As a result, the unitary conception of the 'secondary teacher' was displaced by one that emphasised clearly differentiated, specialised career patterns, each with different 'continuing education' needs. For the 65 per cent who were assistant teachers, 'a wide variety of continuing education courses in the various subject areas, classroom management, modern teaching techniques and evaluation, need to be provided' (ibid.: 33). After 'five to ten years' of teaching experience, 'more able teachers will be appointed to positions of responsibility' (ibid.) and, for a small minority, then to senior school management, advisory service or inspectorate roles. However, it was also argued that 'the qualities which make for good teaching do not necessarily imply managerial ability and it follows that formal preparation is needed for teachers to accept new administrative roles with confidence and perform them adequately' (ibid.: 12).

In order to cope with this expanded programme of continuing education for teachers, a national system of teachers' centres was proposed to provide local training and resources, and the teachers' colleges, previously concerned only with pre-service education, were to be permitted to offer in-service courses. It was also recommended that the responsibility for approving programmes should be exercised by the inspectorate and Curriculum Development Unit in collaboration with the NZPPTA and subject organisations. Between 1977 and the early 1990s programmes of specialised courses for teachers burgeoned and became institutionalised within the education system as a whole.

In the late 1970s and early 1980s the image of the model teacher changed markedly as a result of a combination of pressures caused by economic crisis and burgeoning youth unemployment and labour market changes, vocal lobby group dissatisfaction with the standards of schooling manifested as a 'back-to-basics' campaign, and an interest in the results of school effectiveness studies from overseas (Nash, 1983). In contrast with the liberal progressive consensus that appeared to exist between the Department and the NZPPTA, popular dissatisfaction with schooling had been building during the 1970s, and was articulated through a number of influential groups, including the New Zealand Chamber of Commerce, the New Zealand Employers' Federation, the Concerned Parents' Association and the Educational Standards Association. According to Nash, the Department of Education's position was first to 'decline to recognise' the concerns and then to refute them (ibid.: 28). In 1978, however, the change in official position could not have been more abrupt or unambiguous:

> *The appointment of a new Minister of Education in 1978 marked a sharp change in the attitude taken by the Department. Early in 1979 the Department's inspectors addressed a series of regional meetings at which teachers were advised that the 1980s were to be a time of consolidation rather than experimentation and that their efforts would be best applied to maintaining and improving basic skills.*

> (Ibid.: 29)

The growth of accountability measures

From this time, also, discourses of teacher development and education were to become interwoven with, and, by the mid-1990s, subordinate to, those of teacher quality and performance. In November 1979, in a graduation cere-mony address, the Director-General of Education (and opponent of the 'back-to-basics' calls), W.L. Renwick (1980), argued for a redefinition of teach-ers' professional status. In its argumentation and choice of terminology, the address sought to reconstruct the model of the professional teacher in two key respects. Teachers were described as public servants who provided a public service to their clients at public expense. While Renwick expressed no desire to circumscribe the right of the teacher to exercise his or her professional judgement, he argued that the traditional professional expectation of autonomy and self-regulation was not tenable in the case of teachers. Because of their working circumstances, teachers 'for whom co-operation, teamwork and the sharing of expertise have always been of central importance' needed to be more accountable to their professional peers. Equally, given the growing complexity of their work and its importance to the community, public as well as professional interests needed to be represented 'in the control and regulation of the teaching profession' (ibid.: 21).

The standards, accountability and school effectiveness texts that became more widespread in this period are clearly present in the arguments of the Education and Science Select Committee in its *Report of the Inquiry into the Quality of Teaching* in 1986, and in the *Tomorrow's Standards* report of 1990. Indeed, the Select Committee report contained, among others, specific sections on teacher professionalism, accountability and quality. Accountability measures were argued to fulfil a range of functions including the monitoring of teacher standards and assisting 'teachers to perform better by providing a critical appraisal of how teachers are performing' (ESSC, 1986: 39). The Select Committee also believed 'that a balanced case has been put together for pupil achievement to be used as one measure of accountability' (ibid.: 41). The *Tomorrow's Standards* ministerial working party investigated a wide range of assessment purposes and methods, as the subheadings of the final report show: 'monitoring national performance', 'assessing the effectiveness of schools', 'assessment of students in secondary schools', 'assessment and New Zealand's dual cultural heritage', 'the assessment of teachers and their professional development' and 'pre-service and in-service training in assessment techniques'. By 1990, then, the primacy of assessment in promoting accountability and standards had been established in official policy texts, and teachers' preferred position as proficient assessors of students', their own and each others' learning made explicit.

In the period from 1990, a host of co-ordinated assessment and accountability policy texts have been developed against which individual teachers, workgroups and schools may be held ever more precisely accountable for their students' outcomes. These developments mark a shift in emphasis within official discourses of teaching from 'professional' to 'contractual' forms of accountability. Moreover, students, teachers, curriculum leaders, principals, parents and trustees are now *all* involved in various aspects of these linked planning, policy writing, assessment, record keeping, review and quality assurance mechanisms. The policy texts to which schools are obliged to develop responses include prescribed curriculum and qualifications frameworks, individual curriculum subject documents, school charters, National Education Goals and National Administration Guidelines, Assurance Audits and Effectiveness Reviews (since 1998, combined Accountability Reviews) conducted by the ERO and Performance Management Systems for the employment, appraisal and professional development of teachers and principals.

Notably, however, the emphasis in these texts is clearly that of 'steering at a distance' (Kickert, in Ball, 1993: 111) by the state with teachers, workgroups and schools monitoring and recording their own performance, in the knowledge that some form of either internal review or external inspection will be conducted at some stage in the future. In this regard, the 1990s in New Zealand schooling arguably mark the final abandonment of official policy texts in which teachers were considered to be 'the central actors in this process of innovation' (*Improving Learning and Teaching*, 1974: 34) and their replacement with others which attempt to position teachers along with their students, workgroups, schools and local communities as simply one component part within a panoptic structure (Foucault, 1995: 195) of contractual responsibilities.

Conclusion

In this chapter, I have tried to show how the current approach to performance management in New Zealand is not a 'big bang' attempt to promote change in schools but the latest stage in a more gentle evolution of efforts to address longer standing issues and tensions of educational practice, informed by topical theories of 'social efficiency'. In some respects New Zealand's current version speaks to teachers' historical needs and aspirations, in others' to those of politicians and bureaucrats. In attempting to predict its potential for 'enculturation' and to explain the demise of previous, looser versions of what we are here calling 'performance management', I keep asking myself a beguilingly simple question:

To what extent is this approach to performance management based on our knowledge of how teachers learn to develop their individual and collective practice?

References

Advisory Council on Educational Planning (ACEP) (1973) 'The continuing education of teachers'. Mimeo.

Ball, S. (1993) 'Policy, power relations and teachers' work', *British Journal of Educational Studies*, 41 (2), 106–21.

Campbell, E. (1978) *Realities of curricula*. Wellington: Department of Education.

Collins, G. (1997) 'Performance management – development and implementation issues', in J. O'Neill (ed.), *Teacher Appraisal in New Zealand: Beyond the Impossible Triangle*. Palmerston North: ERDC Press.

Education Amendment Bill (No. 2) (2000) NZ Parliament, December.

Education and Science Select Committee (ESSC) (1986) *Report of the Inquiry into the Quality of Teaching*. Wellington: Government Printer.

Education Forum (1992) *Better teachers for better learning. Teachers' employment conditions: current and prospective*. Auckland: Education Forum.

Fancy, H. (1996) 'Performance management in schools. Go 8128', *New Zealand Gazette*, 12 December, 4724.

Foucault, M. (1995) *Discipline and Punish*. 2nd edn. New York: Vintage Books.

Habermas, J. (1975) *Legitimation Crisis*. London: Heinemann.

Hamilton, D. (1989) *Towards a Theory of Schooling*. Lewes: Falmer Press.

Hargreaves, A. (1994). *Changing Teachers, Changing Times*. London: Cassell.

Improving Learning and Teaching (1974) Wellington; Government Printer.

Jesson, B. (1989) *Fragments of Labour: The Story behind the Labour Government*. Auckland: Penguin.

Lange, D. (1988) *Tomorrow's Schools*. Wellington: Government Printer.

McLaren, I. (1974) *Education in a Small Democracy: New Zealand*. London: Routledge and Kegan Paul.

Meikle, P. (1961) *School and Nation: Post-Primary Education since the War*. Wellington: NZCER.

Ministry of Education (MoE) (1995) *Draft National Guidelines for Performance Management in Schools*. Wellington: Learning Media.

Ministry of Education (MoE) (1999) *Teacher Performance Management: A Resource for Boards of Trustees, Principals and Teachers*. Wellington: Learning Media.

Nash, R. (1983) *Schools Can't Make Jobs*. Palmerston North: Dunmore.

New Zealand Education Gazette (NZEG) (1999) 'National Administration Guidelines', 29 November, 25.

New Zealand Post-Primary Teachers' Association (NZPPTA) (1961) *The Critical Situation in Post-Primary Schools*. Wellington: NZPPTA, November.

New Zealand Post-Primary Teachers' Association (NZPPTA) (1969) *Education in Change*. Auckland: Longman Paul.

New Zealand Post-Primary Teachers' Association (NZPPTA) (1974) *Teachers in Change*. Auckland: Longman Paul.

New Zealand Education Gazette (NZEG) (1991) 'What's all this about accountability?', 14 June, 1–3.

New Zealand Education Gazette (NZEG) (1998) 'Introduction of interim professional standards for primary school teachers and primary school deputy and assistant principals', 5 October, 1–2.

New Zealand Education Review (NZER) (2001) 'Performance queries', 16 March, 4.

O'Neill, J. (1998) 'ERO's capable teacher: a science of control', *Delta*, 50 (2), 201–24.

O'Rourke, M. (1993) 'School charters and the revised national education guidelines', *New Zealand Education Gazette*, 30 April, 3–4.

Openshaw, R. (1980) 'The politics of "back to basics"', *New Zealand Journal of Educational Studies*, 15 (2), 127–36.

Rae, K. (1991) 'Industrial relations for New Zealand teachers', *Access*, 10 (1), 21–34.

Renwick, W. (1980). 'Teachers and professional status', *Education*, 29 (5), 18–21.

Report of the Commission on Education in New Zealand (Currie Report) (1962) Wellington: Department of Education.

Shallcrass, J. (1973) *Secondary Schools in Change*. Wellington: NZPPTA/Price Milburn.

Simkin, G. (1995) 'Overcoming the bulk funding blockage. The Ministerial Reference Group on School Staffing', *New Zealand Annual Review of Education*, 5, 57–74.

Smyth, J. and Shacklock, G. (1998) *Re-making Teaching: Ideology, Policy and Practice*. London: Routledge.

Today's Schools: A Review of the Education Reform Implementation Process (1990). Wellington: Learning Media.

Tomorrow's Standards. Report of the Ministerial Working Party on Assessment for Better Learning (1990). Wellington: Learning Media.

The Post-Primary School Curriculum (Thomas Report) (1959). Wellington: Department of Education.

Webster, B. (1981) 'The politics of the New Zealand Post-Primary Teachers' Association', in M. Clark (ed.), *The Politics of Education in New Zealand* Wellington: NZCER.

Whitehead, C. (1974) 'The Thomas Report - a study in educational reform', *New Zealand Journal of Educational Studies*, 9 (1), 52–64.

16

■ ■ ■

Performance Management of Teachers in the USA: the Multidimensional Approach

David Weller

Performance management in the USA comes in different 'shapes and sizes' and is a result of state governments, not the federal government, having jurisdiction over public education. Each state in the USA is responsible for educating its own citizens and, therefore, each passes legislation governing all aspects of schooling. As long as state law does not violate federal law, states virtually have a free rein on how public education is conducted and how accountability is maintained within their borders. As such, performance management methods among states differ based on the needs and expectations of the constituency of each state. Compounding the lack of uniformity in performance management is the power of the local government within each state. In states having no uniform system for evaluating teacher performance, local school systems are responsible for developing and adopting their own teacher assessment criteria and methods. In states having statewide legislated assessment procedures, local school systems are free to develop and use their own assessment standards and methods as supplements to state-mandated teacher evaluation instruments. However, within this highly diverse approach to teacher evaluation, two broad goals seem to emerge which drive state and local mandates for accountability and the overall approach to teacher evaluation.

First, providing a fair, valid and comprehensive system for managing teacher performance is believed to be the single most important responsibility school administrators have (Duke, 1987). The evaluation of teacher performance and the improvement of classroom instruction is central to effective outcomes of schooling because it directly correlates to improved student learning (Popham, 1988).

Second, any teacher evaluation process which lacks teacher input on how their classroom performance should be evaluated, on the type of instruments or methods used to evaluate their performance, on the process used to remediate any identified weaknesses, and on the type of rewards and recognition teachers should receive for exemplary performance is less than adequate for an effective performance management process (Weller, 1999).

Historical background

Before the 1900s, the evaluation of teacher classroom performance was an 'inspection' process. That is, teachers were observed and rated on their classroom performance by administrators who checked on teacher conformity to established local school board standards and who had no training in classroom observation techniques. Criteria for inspection of teacher performance were mostly personal as opposed to professional standards, with appearance, diction, and professional behavior being the prevailing criteria.

(Weber, 1987)

By the early 1900s, 'inspection' of personal characteristics associated with effective teacher performance gave way to 'standards of efficiency' as schools began to adopt the principles of Taylor's scientific management. Interest in the efficient use of time and materials in the classroom consumed much of the school administrator's time and effort. Developing a set of rules and regulations to promote economic efficiency in the classroom and ensuring that teachers adhered to these procedures was the focus of performance management until the 1950s.

During the 1950s, researchers began to investigate significant teaching behaviours which could be targeted as 'effective' teaching practices and, when grouped together, could provide teacher training institutions with programmes to train a species of 'effective teachers'. Popham (1988) notes that the focus of teacher effectiveness research during the 1950s and 1960s was on anything *but* 'devising assessment techniques to yield information for making decisions about individual teacher effectiveness' (ibid.: 274). With the pressure for teacher accountability, the theme for research during the 1970s, came the development of teacher assessment instruments designed to ensure that minimum standards are met, that deficiencies are identified and that the evaluation process provides sufficient information to help teachers grow personally and professionally.

Currently, after more than two decades of research, it is clear that no single best way exists to evaluate teachers for effectiveness. The pluralistic nature of teaching does not allow for a 'one-size-fits-all' approach to teacher evaluation.

Moreover, if performance assessments are to accurately assess teacher effectiveness, they must be multidimensional in scope and be mutually agreed upon by both teacher and administrator. Only when these criteria are met can evaluation results be used to make objective decisions about continuing employment, granting of tenure and promoting teachers to positions such as department head or assistant principal.

Assessing teacher performance

The primary goal of assessing teacher performance is to improve teaching so as to maximise student achievement. To this end, teacher assessment instruments should be valid and reliable, they should be both formative and summative in scope, and they should assess individual teacher performance on job related objectives. Meaningful and individualised remediation programmes, based on appraisal results, should be provided to teachers who fail to meet acceptable performance criteria levels.

Because enhancement of job performance is the overall goal of teacher assessment, teacher evaluation should be viewed as a non-threatening process designed to improve classroom performance and assist teachers to develop personally and professionally. Administrators can create positive attitudes on the part of teachers towards performance assessment by administrator emphasis on the positive aspects of evaluation for both teacher and student.

Also important to a positive attitude towards assessment is the type of relationship administrators have with their teachers and the manner in which performance appraisal is conducted. When administrators are respected, are trusted and have the best interests of teachers at heart, teachers are more likely to view performance assessments in a positive light, take recommendations for improvement more seriously and have a greater commitment to improve (Duke and Stiggins, 1993). Hoenack and Monk (1990) found a positive correlation between teacher evaluation results and teacher improvement when performance appraisals and their results are considered to be fair and accurate. However, when teachers view evaluation results as unfair, inaccurate or invalid, they feel threatened, are less open to improvement and are likely to have low morale.

Teachers also view performance appraisal more positively when they know the results will be used to develop staff development programmes to build individual improvement plans, to realign job descriptions and job requirements, and/or to recognise achievement (Weller and Weller, 2000). When assessment is used as a vehicle which allows a teacher to improve continuously as a professional and as a person, teacher evaluations are less threatening and more satisfying.

Negative outcomes of performance appraisals come under the 'threat' and 'control' factor headings. Teacher assessment conducted with these factors as primary objectives serve only to make teachers conform to organisational or administrative expectations, to punish or belittle teachers, or to 'motivate' through threat. Castetter (1996) relates that when performance appraisals are used to control teacher behaviour through administrative authority, they serve to cause the resentment of teachers and thwart teacher inclination to be creative and try innovative practices. When teachers are evaluated on unrealistic criteria or when subjective judgements are made about their teaching, teachers become distrustful of and dissatisfied with the evaluator and the assessment process.

Negative views of evaluation may also be caused by personality differences or past, unpleasant events involving the evaluator and the teacher. Both cases may distract from the evaluator's objectivity and create a level of anxiety on the part of the teacher which negatively impacts performance. In such cases, teachers should have the right to expect a fair and impartial assessment of their teaching performance through the selection of an unbiased evaluator. Negative views of evaluation may also be caused by the attitude the teacher takes towards the assessment instrument and the assessment process. When assessment instruments and the assessment processes are unexplained, when they are deemed unfair or when they are considered unlikely to provide the evaluator with an accurate assessment of a teacher's instructional ability, evaluation becomes a threatening and unrewarding experience.

Teacher evaluation instruments

Teacher evaluation instruments are usually prescribed by the state or the local board of education. Procedures for assessment typically include a prescribed number of classroom observations, the conditions under which evaluation is to take place, and a knowledge of the criteria used to assess performance. Sometimes training and evaluation certification are required, especially on state-mandated instruments. Two overarching questions concerning teacher performance are usually embraced in all teacher evaluation instruments: (1) 'Is the teacher able to demonstrate satisfactory performance on the assessment criteria?' and (2) 'Does the teacher demonstrate and apply the required knowledge and skills in an appropriate manner?' The first question calls for the evaluator to assess the overall knowledge and ability levels of the teacher, and the second question requires judgement decisions on the appropriate application of essential knowledge and skills. For teacher evaluations to be valid and reliable, the following must occur:

1   Teachers must understand and be familiar with the assessment criteria and the formal procedures designated to conduct teacher evaluations. Evaluators

should conduct periodic seminars for all certified teachers and annual seminars for new teachers on the teacher appraisal process.

2 Evaluators must know and understand the goals and objectives of the lessons being observed, the types of students being taught, and the fact that instruction is a cumulative process, not an incremental condition.

3 Evaluators must have training on scoring the assessment instrument. Lack of training in the use of the instrument calls into question the reliability of the evaluation findings.

4 Many evaluation models provide guidance for developing a fair and informative process to evaluate teachers. The generic six-step model presented below is holistic in scope and is a structured, professional, non-threatening approach evaluators can use in the teacher appraisal process.

Step 1

During preplanning time, meet with all teachers and discuss the purpose of evaluation, share your philosophy of teacher evaluation, and provide teachers with copies of the assessment instrument(s). Teachers should have the opportunity to ask questions and they should be provided with a time line for classroom observations. In regard to announced and unannounced classroom observations, philosophies differ and which type is used in the evaluation may be prescribed by local or state policy. Those who support announced visits argue that they want to see teachers perform at their best. Those favouring unannounced visits hold that teachers should be performing at their best at all times. Unannounced visits can cause much anxiety among both experienced and beginning teachers alike.

Step 2

About one week prior to a classroom observation, meet individually with the teacher and obtain a copy of the teacher's weekly lesson plans. Review the assessment criteria with the teacher and discuss any personal or student related problems. This pre-observation conference should be conducted in a teacher-friendly environment, the conference should not be rushed, and teachers should be encouraged to discuss problems or extenuating circumstances which may impact their performance. Agree on a specific time or span of time in which the observation(s) will occur.

Step 3

Carefully read the lesson plan for the observed lesson and evaluate the teacher on the agreed upon criteria and procedures. Be on time and *do not* deviate from the procedures discussed and agreed upon in the pre-observation conference with the teacher.

Step 4

Meet with the teacher within two days of the observation and jointly discuss observation results using the scored evaluation instrument to focus discussion. Always present positive findings first and then discuss those areas needing remediation. Allow teachers time to present their perspectives of the lessons and be willing to review your assessment if appropriate. Revisions and/or corrections to scored evaluation instruments indicate personal strength, openness and fairness on the part of the evaluator; and they indicate to the teacher that, regardless of the position of the evaluator, human error is possible. Understanding and flexibility on the part of the evaluator raise teacher respect for the evaluator and enhance morale. Conferences may be tape recorded to serve as the basis for a written post-evaluation conference. Taking notes during the conference is a distraction for both teacher and evaluator, and it lengthens the conference unnecessarily.

Step 5

Within two days of the post-observation conference, provide the teacher with a written record of conference results. If an improvement plan is called for and has been mutually agreed upon during the conference, you should provide a copy of the plan to the teacher. Both parties should sign the written results of the post-observation conference and remediation plan. Any remediation plan must include adequate time, support and resources for the teacher to complete the jointly agreed upon improvement process.

Step 6

For a teacher working under an improvement plan, the evaluator must follow the plan as agreed upon. Any deviation from the plan or failure to provide needed resources or support will call for a new improvement plan or an adjustment in the original plan that is mutually agreeable. New or adjusted improvement plans must be in writing and be signed by both parties. Periodic conferences should be held to assess teacher progress and to identify any difficulties encountered by the teacher. Peer coaching or any other mentoring-type programmes should be made available to assist teachers as they work to improve their classroom performance.

Performance assessment criteria

State and locally mandated assessment instruments vary from state to state and school system to school system. Most state-mandated instruments are non-criterion referenced assessments. As norm-referenced instruments, they use teacher performance criteria of groups of teachers or the average performance of a large group of teachers to obtain criteria for 'acceptable' teaching performance. Criterion referenced tests are tests which use local standards as the basis for performance assessment and take into account the actual job responsibilities and expectations for each local school system. Figure 16.1 presents an example of criteria used by one state for assessing teacher performance (Georgia Department of Education, 1993). These criteria were state-mandated until 1996 when Georgia law allowed for local school boards to adopt their own teacher evaluation criteria and procedures.

Teaching Task I: Provides Instruction

Dimension A: Instructional Level – The amount and organisation of the lesson content are appropriate for the students based on their abilities and the complexity and difficulty of the material.

Dimension B: Content Development – Content is developed through appropriate teacher-focused or student-focused activities.

Dimension C: Building for transfer – Lesson includes initial focus, content emphasis or linking, and summaries that build for transfer of learning.

Teaching Task II: Assesses and Encourages Student Progress

Dimension A: Promoting Engagement – Instructional engagement is promoted through stimulating presentations, active participation, or techniques that promote overt or covert involvement.

Dimension B: Monitoring Progress – Progress, understanding, and bases of misunderstandings are assessed by interpreting relevant student responses, contributions, performances or products.

Dimension C: Responding to Student Performance – Students are provided reinforcement for adequate performances when appropriate and specific feedback or correctives for inadequate performances.

Dimension D: Supporting Students – Support for students is conveyed by using techniques such as providing encouragement, lowering concern levels, dignifying academic responses and by using language free of sarcasm, ridicule and humiliating references.

Teaching Task III: Manages the Learning Environment

Dimension A: Use of Time – Use of instructional time is optimised by techniques such as providing clear directions and using efficient methods for transitions, materials distribution and other routine matters and by techniques such as focusing on objectives and providing sufficient instructional activities.

Dimension B: Physical Setting – The physical setting allows the students to observe the focus of instruction, to work without disruption, to obtain materials, and to move about easily. It also allows the teacher to monitor the students and to move among them.

Dimension C: Appropriate Behaviour – Appropriate behaviour is maintained by monitoring the behaviour of the entire class, providing feedback, and intervening when necessary.

Figure 16.1: Teacher performance criteria (formerly state-mandated) in Georgia
Source: Georgia Department of Education (1993)

Supplemental evaluation material for assessing teacher performance should be used in conjunction with mandated evaluation instruments to provide the most comprehensive picture of teacher knowledge and skills possible. Supplemental materials included in the evaluation process should be jointly determined by teachers and evaluators and a joint decision should be made regarding the weighting of each supplement (Weller and Weller, 2000). The most common forms of supplemental teacher evaluation materials are as discussed below.

Lesson plans

Lesson plans are performance criteria which can be objectively evaluated according to local expectations or standards. Goals and objectives, teaching methods, the use of technology and/or teaching materials, and student learning processes and outcomes should be stated in the plan and they can then be evaluated as a measure of performance. Figure 16.2 presents an example of a lesson plan which can be objectively evaluated. The figure presents a comprehensive lesson plan for a ninth grade English class whose goal is understanding the multiple uses of a thesaurus. Local standards dictate the inclusion of each item found in the lesson plan, and the evaluator's assessment of this supplemental document for assessing teacher performance would be the highest possible mark allowed.

Grade:	*Nine*	Date: *15 March 2001*
Period:	*Three*	
Student Ability Group:	Mixed (low to high)	
Goal:	Students will understand multiple uses of a thesaurus.	
Objectives:	1) Students will be able to distinguish the difference between synonym and antonym (text pp. 93-96; Curriculum Guide p. 21).	
	Students will locate 10 synonyms and 10 antonyms in the thesaurus.	
	Students will write 10 sentences, correctly using synonyms and antonyms.	
Teaching Methods:	Lecture, exercises in workbook, use of thesaurus, use of blackboard.	
Technology:	Overhead projector and computer program learning series for remediation.	
Homework:	Students will write a five paragraph paper on a favourite summer experience using a minimum of 2 antonyms and 2 synonyms per paragraph.	

Figure 16.2: Lesson plan for supplemental evaluation of teacher classroom performance

Self-evaluation

Teachers have important information about themselves to share with others which is valuable to the overall performance appraisal profile. When self-evaluations are used in a teacher's assessment profile, administrators have a more complete picture of the variables impacting teaching performance. Koehler (1990) relates the positive psychological effect self-evaluation has on teachers and its high value when developing self-improvement plans. Self-evaluations, when completed objectively, can minimise the 'halo effect' that may result from classroom observations. Halo effects can be minimised by training and experience, by having more than one evaluator rate observed performance and by conducting several observations.

Examples of self-evaluations include logs, self-rating scales and portfolios with documented student and parent comments and rewards and recognition for achievement. Records such as these provide evaluators with a more personalised view of teacher performance and often allow evaluators access to little known facts about the teacher.

Peer appraisals

Peer evaluations can be valuable and important as an additional piece of information in a holistic assessment package. Seyfarth (1996) relates the value of master teachers' evaluating beginning teachers or teachers with identified weaknesses from previous evaluations. Castetter (1996) notes the importance of peer evaluation and calls for more of this type of assessment because of their 'expert judgement'. Principals cannot be experts in all fields, nor are all principals 'excellent' teachers. Master teachers can best provide the 'expert judgement' needed to make peer appraisals a valuable and reliable data source for teacher evaluation.

> When mentoring or coaching programs exist, mentors are natural choices for peer evaluation responsibilities. Mentors can provide immediate, objective feedback on teacher performance and model the desired behaviors deemed essential to strengthen teacher performance. Some argue, however, that mentors can be biased in their evaluation of teachers. Working closely with peers may result in friendships or personality conflicts which may cause lack of objectivity on performance evaluations. Also, mentoring can be costly, often requiring substitutes to cover classes while mentoring activities take place. When mentors are aware of their professional responsibilities and have the time and resources to meet the objectives of the mentoring program, however, objective performance ratings are the most frequent outcomes.
>
> (McCarthy and Peterson, 1988)

Parent and student appraisals

Evaluation of teacher performance *should not* be connected to student and parent evaluation instruments. Debate exists as to whether or not either population has the knowledge or background to appraise effective teaching and/or mastery of content. Both parents and students *can* assess certain behaviours of teachers, such as interpersonal relationships and human relations skills. Student evaluations are primarily criticised as being 'popularity contests'. Students cannot know the requirements for good and effective teaching, nor can they assess the teacher's command of subject matter. Parents are also in a poor position to evaluate teaching performance and command of subject matter. Parent evaluations are often criticised as being 'accommodating contests' – teachers who placate parents the most receive the highest evaluations. Often, objective analysis falls to personal bias and when this happens student and parent evaluations lose reliability. Popham (1988: 278) relates that great care should be taken if student evaluations are used to assess teacher performance because 'the students' estimates of a teacher's instructional skills are often contaminated by the teacher's popularity or the student's interest in the subject matter being taught'. Therefore, if student evaluations are used, students should be asked to assess areas that are not related to knowledge of subject matter or to effective teaching behaviours. Moreover, any type of student evaluation data *should not* carry as much weight as other teacher evaluation data.

How, then, can student and parent evaluation information be used to improve teaching in a way that ensures the professional fate of teachers is not in the hands of students and parents who may carry a grudge and see the evaluation process as a way to get even? One way is to make student and parent evaluations the prerogative of the teacher. Teachers may opt to use this type of evaluation as a means for developing their own improvement plans, and may or may not share the results with the administration. When evaluations are used in this way, parents and students will provide more appropriate feedback. Teachers should let parents and students know that their input will be used for personal/professional development and that the results are important for enhancing their overall performance. If teacher evaluation instruments for students and parents are used, they should be developed by teachers and administrators, pilot-tested prior to use, and evaluated yearly for reliability and validity.

Finally, administrators should realise that informal feedback from parents and students may be influenced by a variety of variables and that this data source should be carefully considered before forming an overall opinion about a teacher. Looking for consistent 'patterns' over time about teacher behaviour is the best way to form an overall opinion about teacher performance. Administrators should keep ongoing logs about teachers from student and parent conversations, and they should periodically analyse these logs for behaviour patterns. Taken together, parent and student feedback of this nature may be the most reliable source of evaluation data on teachers from these two populations.

Teacher portfolios

The use of teacher portfolios is another way to evaluate teacher performance. Seyfarth (1996) provides a teacher portfolio model, which is document focused, is assembled by teachers and can be evaluated by administrators. Portfolios allow teachers control over what is being assessed, but the task is time-consuming and requires organised record keeping. Perhaps one of the best pieces of documentation in a portfolio are videotapes of class sessions especially when the videotapes are accompanied by copies of lesson plans, tests and handouts, and grade distributions. Videotapes take away much of the tension associated with classroom observations, and having several tapes of a teacher provides a documented 'pattern' of a teacher's performance behaviour. Other information sources to include in the portfolio are parent comments and student evaluations, a list of workshops and staff development sessions attended that lists new ideas or information and their documented application to teaching, professional improvement plans and documented progress towards meeting objectives, peer or mentor evaluations and creative projects, publications or awards.

Evaluating portfolios is time-consuming, calls for subjective judgement, and can trigger teacher–administrator conflict when no clear evaluation criteria exist. If portfolios are used for teacher evaluation, and they should be because they are the most comprehensive form of assessment available (Wolf, 1991), then teachers and administrators must jointly agree on the criteria to evaluate the work, the documents to be included and the weights to be assigned to these documents. Without this clear understanding, the use of portfolios for evaluating teacher performance should be discouraged.

Using student achievement test scores to evaluate teachers

Using student achievement scores to evaluate teacher effectiveness is currently causing much debate. Some hold that test scores should be part of the evaluation profile because the 'bottom line' for assessing teacher effectiveness is increased student test scores. This is the popular view held by most parents, community members, business leaders and government officials (Weller, 1999). However, the use of standardised tests results in the evaluation process attributes too much credibility to instruments having inherent limitations, which lay people fail to realise. Use of these tests without consideration for their inherent weaknesses is unfair to teachers because they provide an inaccurate measure of teacher performance.

Major weaknesses of standardised tests, whether norm referenced or criterion referenced, are discussed by Popham (1988). One weakness is the possibility of *cultural bias*. A second weakness is the mismatch between teaching and testing. A mismatch is the difference in what the test measures and what is actually being taught in the curriculum. Another weakness is the 'high generality' test makers build into tests for marketing purposes. This factor often omits items, major concepts and/or content deemed important by teachers or local curriculum guides, and includes items or concepts not deemed essential for teaching by these sources. A fourth weakness is the possibility of inadequate or low reliability and/or validity of the test. Careful attention should be given to selecting tests with exceedingly high validity and reliability coefficients. Fifth, standardised tests do not adequately measure the effectiveness of teaching. Sixth, some students naturally do poorly on standardised measures, regardless of their accumulated knowledge and skills.

While learning is correlated with teacher performance, Popham (1988) notes the quandary that exists for educators in the area of standardised testing. Standardised tests are 'handy' and have public appeal; on the other hand, they have many inherent weaknesses, such as reliability and validity issues and their accuracy in making generalisations from one population to another. Weller (1999), however, maintains that when teachers establish content validity and reliability on their own tests, they can use this data to support their findings to others. Teacher-made tests then become the *best* and *most practical way* to assess teacher performance if one is using test measures for evaluation purposes. When teacher-made tests are used in conjunction with other teacher assessment data (portfolios, videos etc.), a more comprehensive profile exists and the safer the administrator is in the identification of the 'true' strengths and weaknesses of teachers.

Developing a model for teacher appraisal

Teacher evaluation in the USA is a situation-specific phenomenon that must take into consideration a variety of local impacting variables if an accurate picture of performance is to result. Although it is impossible to control for all variables impacting teacher performance, some of those variables can be identified and steps can be taken to either mitigate or lessen the impact of these variables. When developing a situation-specific, school-based model for teacher appraisal, the following variables should be considered:

1   Local school board standards and expectations for performance must provide the foundation for a teacher assessment model. State standards, if they apply, must also be incorporated into the model. Local standards include the overall goals and objectives of the school system, information found in the school system curriculum guide, vision and mission statements of the

school, and standards set by the department to which the teacher is assigned. Teacher job descriptions provide the final source for developing a teacher performance instrument.

2 The school's student ethnic composition; its student distribution in regards to socio-economic status, IQ and range of students, and other student-associated variables unique to the school must be taken into consideration.

3 Specific abilities of students in each classroom being observed regarding IQ range, student knowledge and skill levels in relation to peers in other classes, and resources available for teachers to teach the lesson(s) observed must be considered.

4 Test measures for students must have validity and high reliability.

5 Teacher evaluation measures must be made known to teachers and teachers must be assessed on the criteria that are made known to them.

6 Teacher performance evaluation should be based on a variety of assessment measures to provide the most complete and comprehensive profile of teacher performance.

References

Castetter, W.B. (1996) *The Human Resource Function in Educational Administration*. 6th edn. Englewood Cliffs, NJ: Prentice-Hall.

Duke, D.L. (1987) *School Leadership and Instructional Improvement*. New York: Random House.

Duke, D. and Stiggins, R. (1993) 'Beyond minimum competency: evaluation for professional development', in J. Millman and D. Darling-Hammond (eds) *The New Handbook for Teacher Evaluation*. Newbury Park, CA: Sage.

Hoenack, S. and Monk, D. (1990) 'Economic aspects of teacher evaluation', in J. Millman and D. Darling-Hammond (eds) *The New Handbook for Teacher Evaluation*. Newbury Park, CA: Sage.

Koehler, M. (1990) 'Self-assessment in the evaluation process', *National Association of Secondary School Principals Bulletin*, 74 (527), 40–4.

McCarthy, M.M. and Peterson, K.D. (1988). Peer 'review of materials in public school evaluation', *Journal of Personnel Evaluation in Education*, 1, 259–67.

Popham, W.J. (1988) *Educational Evaluation*. 2nd ed. Englewood Cliffs, NJ: Prentice-Hall.

Seyfarth, J.T. (1996) *Personnel Management for Effective Schools*. 2nd edn. Boston: Allyn and Bacon.

Weber, J.R. (1987) *Teacher Evaluation as a Strategy for Improving Instruction*. Eugene, OR: University of Oregon (ERIC Clearinghouse on Educational Management).

Weller, L.D. (1999) *Quality Middle School Leadership: Eleven Central Skill Areas*. Lancaster, PA: Technomic.

Weller, L.D. and Weller, S. (2000) *Quality Human Resources Leadership: A Principal's Handbook*. Lanham, MD: Scarecrow Press.

Wolf, K. (1991) 'The school teacher's portfolio: issues in design, implementation, and evaluation', *Phi Delta Kappan*, 73, 129–36.

17

■ ■ ■

Performance Management in England

Mike Brearley

The British government is committed to raising standards in education and one of the major issues at the 1997 election was 'Education, Education, Education'. The political map of Britain is such that there are different arrangements for the delivery of state education in England, Scotland, Northern Ireland and Wales. This chapter will focus on the specific programmes in performance management in education that have been developed for England since the 1997 election and which came into force in September 2000 through *The Education (School Teacher Appraisal) (England) Regulations 2000.*

Purpose of the chapter

This chapter will describe in detail the programmes of performance management which are part of a package of measures introduced through the Standards and Effectiveness Unit (SEU), which is part of the Department for Education and Employment (DfEE). The unit has not been slow in responding to its task since the 1997 election, introducing amongst other things, the National Literacy Strategy, National Numeracy Strategy, Specialist Schools Initiative, City Academies, Education Action Zones, Fresh Start Programme for failing schools and so on.

The process of performance management in English schools is part of this wider programme of measures designed to raise standards. The DfEE believe that performance management will play its part in this process through an elaborate appraisal system linked to performance related pay. They state that this will be successful when:

- appraisal is well integrated into the school's improvement plans;
- appraisal is complementary to other systems of monitoring and review being used in the school;
- the process of appraisal takes place in a clear and coherent way;
- there is agreement between all those involved in raising standards in schools about what appraisal looks like;
- the targets used in the appraisal process are prioritised and SMART (Specific, Measurable, Attainable, Resourced, Time-constrained);
- appraisal leads to high-quality staff training and development;
- appraisal can be seen to contribute to higher standards and is not just a bureaucratic burden.

The introduction of performance management into English schools has not been without its problems, and at the time of writing there has been no effective evaluation of its success. There are certainly some aspects of the programme that will call into question whether it will have the sustained and integrated impact to which the SEU aspires.

Background

The backdrop to performance management in England was the limited progress made by the appraisal process introduced in 1991. Sightings were still being reported as late as 1999 though effectively it had ceased to be a credible part of school development by the middle of the decade.

Dogged by heavy bureaucracy, opposition from the teacher unions and failure to make a positive impact, the appraisal process declined from ambition, to irritant to guardian of inertia. As a deputy head of a large comprehensive in the early 1990s I watched the process at close quarters and saw how the eventual collusion between appraiser and appraisee that was often endemic in the process made sure that nothing changed.

The context in which the current programme of performance management is set is now far more supportive than was the case in the early 1990s. What is taught in English schools is now clearly defined through the National Curriculum, which has been on a cycle of continual development since the 1988 Education Act. The standards expected in both teaching and leadership are defined in the National Standards for Teachers (TTA, 1998). The performance management programme is now expected to be the process that will deliver the National Standards in leadership and learning of the National Curriculum.

Timetable for introduction of performance management

The initial timescale for the introduction of performance management was:

- 1 September 2000 – revised performance management arrangements will come into effect for teachers and headteachers in England;
- 31 December 2000 – schools should have put in place their performance management policy and headteachers should have met with governors to discuss and agree objectives;
- 28 February 2001 – headteachers should have discussed and agreed objectives with their team leaders.

The timetable has slipped because of a successful legal challenge by two of the teacher unions which led to a revision of parts of the process and difficulties in recruiting External Advisers and Threshold Assessors. The first round of the process may not be completed until July 2001. One of the problems that occurred was that many headteachers seeking to find out more about this process put themselves through the training as External Advisers and Threshold Assessors without intending to fulfil the role. The company contracted to the DfEE to deliver the training was then left believing that it had enough trained people to make the performance management process work, whereas only a proportion of them were willing to undertake the tasks. With a wonderful sense of 'process myopia' the company said that anyone doing the training for any of the three posts and not undertaking a minimum number of school visits, would lose their accreditation. They were in effect threatening to take away the very thing a large minority of those trained did not want.

What is performance management in England?

The DfEE (2000: 3) describes performance management as

a way of helping schools improve by supporting and improving teachers work, both as individuals and as teams. Teachers and their team leaders – and Heads and their Governing Bodies – will agree and review priorities and objectives within the context of the school development plan. The outcomes of performance reviews will help set priorities for future planning and professional development and will inform governing bodies decisions about discretionary pay awards.

The DfEE describes the purpose of performance management as being to benefit both pupils and teachers. It reports that (ibid.):

The pupils will benefit because their teachers will have a more sharply focused picture of what, with encouragement, support and high expectations, their pupils can achieve.

Teachers have the right to expect that their performance will be regularly assessed and that they will have a proper opportunity for professional discussion with their team leader about their work and their professional development.

This is to be achieved through three distinct processes (Figure 17.1).

The programme will not be the responsibility of individual schools in the way it was in the 1990s. There is external verification through the recruitment and training of Performance Management Consultants, External Advisers to Governing Bodies and Threshold Assessors. This is to ensure consistency and high expectation in each of the constituent parts of the process.

Performance Management Consultants are nationally trained and accredited to advise schools in the early stages of developing the process. The training programmes for these consultants were designed to give a clear and consistent message. They were heavily scripted, which achieved a consistent message at one level, though made deeper development more difficult. There is a paradox in scripted training, in that its quality becomes even more dependent on the ability of the trainer rather than the skill of the scriptwriter. The quality of the training varied more than might have been expected and anecdotal evidence suggests that there has not been the level of consistency that was hoped for.

External Advisers are again nationally trained and accredited, and their role is to advise and support the governing body in reviewing the head's performance. Every school is entitled to one day of the adviser's time, though they are expected to pay if they want more than one day. The process of objective setting for headteachers is described later in this chapter.

The Threshold Assessors validate the evidence collected in school that demonstrates that a teacher has sufficient competence to go through the 'pay threshold' and on to a separate pay spine.

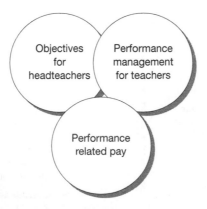

Figure 17.1: The components of performance management

Performance management in school

The central core of the performance management process is the introduction of individual policies within schools. There is a tight structure within which the schools have to operate and many just adopted the 'model' offered by the DfEE (Figure 17.2).

The purpose and the process of the school policy

The rationale

The rationale is described by the DfEE (2000b: 1) as being:

> *A shared commitment to high performance. To focus attention on more effective teaching and monitoring. To raise the quality of teaching and to benefit pupils, teachers and the school. It means providing appropriate and effective personal training and development to ensure job satisfaction, a high level of expertise and progression of staff in their chosen profession.*

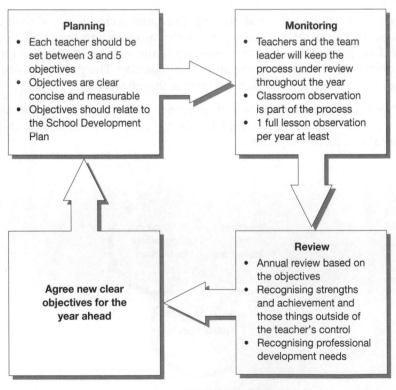

Figure 17.2: The planning, monitoring and review cycle

Roles

The emphasis of performance management in England is to have it integrated into school life. To this end the governors have a strategic view in agreeing the school policy and ensuring that the performance of every teacher is reviewed regularly. The governors also have a particular role in the setting of objectives for headteachers, which will be covered later. The headteacher is responsible for ensuring that the reviews take place and in an appropriate way. Team leaders, working with a group of between four and six other staff, conduct the objective setting, monitoring and review of individual teachers.

Timing of reviews

The review cycle will last for one year. The choice for the first cycle is to have it last either nine or 18 months. This choice was provided because the initial deadline for setting the first round of objectives was February 2001 and out of synchronisation with the cycle of the school year. The flexibility allowed the process to be brought back in line with the academic cycle. The same discretion was not open to the objective setting process for headteachers and so some will set objectives in the summer term and then review them and set new ones the following autumn (Figure 17.3).

Planning

In the planning process the objectives for an individual teacher are set with their team leader. In some smaller primary schools this may be the headteacher, in larger primaries and secondary schools this role would devolve through the school to deputy heads, heads of department and deputy heads of department. The objectives should be challenging, though realistic

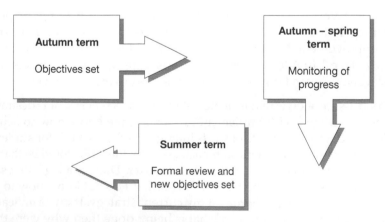

Figure 17.3: The performance management cycle

and take into account the nature of the job description of the teacher. Examples given by the DfEE (2000c) give a strong insight into their expectations and perhaps highlight a significant flaw in the process. The following examples are taken from the DfEE's booklet *Performance Management – Guidance for Governors*.

Example 1

'To raise the percentage of pupils attaining 5 or more GCSE passes at A–C from 69% to 75% over the next three years and to raise the percentage of pupils achieving A grades at GCSE by 5% over the next 3 years.'

Example 2

'To increase the number of year 2 pupils attaining level 2 in their Key Stage 1 SATs results for maths and science by 2% in the academic year 2001 and by 5% in 2002.'

In order to make the process measurable there is a strong emphasis on statistically based targets, which in some instances appear to be based on some rather weak assumptions. The first assumption seems to be that there is a consistent level of ability from one cohort of pupils to another and therefore incremental raising of levels of achievement year on year is possible. This may be appropriate when you are looking at the national picture and the holistic statistical sample that this includes. It may be less appropriate at a local level. The levels of ability in an average sized secondary school in England (750 pupils) do vary from one year to the next by up to 30 per cent. The situation is more dramatic in small primary schools (average 230) where the cohort of students in one Key Stage could be a single figure and offer wild swings in ability, year on year.

Basing objectives on annual incremental improvement may not be possible. This approach does reflect the National Targets for education that expect an annual improvement. Nationally this has been achieved through the full range from Key Stage 1 to A level. The question remains as to whether this national statistical analysis can be successfully transferred to the local level.

The second assumption is that incremental raising of achievement is desirable and that those concerned with implementing this change know how to achieve it. There is considerable evidence of stress in English schools, both for students and teachers. One consequence of the approach taken by the DfEE could be that people are encouraged to work harder rather than smarter. There is a logic that says, if I knew how to do something better then I would. If I do not know how to do that then I am left with working harder at my current strategy. If my team leader has good ideas about how to improve what is being done then why were they not shared earlier? If he or she is not aware of how things could be done differently, then we are back to working harder. As Captain found to his cost in Orwell's *Animal Farm*, working harder does not always bring the expected rewards.

The value of using national statistics is that they offer a ready point of measurement and an opportunity to integrate national targets into the objectives for individual teachers. It is still possible to use national statistics in the objectives though in a different way. Rather than seeing them as the point to be reached in the future they should be used as a retrospective way of benchmarking performance. In order to do this you 'step up' the objective above the statistical measure.

I can apply this principle of 'stepping up' to one of the objectives set by the DfEE. In stepping up, I would ask the following question: When I have raised the level of GCSE success by 6 per cent, what will I have changed? The answer will be focused on the learner and will identify the change that will bring about the improvement. It may be that the answer would vary from school to school, though would probably include issues covering motivation, self-esteem, the ability to revise, the ability to organise work for learning and so on.

Whatever needs to change in order to raise the levels of GCSE success then becomes the focus for the objective. The objective would then read: 'To raise achievement at GCSE by 6 per cent through the development of revision strategies and raising the self-esteem of the students in Year 11'. The objective then focuses on the process of bringing about the raising of standards rather than the change in the level of achievement itself. When we do something different that involves people we cannot know what the outcome will be. We may have hopes, expectations or even prayers, but we can have no certainty. The 6 per cent rise in GCSE levels is therefore no more than one of these things. The point is that the objective reflects something new being done, which in the professional judgement of those concerned will make a difference. It may have the desired impact, or like Edison when inventing the light bulb, it may be just one of '10 000 ways that I successfully discovered that didn't work'.

Monitoring

When objectives are stepped up from the statistical measure the monitoring becomes a more supportive process of asking:

1 When will the programme be devised?
2 How will it be taught to the students?
3 How and when will you monitor the impact of the programme?
4 Has the programme had the hoped for impact on achievement at GCSE?

The matter of examination achievement then becomes an issue of retrospective analysis rather than a predictor of future achievement and the focus is rightly placed on the process and not the outcome.

Part of the monitoring process of performance management will take place through classroom observation as well as the use of other relevant information. The role of classroom observation is stressed, and although not currently common practice in secondary schools it is commonplace in the primary sector. In the DfEE's (2000b: 5) model of performance management policy they stress: 'Classroom observation is accepted good practice with a minimum of one observation each year required by regulations.' They go on to say that:

1 'Successful observation requires preparation and training.'
2 'The nature of the observation will depend on its purpose.'
3 'Full, constructive and timely feedback is required.' (2000b: 5)

Review

The review part of the process of performance management will include:

- confirming the teacher's tasks and objectives;
- recognising strengths;
- confirming action agreed with the teacher;
- identifying areas of development;
- recognising personal development needs;
- agreeing new clear objectives.

Within ten days of the review meeting the team leader will provide a written report for the teacher. Within ten days of having received the report the teacher can add anything they wish in writing.

Complaints procedure

If a teacher wishes to make a complaint about the process or the outcomes, then it should be done within ten days of them receiving their written report. If the team leader or the head cannot resolve the difficulties, then the complaint passes to a 'Review Officer' who will investigate the complaint. The choices available to the Review Officer are:

1 The review statement remains unchanged.
2 He or she may add observations of their own.
3 The review statement may be changed with the agreement of the person responsible, or in the head's case, of the appointed governors.
4 The Review Officer could declare the review statement null and void; in which case the process will be repeated. For heads this will mean the appointment of new governors and in the case of the teaching staff, the head will appoint a new team leader. Any new review or part review will be conducted within a further 15 days.

Access and confidentiality

Access to the reports is limited to the teacher themselves, the team leader, the headteacher and any governors who have concerns with teachers' pay. There is also a need for the person responsible for training and development in school to be given information about the professional development needs of the teacher.

The head has also to report annually to the governing body on the performance management in school.

Reviewing the headteacher's performance

Rationale

The rationale for this aspect of the process (Figure 17.4) is described in the training manual for External Advisers as being:

1 Heads are the key to the performance of the school.
2 In the most successful schools, the governors and SMT provide a clear sense of direction with emphasis on raising standards.
3 Good management and clear objectives are central to raising educational standards.
4 The agreement of performance objectives is a powerful means of focusing the work of the headteacher.

Planning

The objectives for the headteacher are to be 'clear, concise, measurable and appropriate' (DfEE, 2000c: 29). The minimum legal requirement is that objectives are set for:

- School Leadership and Management;
- Pupil Progress.

In some sense this is a false dichotomy because if the head is doing something that is not concerned with pupil achievement, then the question might be raised about why they are spending their time on this project. Equally, if what they are doing is not connected with leadership, then similar questions need to be raised. Whatever a head does will be perceived by others in a leadership context because they are the head. The distinction is made, not by what you do but by what you measure. A literacy project could be about pupil achievement if what is measured is the impact on standards of literacy. If what is measured is the developing capability and commitment of the staff towards the project, then it becomes a leadership objective.

213

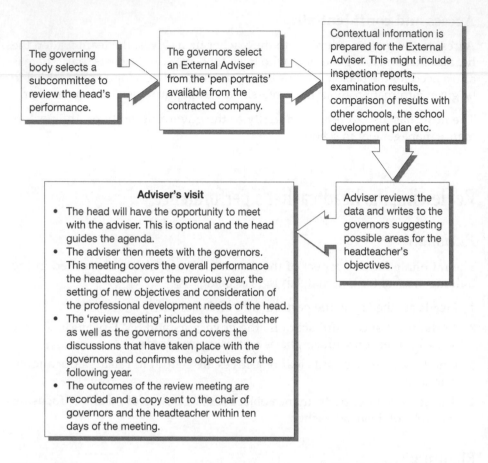

The governing body selects a subcommittee to review the head's performance.

The governors select an External Adviser from the 'pen portraits' available from the contracted company.

Contextual information is prepared for the External Adviser. This might include inspection reports, examination results, comparison of results with other schools, the school development plan etc.

Adviser's visit

- The head will have the opportunity to meet with the adviser. This is optional and the head guides the agenda.
- The adviser then meets with the governors. This meeting covers the overall performance the headteacher over the previous year, the setting of new objectives and consideration of the professional development needs of the head.
- The 'review meeting' includes the headteacher as well as the governors and covers the discussions that have taken place with the governors and confirms the objectives for the following year.
- The outcomes of the review meeting are recorded and a copy sent to the chair of governors and the headteacher within ten days of the meeting.

Adviser reviews the data and writes to the governors suggesting possible areas for the headteacher's objectives.

Figure 17.4: The process of reviewing the performance of the headteacher

As with the objectives set in school for individual teachers, there is ambiguity about the juxtaposition between process and outcome. Should the issues of being 'clear, concise, measurable and appropriate' be applied to the *process* of objective setting or the *outcome*? The dangers in focusing on the outcomes are the same as described for individual teachers. 'Stepping up' the objectives for headteachers in the same way as for classroom teachers will generate the motivation and creativity that is sought.

An example of a leadership objective is given in the DfEE paper (2000c: 18). Set in the context of a deputy head in a secondary school: 'To reduce the number of exclusions by 30% in the course of the year.' Step this up and ask 'When you have reduced exclusions by 30 per cent, what will have changed?'

The answers would depend on local circumstances though could include better counselling, changed teaching methods, a behaviour management policy and so on. The objective then becomes 'To reduce the number of exclusions by 30 per cent by introducing a new behaviour policy for the school'.

Monitoring

The monitoring by the appointed governors is then focused on the process. The headteacher's competence is judged by what he or she does. The measuring of the impact of what they do is merely the way of benchmarking whether to carry on with the project or to try something different. Edison was not a bad engineer 10 000 times and then suddenly a good one. The expectations of governors on a headteacher may not stretch to the extent that Edison experimented, but the principle remains.

Access and confidentiality

Complaints and confidentiality are in part overlapping. If a headteacher wishes to complain about the objectives they are being set then there will need to be a 'Review Governor' available to hear the complaint who is not 'tainted' by knowing what the objectives are before a formal hearing. It may be that knowledge that a particular programme of development in school is part of the objectives set for the headteacher may or may not inspire others to support the initiative.

There is a difficulty with confidentiality, which may come into conflict with the leadership style of the head or the political culture of the school. There may be heads who want to let those in the school know what their targets are in order to have an open and supportive process. There may be governors who are more used to working openly and for whom the levels of confidentiality are anathema. The issue is something that individual schools need to be aware of and work through.

Performance management – pay, promotion and dismissal

The process of performance management is tied to the concept of performance related pay. If a teacher is below the ninth point on the incremental scale of teachers' pay then they can expect to have an incremental increase in their pay every year until they reach that ninth point. Performance management allows for the possibility of a double move in which a teacher might pass through two incremental points in one year. It also allows for the possibility of a teacher being refused their incremental rise because they have not completed their objectives.

Once at the ninth point a teacher can apply to go 'through the pay threshold' which will take them on to another pay spine and is intended to provide an incentive for good teachers to be rewarded for staying in the classroom rather than seeking management and leadership posts.

In order to go through the threshold a teacher has to complete a detailed form demonstrating that they are competent in each of the threshold standards. These standards are:

1 *Knowledge and understanding*: teachers need to demonstrate that they have a thorough and up to date knowledge of their subject.

2 *Teaching and assessment*: teachers must demonstrate that they consistently and effectively
   (a) plan lessons and the sequence of lessons to meet the individual needs of students;
   (b) use an appropriate range of teaching strategies;
   (c) use information about prior learning to set well-grounded expectations.

3 *Wider professional effectiveness*: teachers should demonstrate that they
   (a) take responsibility for their professional development;
   (b) make an active contribution to the policies and aspirations of the school.

4 *Professional characteristics*: teachers should demonstrate that they are effective professionals who challenge and support their pupils through
   (a) inspiring trust and confidence;
   (b) building team commitment;
   (c) engaging and motivating pupils;
   (d) analytical thinking;
   (e) positive action to improve the quality of pupils learning.

If a teacher is able to demonstrate their competence in each of these areas and that view is supported by their headteacher and an external Threshold Assessor, then the teacher will move on to the new pay spine with an initial pay rise of £2000 per annum.

The governors who are responsible for setting the objectives, monitoring and reviewing the performance of a headteacher can use their findings as part of the process of review of the headteacher's pay. The governors have discretion about the response they make.

Conclusion

The process of performance management is part of a far wider agenda of accountability in education in Britain – accountability in both leadership and learning. The process of developing accountability has been ongoing since the

1988 Education Act and continues today, with models being developed by Hay Management that include the use of pupil evaluation of teacher performance as well as the league tables that purport to offer an insight into organisational effectiveness.

There may be a danger of breaking education into its component parts and then trying to reassemble them to create the whole picture. Perhaps there are lessons to be learnt from the physicist David Bohm who is quoted by Peter Senge in his book *The Fifth Discipline* (1990) saying: 'the task is futile – similar to trying to reassemble the fragments of a broken mirror to see a true reflection'.

In large part I judge the effectiveness and success of my local school by the conversations I have with my children at the dinner table. Conversations about their day in school and how they enjoyed, were excited by or enthralled by what they had done that day. How far performance management will contribute to those conversations remains to be seen.

Reference

Department for Education and Employment (DfEE) (1997) *Excellence in Schools*. London: DfEE.

Department for Education and Employment (DfEE) (2000a) *Performance Management in Schools*. London: DfEE.

Department for Education and Employment (DfEE) (2000b) *Performance Management in Schools – Model Performance Management Policy*. London: DfEE.

Department for Education and Employment (DfEE) (2000c) *Guidance for Governors*. London: DfEE.

Department for Education and Employment (DfEE) (2000d) *Performance Management. Training for Advisers*. London: DfEE.

Department for Education and Employment (DfEE) (2000e) *Performance Management Framework*. London: DfEE.

House of Commons (2000) *The Education (School Teacher Appraisal) (England) Regulations 2000*.

Senge P. (1990) *The Fifth Discipline*. London: Century.

Teacher Training Agency (TTA) (1998) *National Standards in Teaching*. TTA.

Index

∎ ∎ ∎